FINDING THE ARCTIC

HISTORY AND CULTURE ALONG

A 2,500-MILE SNOWMOBILE JOURNEY

FROM ALASKA TO HUDSON'S BAY

FINDING THE ARCTIC

MATTHEW STURM

UNIVERSITY OF ALASKA PRESS
FAIRBANKS, ALASKA

University of Alaska Press
P.O. Box 756240
Fairbanks, AK 99775-6240

Publication of this book was supported in part by a generous grant from the
U.S. Army Cold Regions Research and Engineering Laboratory

Library of Congress Cataloging-in-Publication Data

Sturm, Matthew.
 Finding the Arctic : history and culture along a 2,500-mile snowmobile journey
from Alaska to Hudson's Bay / Matthew Sturm.
     p. cm.
 Includes bibliographical references and index.
  ISBN 978-1-60223-163-4 (pbk. : acid-free paper)—ISBN 978-1-60223-164-1
(e-book)
 1. Snowmobiling—Arctic regions. 2. Arctic regions—Description and travel.
 3. Arctic regions—History. 4. Arctic regions—Social life and customs.
 I. Title.
 GV856.7.A73S78 2012
 796.94097--dc23
                              2011033430

Cover design by Kristina Kachele
Text design by Paula Elmes, ImageCraft Publications & Design

This publication was printed on acid-free paper that meets the minimum require-
ments for ANSI / NISO Z39.48–1992 (R2002) (Permanence of Paper for Printed
Library Materials).

Printed in China

CONTENTS

Preface vii
Introduction ix

01   TRACKS NORTH 1
Ballad of the Arctic Science Bandits 11
Changes North 12

02   ROSEBUD REALITIES 17
Quest's Older Cousin—The Iditarod 22

03   PORCUPINE HOSPITALITY 37
Quarantine Island 45

04   POIGNANT PASSING:
THE MAD TRAPPER OF RAT RIVER 55
Who Was the Mad Trapper of Rat River? 64

05   BIG MAC 75
Snow and Ice Roads 82

06   FINDING THE DOUGLAS CABIN 93
Black Lake Ice 100
The Shield and the Cordilleran 106
Fort Confidence 112

07 THE NORTHERN CROSS 115

08 KUGLUKTUK 137
    Inuksuk 148
    Sea Ice Going, Going, Gone 150

09 THE STARVATION TRAIL 153

10 THE DIAMOND CONFLUENCE 173
    The Complex Calculus of Barrenlands Diamond Mining 185
    The Oldest Rocks in the World 193

11 BRAIDED STRANDS: THE FIRST INTERLOPER 195
    Whiteout on Aylmer Lake 206
    Strange Wooly Attractors 211

12 BRAIDED STRANDS: THE LAST REFUGEE 217

    Acknowledgments 235

    Another Arctic Story 239

    Recommended Reading 241

    Index 247

I have lived and traveled in the Arctic since 1973. I love the land and the people. I like the weather, particularly the cold. After thirty-eight years, the place still surprises me. To outsiders it can seem bleak and barren, but I find it complex, with unexpected facets. I wrote this book because I wanted to shine a light on these. I also wanted to collect in one place some of the human history that has shaped the culture and the people who make their lives in the Arctic today. It is a history braided from two cultural strands, Western and Native. Like everything else about the Arctic, it is rich and nuanced. Sadly, many of the best stories seem to be fading from memory. My qualifications, if any, for writing this book are the passion I have for the Arctic and some unusually long winter trips I have taken across arctic Canada and Alaska. Between those trips, and endless reading of arctic books, you might say I have been trying to find the Arctic, or at least my place in it, for many years.

So here is a selection of stories about arctic exploration, culture, commerce, and adventure that, to me, capture the spirit of the North, or at least that aspect of the spirit that lured me here nearly forty years ago. The skeleton that connects these stories is a 2,500-mile snowmobile trip I led in 2007, but the muscle and sinew are the deep-rooted interest in the past, present, and future of the Arctic that I shared with my companions on that journey. It is my hope that as you travel with us, this austere but fascinating land will glitter and shine as brightly for you as it does for me.

Matthew Sturm
Fairbanks, June 22, 2011

INTRODUCTION

I started looking for the Arctic from the moment I arrived there. I first crossed the Arctic Circle in 1973 while serving on the United States Coast Guard icebreaker Northwind. *The year before I had crossed the Antarctic Circle during a cruise to McMurdo Sound. My journey toward the poles started at age seventeen, when, thoroughly bored with high school, I enlisted in the Coast Guard. My first posting was on the 255-foot cutter* Klamath. *It turned out to be even more boring than school. The* Klamath's *job was to sail to Ocean Station Papa (50°N, 145°W) halfway between Seattle and Hawaii, and then to float there for a month, a manned navigational aid for jets flying to and from Hawaii. For days on end we turned the engines off and drifted, wallowing between the swells. My job was navigating, which is pretty easy when you are hardly moving.*

Compared to that assignment, serving on an icebreaker sounded like an adrenaline rush, so I transferred to the *Northwind*. At the time I didn't know she was one of a select group of ships that had traversed the Northwest Passage (and done so twice in one season). Indeed, I was woefully ignorant of all arctic history. After breaking ice in Antarctica, we sailed north to Nome, Alaska, then up to the Diomede Islands in the Bering Strait. We eventually worked our way into the pack ice of the Chukchi Sea and even briefly steamed into Russian territory, running a risk of being detained.

North to Alaska! This stirred something in my teenage soul. From the ship's bridge I could see the arctic tundra stretching away into a distant blue haze. I knew there was adventure out there, and I wanted it.

USCGC *Northwind* off Greenland in the summer of 1986. Inset: Bob Irissari (left) and me on board in 1973. *Tech Sgt. Jose Hernandez, U.S. Air Force* (Northwind).

I was hardly the first. At least six hundred years earlier, intrepid Europeans such as Leif Eriksson, John Cabot, Martin Frobisher, John Davis, Henry Hudson, and Jens Munk had begun to push west and north into the icy seas around Greenland in frail little sailing ships. They were looking for fame, furs, precious metals, and a shorter route to the Orient, and—just my hunch—they may also have been seeking adventure, which they got in spades. Of course, people were already living in the Arctic when Westerners got there. During the last ice age, unknown and unsung hunter-travelers had pushed across Siberia and entered what is now Alaska via the Bering Land Bridge, a continental link now submerged under the Bering Sea. They were probably looking for better hunting, but I fancy that curiosity about this new world may have been mixed in with more practical motives.

It wasn't just the land that got to me. The people who worked and chose to live in this harsh and difficult place intrigued me as well. My first encounters with arctic residents took place somewhere north of St. Lawrence Island. The *Northwind* was working its way through thick pack ice in misty weather when we came upon an *umiak* with four hunters in it. The skin boat seemed to materialize from between two ice floes. It ghosted alongside our white-painted steel hull, a tiny thing floating a good fifteen feet below our taffrail. We had a brief parley, then the hunters ghosted away, disappearing into the maze of ice whence they had come. The *umiak* was of traditional design and construction: walrus hide laced with gut thongs, but the hunters had mounted a 25-horsepower Evinrude motor on the back. Modern plastic orange floats lay in the bottom of the boat, alongside brass harpoons, modern rifles, and unruly coils of rope. For days the incongruous juxtaposition of steel and hide, harpoon and Evinrude, remained in my head.

A few days later at Nome we got a brief shore leave. I wandered out on the tundra where I was attacked by so many mosquitoes that I had to put my jacket over my face to be able to breathe. I twisted my ankle while trying to hike across a swampy field of tundra tussocks, getting soaked in the process. I climbed on a gold dredge built around 1910 and felt the polish that thousands of hands had imparted to the wooden stair railings. I participated in the annual Fourth of July raft race—a drunken melee that finished near midnight—marveling that the sun was still streaming down on us so late at night. I wandered into a Front Street bar and drank with the locals. The weather, the waves, and the powerful land had already begun imperceptibly seeping into my soul until I knew that I needed to stay and learn more about this place. My initial attraction may have been a young man's desire for adventure but I sensed there was clearly more to be found in the Arctic if one could learn to look and listen.

I have spent most of the intervening years trying to do just that. Too often the histories and the novels I have read, the TV documentaries and movies I have seen, served up cliché and myth, with two basic story lines dominating. One is the harsh-but-exquisite-wilderness story, wherein visitors are challenged by distance, blizzard, and mosquitoes, but are ultimately rewarded with beauty and solitude. The other is the bad-place-to-live story, in which arctic life is tough and darkness and isolation lead to madness, alcoholism, drug abuse, and violence. Neither story is wrong, but each misses what is to me a more compelling story: the interplay between a beautiful, frigid, and inhospitable land and its spirited people.

To understand that bond, we needed to get out there. When my six companions and I decided to travel across northern Alaska and Canada on

This *umiak*, a traditional whaling boat wrapped in walrus hide with hand-carved wooden paddles, blends old and new with its steel screws, modern float, and black nylon rope.

snowmobiles in the winter of 2007, we picked a route that ran through as many historic and significant places as possible. By actually standing where the old adventurers stood, while recalling the old stories, we hoped to get closer to something unique and elusive—call it the soul of the Arctic. Perhaps we would even come to understand how we had been drawn to the North, why we had chosen to stay, and how we fit into the larger sweep of northern history.

Of course the Artic is not frozen in time. The newest arctic story is climate change. Just when I arrived in the North, its climate started to warm. The transformation has been slow and almost imperceptible in places, but a large body of evidence confirms it is real. In media reports, and perhaps even in the minds of some Arctic dwellers, there is the idea that warming will take the sharp edge off a cold and hostile place, softening it and making it more like the rest of the world. For instance, the Arctic Ocean, currently inimical to shipping, might become another Baltic Sea as it loses all of its summer sea ice in the next two decades. These climate-driven changes have rekindled interest in the Arctic worldwide. More than ever, people—including many who have never been there and may never go—want to know the arctic story. Perhaps they fear that the Arctic might soon disappear, that its essential qualities will evaporate.

I don't think so. It may get a little warmer and milder but ice, snow, cold, and darkness will remain part of the arctic story for many years to come. The soul of the Arctic, if it has one, will continue to leave a unique mark on the people who make their lives there. As many of the classic tales retold here will illustrate, while technology and commerce have already drawn the modern Arctic closer to the rest of the world, what we saw during our SnowSTAR expedition taught us that some things never change. So, like many of the old stories ours has ice and snow, wind and cold, but it also includes the smiles of students in distant villages, strange diamond mines out on the tundra, satellite phones and CNN, snow knives, and six good companions.

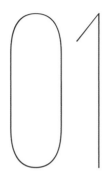

TRACKS NORTH

We thought our expedition would be about finding The Soul of the Arctic. What hubris! We should have known that it would end up being about practical things. How much gas do we have? Are our clothes warm enough? Did the handle fall off the camera? Can we fix it? Very soon into the trip we were forced to admit that our original goal was too vague and pompous. The soul of a place has to seep in, if it does so at all, like a marinade, unnoticed. Look for it and it's gone. So instead we agreed we would focus on getting from Point A to Point B—Point A being Fairbanks, Alaska, and Point B being Baker Lake, Nunavut.

The plan was simple: start in Fairbanks; drive snowmobiles to Hudson Bay. Our constraints along the way were equally simple: don't run out of gas or food. It turns out the limited number of towns and villages between Fairbanks and Hudson Bay provided few choices: a southerly path across Great Slave Lake or a northerly trajectory across Great Bear Lake. We chose the latter. Deciding where to end up on Hudson Bay was also easy. Tales of terribly rough moraine rock south of Baker Lake kept us well to the north. Our timing was heavily restricted, too. We needed about two months for the journey. Snow would start melting in May, but the dark and cold of midwinter would not give way to the returning sun until the beginning of March, so that's when we would leave.

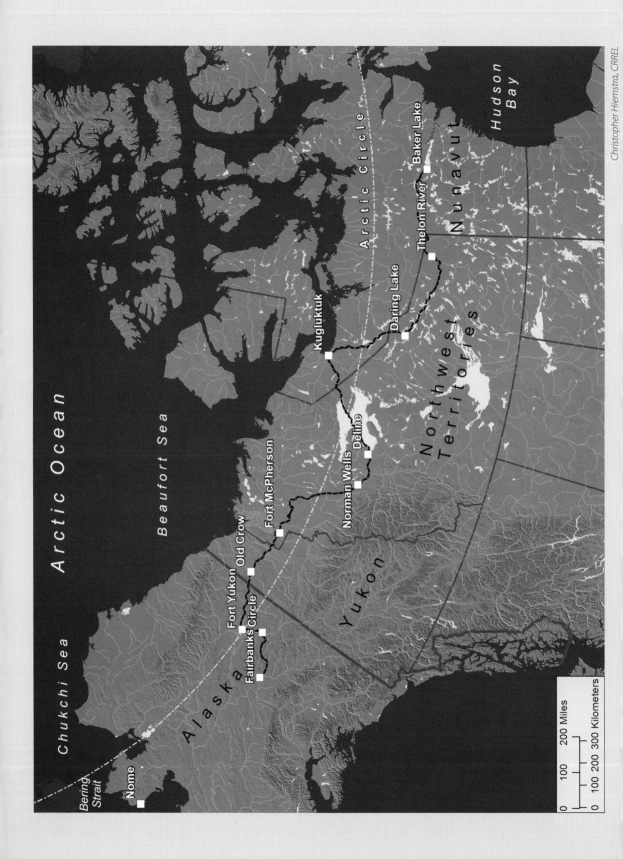

Arctic Ocean

Chukchi Sea

Beaufort Sea

Bering Strait

Hudson Bay

Arctic Circle

Nunavut

Northwest Territories

Yukon

Alaska

Nome

Fairbanks

Circle

Fort Yukon

Old Crow

Fort McPherson

Norman Wells

Deline

Kugluktuk

Daring Lake

Thelon River

Baker Lake

0	100	200 Miles
0	100	200	300 Kilometers

AS IS SO OFTEN THE CASE, the idea for a trek across a bleak frozen wilderness surfaced in a warm place: the back room of Jon Holmgren's machine shop. Jon and I met the first summer I arrived in Fairbanks, 1981. A lanky twenty-five-year-old living at the Sandvik House, the local hangout for mountain climbers, Jon was renting the closet behind the stairs as a bedroom. I was a new graduate student looking for climbing partners and we hit it off immediately. Our first big climb together was a winter ski ascent of Mt. Sanford, a 16,237-foot glacier-covered volcano in southcentral Alaska. High on the peak, when a third member of our expedition became ill and things looked grim, I first learned that Jon was calm in a crisis and wise beyond his years. We got our sick partner down the mountain intact and went on to climb several more big Alaska mountains, cementing a thirty-year friendship.

Growing up in Fairbanks, Jon showed an early interest in things mechanical, but he's tried his hand at a number of professions over the years. A high school summer job crushing rocks and assaying minerals for a local mining exploration firm led to staking mining claims, then to building drill pads in the Alaska Range, and eventually to running a gold mine in western Alaska. Along the way, Jon picked up a degree in geophysics. When the two of us took physics classes together at the University of Alaska, I learned that in addition to being a solid climbing partner, he was also the smartest guy in the room.

Some years back Jon was running a car shop, fixing mostly Subarus, and after he had sufficiently beaten up his hands at that job, I was able to entice him to come to work with me as a snow scientist. He developed a radar that could measure snow depths, as well as several other specialized snow instruments. But the mind-numbing tedium of writing scientific papers and proposals was not really his thing. So he built a big shop in Fox, Alaska, and began a career as a machinist. Jon now has a worldwide reputation for making top-notch specialty scientific equipment such as permafrost drills. His shop is a magnet for some of the most interesting Alaskans I know. On a recent summer day, a pilot from Coldfoot came by needing a camera mount for his small bush plane, a miner showed up with a broken hydraulic piston, a master

Jon Holmgren, machinist, mechanic, miner, geophysicist, traveler, and arctic philosopher.
D. Solie.

carpenter was building a riverboat in the back of the shop, and a constant stream of people stopped by to ask the best way to fix, build, or modify their respective cars, contraptions, and inventions.

In Jon's small office we hatched plans for the expedition. They grew from our shared desire to travel through the Arctic doing more than just measuring snow. All of our previous trips had been science-driven expeditions, with extensive data-gathering quotas that required both fast traveling and dull, repetitive work. Long before the trip we would choose equally spaced points along a route, each representative of surrounding landscape, which in most cases meant they were flat, boring spots devoid of cultural or historic interest. At each site, we would spend hours measuring the snow depth, density, and crystal properties, with our heads down in the snow rather than looking at our surroundings. I had started these studies decades earlier during my doctoral dissertation. My goal was to understand the role of snow in climate, particularly in the Arctic where it lingers on the ground for seven to ten months of the year. As the world became increasingly aware that a warming climate was altering the arctic environment, these snow studies had taken on a new sense of urgency and importance, and the results of the work made their way into computer models designed to predict global warming.

Intellectually, these working trips were satisfying but both of us were craving a richer, fuller journey. Steeped in the stories of the men and women who shaped the history of the Arctic and whose lives, in turn, were defined by the place, we wanted to understand their motivations. Jon summed it up succinctly: "This time, we need to see more than just snow. We need to stand in historic places and linger in towns and talk to the people. This trip needs to be about the Arctic, not science." I knew he was right.

That night it was decided. I would handle obtaining funding and research the route. Jon would cover the hard-core logistics, including choosing snowmobiles, figuring out where we would need gas and food caches, and how we would deal with mechanical breakdowns. It would be the longest snowmobile traverse either of us had ever done. The trip was on.

There was no question the next addition to the group would be Glen Liston. Along with Jon, Glen had been on every other snowmobile expedition I had organized. We had been in graduate school together in Alaska, though Glen was now living in Fort Collins, Colorado, where he is a research scientist. While I would love to be known as the strong silent type, hero of so many movies, I talk too much. Glen, however, is the real thing, going about expedition business without fuss or fanfare, and with very few words. Like Jon and me, Glen had come to arctic expeditions by way of mountain climbing, mostly steep ice in the Canadian Rockies. His resume also included a yearlong stint at the South Pole, where I suspect he was known as the most solid and unflappable of all the station personnel. Occasionally, in the tent on a cold night we could get Glen to tell us what it was like to work outside in real cold at 100°F below zero, or to join the elite South Pole 300° club. Membership requires enduring a sauna at more than 200°F, then running outside into –100°F weather, naked except for a single sock to be worn wherever the initiate sees fit.

Unlike most field hands, Glen keeps his gear in immaculate condition and is perhaps the most organized person I know. Where my zippers have a piece of parachute cord tied to them so I can pull on them wearing mittens, Glen's have an intricate Turk's Head lanyard, its color chosen to complement the color of his parka. In his kit, everything has a place and is put back as soon as he is done using it. With his penchant for order, we had come to rely on Glen as the loadmaster on our past expeditions. Many a time I had packed a sled in the morning only to have Glen come along and pull another twelve inches of slack out of tie-down ropes I thought were tight. While both Jon and I must sadly own up to having lost items out of our sleds on long trips, Glen never has.

Quiet, competent, squared-away, Glen is able to stay neat in ways the rest of us cannot. On a 1997 winter expedition down the Kuparuk River, we had been out six weeks, much of the time in cold, windy weather. A television crew was planning to meet us near Prudhoe Bay on the last day of the trip for filming. That morning, as on the forty previous mornings, we got out of our tents and congregated for breakfast around the cook stove. While everyone else was wearing the same grungy and worn parkas as the day before, Glen appeared in a spotless white anorak, tastefully trimmed in fur. How he had managed to keep the garment so dazzlingly clean during the rough and tumble of the previous six weeks amazed us almost as much as the sudden appearance of the anorak itself.

The next two members we asked to join the expedition were Dan Solie and Henry Huntington. Dan had grown up in Fairbanks like Jon, one of three boys in a family that did a lot of hunting and fishing. In high school he started climbing mountains, which led to his working on glacier research projects. In 1982, we measured the flow speed of glaciers on the west flank of Mt. Wrangell, a volcano in southcentral Alaska. The following year, we returned to the mountain to sample the fumarolic gases in its active North Crater. This foray turned into a near-death experience that cemented our friendship.

Mt. Wrangell is 14,163 feet high, which makes it the seventeenth tallest mountain in Alaska. Unlike the fourteen-thousand-foot peaks in Colorado, Mt. Wrangell's upper reaches are covered by glaciers and snowfields, with a polar climate even in the middle of summer. Occasionally, the jet stream blows directly across the summit. The mountain itself is huge: eight times the bulk of Mt. Rainier in Washington state, although it's about the same height. Within the summit plateau, which is actually an ice-filled caldera four miles across, the North Crater is a vapor- and ice-filled pit, about a half mile in diameter and several hundred feet deep. Super-heated steam roars out of black holes in the bottom of this crater, filling it with poisonous chlorine gas. In the summer of 1983 Dan and I flew up to the summit of the mountain with breathing tanks, climbing ropes, ice axes, and specialized glassware designed to capture the effluent from the fumaroles for chemical analysis. Wearing the tanks and rubber face masks, we descended into the inferno. Working rapidly down to the bottom of the crater (our tanks lasted only thirty minutes) we collected our samples by capping a small fumarole with the glassware. The larger fumaroles nearby roared like jet engines. Visibility was nil, in part because steam was swirling around the bottom of the crater, and in part because our masks had fogged in the cold air. Still, I could see that Dan was gazing about like he had arrived in Hell, to which the place bore a striking resemblance. Worse, long before we were done, the timing buzzer on my breathing pack went off, indicating I had five minutes to exit the crater. Reluctant to leave, it was Dan that pushed me up the snow slope. Dan is five feet nine inches tall, not much taller than me, but he has a barrel-chest twice the size of mine, and thick powerful arms. It wasn't hard for him to hustle me up the slope.

Glen Liston, of the Arctic and Antarctic, relaxes in the cook tent.

Our real problems started once we arrived at the crater rim and called the helicopter for pick up. The pilot landed, but as we started to load our gear, he yelled over the roar of the turbine engine and the fumaroles that due to the high altitude he could only take one of us at a time. We hastily sorted gear, but when I tried to get Dan on board, he insisted I should go first. I jumped aboard. The pilot dropped down to the eight-thousand-foot level of the mountain, where I jumped out, then he headed back up to the summit. I expected them back in fifteen minutes, but no sooner had the helicopter passed over the summit than the mountain was capped over by a lenticular cloud, an evil-looking plume signifying whiteout and windy conditions.

Five long hours later, well after I had concluded that the pilot had crashed and that he and possibly Dan were dead on the summit snowfields, I heard the sound of a helicopter coming not from above, but from the valley below. It was Dan and the pilot. They were alive and I was saved: my plight had only been marginally better than theirs, for I was thirty miles of tangled spruce forest away from the nearest road, which was on the far side of the unfordable Copper River. Moreover, by the time they returned it was snowing and the only tent and stove we had were in Dan's pack.

Once safely back at the helicopter base, Dan told his tale. As he heard the helicopter coming back after dropping me off, the mountain capped over with clouds. This took less than five minutes. He could hear the helicopter getting closer, then farther away. Next he heard it shut down somewhere in the fog and blowing snow. At fourteen thousand feet restarting a helicopter is difficult, but the pilot had little choice since he was low on fuel. At the same time, the wind shifted and started blowing chlorine gas over the crater rim toward where Dan was waiting with the gear. He had to move. He started out, pulling a sled across the vast snowfields of the caldera in a virtual whiteout, not sure which direction to go. But then fortune smiled on him. The pilot came up on the same frequency as Dan's radio and asked what they should do. Dan asked the pilot to fire off his shotgun (kept in the helicopter for bear protection). Taking a compass bearing on the sound, he started post-holing through the deep snow, towing all the gear, including the precious science samples. Periodically asking the pilot to fire off another round, Dan made his way toward the helicopter over a period of about four hours, occasionally having to stop when the weather got too severe for him to move ahead.

As the helicopter emerged from the fog and whiteout in front of Dan, the lenticular cloud ripped open above them revealing a startling blue sky. The pilot yelled, "Get in!" and hit the starter switch. Miraculously, the engine sputtered then fired to life. Before Dan was even belted-in or had his headphones on, the pilot took off straight up into the blue hole overhead. Shouting, "What's north of us?" over the sound of the screaming engine, he banked north into the clouds. Fortunately, Dan knew the mountain well and directed the pilot to the northeast, where there were no peaks higher than the summit caldera and they would have a decent shot at getting clear of the mountain in the fog. Trusting to luck they flew blindly for several miles and then began to descend, very quickly dropping out of the bottom of the clouds into clear air space. Cautiously edging toward the north and west, they then circled around and made their way back to me under the cloud deck. With that experience as a bond, Dan was a natural to go on the trip, despite his being a novice at driving a snowmobile.

Henry Huntington was also a novice snowmobile driver at the start of the trip, and new to what was otherwise a group of old friends. Henry and I had collaborated on several scientific papers, attended a number of meetings together, and over a couple of years found that we shared a similar quirky sense of humor. Henry had had an impressive collegiate career, studying at Princeton, where he rowed crew (what else?), then doing his graduate work in arctic social science at Cambridge. Lest his aristocratic academic background suggest that he was unsuited for an expedition, I knew that he had traveled along much of the Alaska arctic coast in a wood and canvas canoe, a journey that sounded thoroughly cold and miserable. He had also lived in Barrow for five years. With his credentials, Henry could have chosen to locate anywhere, and study or work at just about anything, but something about the polar regions had captured his heart. From Barrow, he had moved south, but only as far as Anchorage. We would be relying on Henry to connect us to the folks in the towns and villages, and to keep us from making any social blunders while visiting people along the way.

Dan Solie, physicist, canoe racer, climber, and stout heart in a tough situation.

What I did not know before this expedition was that behind Henry's educated exterior lurked a mind that seemed to run on puns, rhymes, and doggerel. After dinner we would find that he had been whiling away the long hours on his snowmobile making up and memorizing ribald poems commemorating the events of the previous day. Lying back on his sleeping bag in the tent, Henry would reel off his poem with great solemnity, leaving us all in stitches. Sadly, his skill in tying down sled loads was not as impressive. The few times he managed to get underway in the morning without Glen redoing his load, he invariably ended the day by reporting the loss of some strategic piece of gear: a large propane bottle, a component of our cook kit, the better part of five gallons of much needed gasoline. In the last case, he did retain the gas jug itself, which we found empty and trailing behind his sled at the end of a forty-foot rope.

Henry Huntington desperately tries to retain fifty lines of poetry after riding a kidney-punishing snowmobile all day. *H. Huntington*

Three other members rounded out our expedition. Arvids Silis and Chris Derksen are Canadian. From the beginning, we knew the expedition needed to be binational. Arvids and Chris, both snow scientists with Environment Canada in Toronto, had been doing research at Daring Lake in the middle of the Barrenlands of the Northwest Territories for several years. They were trying to understand how to best interpret the information provided by satellites about the properties of arctic snow. They were experienced hands, keen to make a long traverse. The route we had chosen went right through the heart of the area where they were having the most difficulty interpreting the satellite results, so it wasn't hard for Chris to convince his bosses that this was a great opportunity to collect comprehensive data in the middle of their most problematic territory. So we would end up doing a little science after all (see "Changes North" on page 12). A library search suggested ours would be the first scientific measurements of snow cover in the area. We planned to rendezvous with Arvids and Chris at Daring Lake about halfway through the trip.

Chris and I had met several years earlier at a scientific meeting and found we had complementary research interests and outlooks on life. Easygoing and relaxed, he was the youngest member of the group by nearly fifteen years, but he fit in well, even down to his taste for B-rated action videos. His companion from many arctic campaigns, Arvids, was my age, but it did not take long to realize that he was a lot tougher than me. An avid triathlete, Arvids also seemed to have antifreeze for blood. None of us could recall seeing him wearing more than a thin red pile jacket, regardless of the temperature or the wind, during the entire trip. Tireless, always cheerful, but of few words, in the end Arvids was voted the Hardman of the Journey. Both Canadians received the Drink Us Under the Table award for their capacity to consume beer.

BALLAD OF THE ARCTIC SCIENCE BANDITS

Henry Huntington wrote this as we were transiting Great Bear Lake in the Northwest Territories. It commemorates some difficulties we experienced related to bad advice we had received about the type of visas we needed to enter Canada. The threat of jail and deportation was real.

A group of scientists called SnowSTAR
Wanted to drive snowmachines very far
So they sallied forth
To the Canadian North
To see what lay over thar.

At first everything went just fine
On the Quest Trail, Yukon, and Porcupine
The passports were stamped
The schoolkids were amped
And they sped up the Mackenzie in line.

Then they reached the lake of the Bear
And O what a change they had there
A permit they hadn't
Immigration was maddened
No more could they travel without care.

Next stop was the RCMP
And the end to their rogue science spree
Their machines were impounded
Their hopes all confounded
Exoneration was just not to be.

First to trial was good Doctor Sturm
"Not guilty" said he loud and firm
But the evidence weighed
The judge wasn't swayed
And gave Matthew a seven-year term.

Next was the accomplice named Glen
Who had dug snow pits again and again
So he copped a plea
He'll be out in three
If he behaves in the Kugluktuk pen.

Then came the turn of poor Jon
Whose luck it seemed had all gone.
"I'm just the mechanic"
Cried he in a panic
But now he is also a con.

The magnets and compass did in Dan
The Mounties suspected his plan
Though he said that his goal
Was just finding the Pole
He's now serving time in the can.

Henry was the last one in court
In vain did he look for support
The judge wasn't happy
"Social science is crappy
You'll do hard time in Radium's Port."

So ends the tale of the team
And the journey that had been their big dream
The moral is clear
You must bureaucrats fear
No matter how good your outreach and theme.

THE SNOWSTAR EXPEDITION did not start out as a scientific mission, but because we would be traversing 2,500 miles of wilderness for which very little information about snow was available, we could not resist the chance to gather new data. Our trip also coincided with the fourth International Polar Year (IPY; 2007–2009), an all-out international push by thousands of scientists to study both polar regions. The overall goal of the IPY was to determine whether and how the world's frozen areas—the "cryosphere"—are changing, and how those changes might be affecting the rest of the planet. Being snow scientists, our narrower question was, "Is the arctic snow cover changing, and if so what will those changes mean?"

How snow in the Arctic could affect the climate of Florida or Bangladesh may not be obvious, but two properties of snow make it critical to the global climate: it reflects solar energy exceedingly well (sending up to ninety percent back into space) and

it insulates the ground as effectively as a goose-down quilt. These qualities can play against each other—the former promotes cooling of the climate, the latter warming of the permafrost—depending on the depth and nature of the snow cover. Both snow and ice live a precarious existence, however, because even near the poles mean annual temperatures are not far below freezing. A little less snow and ice means a little less reflection of solar rays, and a little more warming of the planet, but locally perhaps cooling of the permafrost.

The radically different geography of the polar regions makes the impact on people of changes in the snow cover very different at either end of the Earth. The Antarctic is a vast continent, centered on the South Pole, where snow has built up over millennia to form the largest and thickest glaciers and ice sheets in the world. But people, other than researchers and a few tourists, have never really lived there. In the Arctic, where an ocean is centered on

Opposites at the ends of the Earth: the Arctic is an ice-choked sea ringed by land, while the Antarctic is an ice-bound continent surrounded by tumultuous oceans. *John Walker, The Living Earth, Inc./ Earth Imaging.*

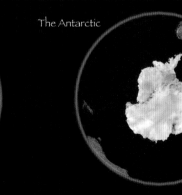

The Arctic The Antarctic

the North Pole and the land is pushed just far enough south so that much of the snow and ice melts away in summer, life is abundant. The snowmelt trickles into innumerable swamps that feed vast lakes and mighty rivers teeming with schools of fish. Summer rain seeps into soils that nurture plants, which sustain vast herds of caribou, large flocks of birds, and hundreds of other animal species. The arctic life forms are tough and scrappy to match their vigorous environment, and because so many plants and animals are there, people have also called the Arctic home for thousands of years.

Now those people, and many others, are worried about the changes sweeping the Arctic as the whole world warms. In the lower latitudes, the effects of warming may be subtle so far, but in the Arctic they are dramatic and hard to miss. And far from being a purely scientific issue or political hot potato, the changes in the North mean the snow, ice, and permafrost on which arctic residents depend for travel, hunting, and sustenance are being rapidly altered. Our measurements would help unravel what was happening to the snow and why.

Consequently, on the trip we made measurements at dozens of points along the route to document the snow and ice conditions. We sampled the snow for mercury and soot, both pollutants with important ramifications for humans and climate change. We cored the ice of the lakes we crossed, measured the water equivalent of the snow pack, did snow depth transects, and measured the snow properties in snow pits, including using a near-infrared camera to document the grain size and stratigraphy for satellite studies. Since the trip we have used these measurements to refine interpretations of satellite data on snow for this part of the Arctic. ■

An Iñupiat seal hunter, Bobby Sarren, is standing on shorefast ice at the edge of the Chukchi Sea. As arctic sea ice diminishes, shorefast ice is no longer reliable or safe, threatening subsistence activities such as sealing and whaling.

Jon Holmgren drills through the ice on Great Bear Lake to measure its thickness. *H. Huntington.*

Bad Boys of the Arctic Arvids Silis (left) and Chris Derksen of Environment Canada.
H. Huntington.

The last member of our team was Dave Andersen, who had made four major snowmobile trips across the Barrenlands. Dave agreed to be our base camp manager, though what possessed him to volunteer for such a thankless job is hard to fathom. We planned to talk to Dave in Fairbanks each evening by satellite phone, and send him trail dispatches and photographs to post on our website for the several dozen schools around Alaska and Canada that would be following our progress. More than anything, Dave was a calm voice at the far end of the satellite connection that anchored us to the "real world."

Despite all that we had in common, it wasn't until halfway through the trip that the real thread binding the eight of us together became apparent to me. Clearly we shared a desire for adventure, but our careful planning and preparation seemed designed to eliminate any potential for things to get out of hand. We also all liked the cold, but our obsessive attention to our clothing and gear was meant to reduce physical discomfort to the bare minimum. So if neither adventure nor cold was what drew us together for the trip, then what was? When Arvids and Chris joined us at Daring Lake the connection began to come into focus. They talked about getting "out on the land," an expression they had picked up working with Inuit guides in eastern arctic Canada.

"Out on the land" meant camping, and traveling, and sightseeing, but also so much more. It meant confronting adversity and hardship with grace. It meant connecting with a past time when only the wild places existed, a time before cities, iPhones, and e-mail. It meant retelling and reliving the history, thereby honoring the heroic feats of those who had come before us. Getting out on the land was all about understanding our place in the natural and human history of the Arctic. And it was about forming bonds of friendship that were made of stronger stuff than the ones that can be forged in towns and malls. Each member of the expedition had been making tracks North throughout his life because of a deep need to get out on the land. And that we did, leaving from Fairbanks on March 16, 2007, perhaps hoping to find the soul of the Arctic, but satisfied if we could just make it to Baker Lake, Nunavut, intact.

Dave Andersen, base camp manager for the expedition. *Dave Andersen.*

02 ROSEBUD REALITIES

Leaving Fairbanks we followed the Yukon Quest trail. While much of the trail is historic, the part we were on was developed in the 1980s for a wilderness sled-dog race and is now heavily traveled by mushers, skiers, and hikers—a considerable contrast with the lightly used historic trails we followed later in the trip. Still, our schooling in tough trails began less than fifty miles from Fairbanks. On the North Fork of the Chena River we encountered nasty overflow ice that stopped us dead. When we tried to climb over Rosebud Summit, double sleds, heavy gear, and a mindset not quite ready for the trail combined to make the steep ascent a struggle. We later crossed paths with a well known race-dog musher who gave us an impromptu lecture on the perils of Rosebud. This section of trail deepened our respect for modern-day extreme outdoor enthusiasts, but also left us wondering how these sporting exploits were connected to the survival-motivated mushing done by hunters, trappers, and explorers in the past.

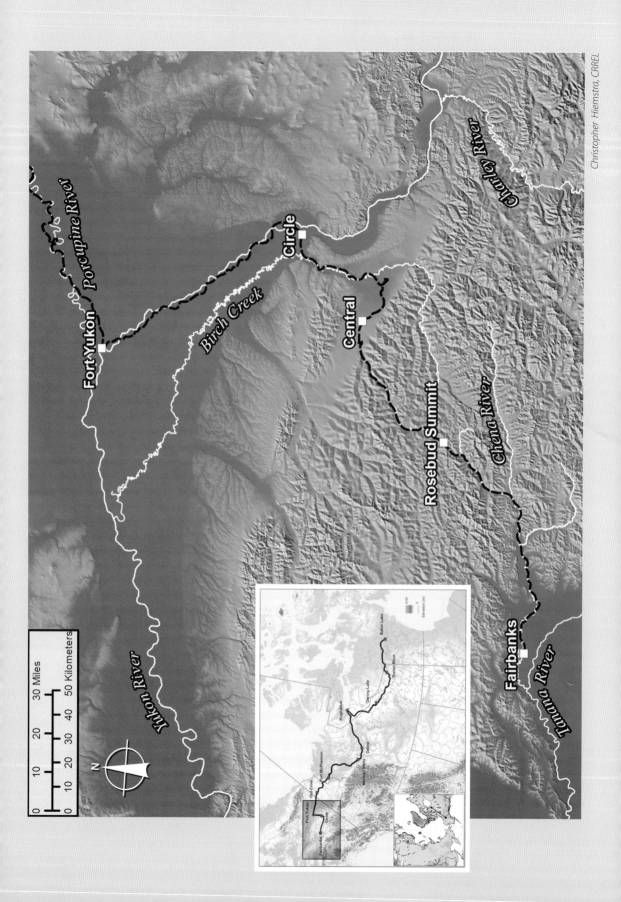

MARCH 16, 9:00 PM:

Everything was packed. Hundreds of gallons of gas had been sealed in red jugs. Food had been sorted into breakfasts, lunches, and dinners, packed into separate black plastic tubs tied on the sleds. Passports were tucked away in Ziploc bags, and each of us had delivered to the staging area two duffle bags, one with clothing and personal gear, the other holding a sleeping bag. I had issued everyone a shining new two-liter stainless steel thermos that we would fill with boiling water every morning so we would not get dehydrated in the cold, dry air. It was time to leave. Several spouses and a few colleagues from work were there, but it was a low-key send-off. Only weeks later we learned that a picture of us departing had made the front page of the *Daily News-Miner*, the local paper. It must have been a slow news day.

Our route out of town was up the frozen Chena River. First, though, we had to cross a busy road then drop down a steep river-bank. Dave, our base camp manager, and another friend, Dick Flaherty, were traveling with us for the first two days. They reconnoitered, then signaled they had found a way down the bank. We were off. I was acutely aware that neither Dan nor Henry had much experience driving a snowmobile and worried that one of them might roll his machine down the embankment, but they both dropped onto the river ice like old pros.

Henry fills six-gallon fuel jugs before the start of the trip.

The river trail we followed all that day is both old and new. It is old in the sense that the rivers of Alaska have always been highways, natural passages through the dense forests. Natives, explorers, and miners traveled Alaska's waterways using boats in summer and dog sleds and snowshoes in winter. The Chena River trail is new in the sense that it is now also the Yukon Quest International Sled Dog Race trail. This thousand-mile race held each February runs from Fairbanks to Whitehorse in Yukon Territory, Canada. The Yukon River was the main artery of commerce during Gold Rush days, and the Quest trail honors that historic transportation corridor, but some of the race route, including a good part of the Fairbanks to Circle stretch, had to be patched together from maps and aerial over-flights in 1983. The Quest organizers were trying to develop a race that was simpler, less expensive to run, and had more of a wilderness flavor than the older and more famous Iditarod Dog Sled Race. A key feature of the Quest race is that the mushers must care for their own dogs: no dog handlers are waiting at the rest stops like on the Iditarod (see "Quest's Older Cousin—The Iditarod" on page 22).

Most of the Quest trail runs either on or alongside the Yukon River, so it is generally quite flat, which is not to say the trail is boring. The river ice can be a jumble of blocks or treacherously thin, with patches of open water hidden by snow. The mushers race around the clock, frequently running in the dark at temperatures that can drop to –50°F or lower. In four places the route leaves the river and climbs above tree line: at King Solomon's Dome near the old gold rush town of Dawson, and at American, Eagle, and Rosebud Summits near Fairbanks. A number of dramas have taken place at Eagle Summit, a wind-swept stretch of alpine tundra with steep slopes leading down to forest on both sides. Particularly in the years when it comes at the end of the race, at least one dog team has balked at the climb and lay down in the snow. Sometimes the unfortunate musher managed to lead or drag his or her team to the top, but other times Eagle Summit was the end of the line and after having successfully covered more than eight hundred miles, the musher had to scratch.

The worst epic occurred the year before our trip. In February 2006, six mushers and eighty-nine dogs were trapped near Eagle Summit overnight in a blizzard. Visibility was less than a quarter-mile and the winds above fifty miles per hour. The mushers could not see the trail markers so they could neither advance nor retreat. Their only option was to huddle in their sled bags through the long bitter night. Their dogs became buried in snow and a tense survival situation unfolded. Because there are checkpoints on either side of the summit, race officials knew that something was terribly wrong and called in a rescue. The

Alaska Air National Guard helicopter returns from Eagle Summit with sled dogs rescued during the 2006 Yukon Quest. *Peter Kamper.*

next morning an Alaska Air National Guard HH-60 Pave Hawk helicopter flew into the difficult conditions at the summit and made five consecutive landings, loading and bringing off all the dogs and mushers without mishap.

For the 2007 race, the Quest crew had marked this section of trail more thoroughly, erecting a series of closely spaced, stout wooden tripods. Nonetheless, in our minds the evil reputation of Eagle Summit was well established. Our iron dogs were unlikely to lie down in the snow during the climb, but they might not be able to haul our heavy double-sled loads up to the top. If they spun out, we would have stuck sleds on a steep hill, a recipe for back-breaking work. Going down the hill's backside could be even more disastrous. Snowmobiles have good brakes, but there is a limit to the incline they can descend before starting to slide. Pulling two heavy sleds that want to push the snowmobile downhill adds the risk of jack-knifing. Then man, machine, and sleds can turn into one ugly tumbling mass. In preparation, we had worked out a system of rough-locking the sleds by running chain underneath them so they would not overtake the snowmobiles, but Eagle Summit still weighed heavily on us as we left Fairbanks. Little did we know that problems would show up much sooner.

QUEST'S OLDER COUSIN—THE IDITAROD

RELATIVELY FEW PEOPLE outside of Alaska have heard of the Yukon Quest sled-dog race, but many know about the Iditarod Trail Sled-Dog Race. Like the Quest, the Iditarod commemorates a historic era and a trail that ran about one thousand miles from Seward on the Gulf of Alaska, northward to the town of Iditarod, where gold was dis-covered in 1909. By 1911, Iditarod had become the largest city in Alaska with almost ten thousand inhabitants. With that many people, mail and freight ser-vices were needed during the winter, so a trail was cleared. Mushers driving teams of twenty dogs would pull sleds carrying half a ton of supplies up the trail, which was eventually extended all the way to Nome on the Bering Sea. As was the fate of so many trails in the North, though, with the arrival of the bush plane in the 1930s, maintenance on the trail stopped and the brush reclaimed it.

The trail's most famous moment came in 1925, when a diphtheria epi-demic threatened Nome. The near-est serum was 675 miles away in Anchorage, but winter aviation was still in its infancy and flying the serum in was impossible. Instead, the pre-cious package was sent up the newly completed Alaska Railroad to Nenana, where a relay of mushers took it down the Tanana River to the Yukon River, then followed the Iditarod Trail to Nome. Each leg of the run was given to the fastest local musher

premier musher, did the critical leg across Norton Sound, using his lead dog Togo. Gunnar Kaasen drove the final two legs into Nome through an eighty-mile-per-hour blizzard with his lead dog Balto. It took a total of six days to deliver the serum, a credible time even for modern mushers with plastic and aluminum sleds. The run garnered worldwide press coverage and the mushers got special gold medals. A bronze statue of Balto, erected a year later, still stands atop a rock outcrop in New York's Central Park.

The first modern Iditarod race was in 1973, although two shorter races were run in 1967 and 1969. Dorothy Page of Wasilla conceived the idea and enlisted the help of Joe Redington Sr., a musher from the Knik area, to organize the race. Twenty-two mush-ers finished in 1973. Today, mushers from all over the world vie for the first place prize of $69,000 and a new pick-up truck. The first musher to Iditarod, about the halfway point, wins a pickup and three thousand dollars in gold nuggets. Prior to 2011, Lance Mackey won the race four years in a row. His father Dick Mackey had won it in 1978 with what may be the most dramatic finish ever. For a thousand miles, Dick had battled Rick Swenson for the lead. The two were tied as they hit Front Street in Nome, where Mackey, look-ing like a wild man, began sprinting to victory, just managing to get his lead dog's nose over the finish line before

Orange-and-black-painted lath still marked the Quest Race trail out of Fairbanks as we headed up the Chena River. The first fifty miles of the trail parallel Chena Hot Springs Road, which I drive many times during the winter to a little cabin I have out near the end of the road. And yet, less than twenty miles from Fairbanks we were lost. What we thought was the trail deposited us in the front yard of a trucking company just off the roadway. While the others idled their machines, I walked over and asked the owner if he knew where the Quest trail was.

One of the new tripods on Eagle Summit. *D. Solie.*

With a bemused smile he said, "Yeah. It's back down the trail about a quarter mile. Head back into the woods, then bear right over the bridge that crosses the little creek." We got lost only a few more times that day before we turned up the West Fork trail toward my cabin, where we planned to spend the night.

The next morning we ate an oatmeal breakfast, then packed up and got underway. The trip down the West Fork of the Chena and back to the Quest trail was uneventful, though we saw a lot of overflow ice we hadn't noticed the night before in the dark. That should have been a warning. Also known as *aufeis*, overflow ice is the bane of winter travel in Alaska. As the season comes on, creeks and rivers freeze from the top down. When channels below the surface get plugged, flowing water blocked from emerging in one place will ooze out somewhere else, then freeze. This freeze-and-migrate pattern continues until a creek that is just ten feet wide and a foot deep in summer produces an ice sheet that stretches from one valley wall to the other.

If the overflow ice is flat and one approaches it with a little momentum, it is usually possible to slide across, though it is not unusual to go gently spinning around like a top. When the overflow ice is not flat, a snowmobile may hit an ice bump and ricochet off like a pinball, spinning and sliding out of

Punch it! Glen discovers overflow ice. *H. Huntington.*

control. A two-foot high wrinkle of overflow ice can be virtually impossible to surmount. But the worst is when oozing water has emerged into an area of snow on top of ice. Invisible at the surface, the water will seep along the base of the snow, saturating it and producing a kind of snow swamp. Several feet of slush may lie concealed beneath a pristine cover of snow or under a thin crust of shiny glare ice that looks solid. An unsuspecting driver will enter the area only to sink into the slush and come to a stop. Getting off the machine means getting soaked feet, not a pleasant prospect at −40°F. Once again the fix is miserable and backbreaking work.

We had gone only a few hundred feet up the North Fork of the Chena River when we found ourselves on wall-to-wall overflow ice. Only the top halves of the orange and black lath markers were sticking out of the ice, indicating the ice had thickened several feet since they were installed. The river is narrow at this point and in summer consists of pools bridged by shallow riffles. We rounded a bend and saw a frozen cascade about three feet high across the whole river. I gunned my machine and hit the cascade going about five miles per hour, but instead of climbing the small icy slope, I rebounded off to the left and slid gently into the snow bank. My sleds followed, spinning slowly around until they were backwards. When everything stopped, the front of my machine was against the back of my second sled. Dan, who was right behind me, had neither time to stop nor room to maneuver. He hit the ice cascade and rebounded, coming to rest tangled up with my sleds. One by one, that little wrinkle of overflow ice stopped all seven of us. When the slow-motion ballet of sliding and spinning sleds and machines was over, we all lay in a big tangle up against the riverbank. Fortunately, no damage was done.

Beyond the ice wrinkle we could see more half-inundated lathe, so we figured we still had to go that way, overflow ice or not. We were just about to try again when we heard someone yell: "Hey, what are you guys doing down there?"

On the high bank to our left was a man on cross-country skis. It turned out to be Bob, a local attorney and avid wilderness racer several of us knew. He pointed out a newer (and pretty obvious) set of Quest trail markers on the bank above the river and said, "The trail is up here. Where are you guys headed?"

When I answered, "across Alaska and Canada," I could see the wheels turning in his head: If these guys couldn't even get three hundred feet off the road system, how are they going to get across Canada?

Embarrassed, but needing to push on, we walked back to the jumble of our snowmobiles and sleds. Under Bob's skeptical eye, and with much slipping and sliding on the slick ice, we hauled our machines around until they were facing downstream, pushed them to get them started on the frictionless surface, then circled back up onto the proper trail. Somewhat chastened, but happy to be moving again, we headed up the North Fork. Our battle with overflow, however, was not done. Throughout the day, we kept coming upon patches of glare ice, often where the trail cut uphill to bypass gullies. There the overflow, a product of seeps and springs, was anything but level. Invariably, someone would hit one of these ice patches wrong and go sailing downhill into the snow below the ice. Several of us would then stop and help the driver get unstuck and back up on the trail. It was slow and painful progress.

The shadows were lengthening when we finally started the climb up to Rosebud Summit, 1,500 feet above the valley bottom. Rosebud is the pass from the Chena to the Birch Creek drainage, part of an extensive alpine ridge system that stretches from Fairbanks all the way to the Yukon River. As the trail emerges from the forest it steepens and narrows. Soon we came to a sixty-foot-long chute on a thirty-degree slope. At the base of the chute several people were working on a broken snowmobile laid over on its side. We chatted with them and learned they had been part of a larger group that climbed the hill about an hour ahead of us. We could see the chute was full of loose snow churned up by the passage of a dozen snowmobiles. Our approach line to the chute would have to be off-angle because of the broken-down machine. What we could not see yet was a snow-covered stump in the trail toward the chute. All these details would normally be of little consequence, but we were heavily loaded with seven snowmobiles and fourteen sleds, each weighing about a thousand pounds. We were about to be tested.

A different, subtler problem was at work, too. We were not yet trail-hardened. We had not mentally accepted the hard work that was the admission price for our journey. We were still thinking of our snowmobiles like our cars back home: jump in, drive to work or the store, motor back. Easy! How often did we have to push our cars out of a ditch, tip them back up onto their wheels after they had flipped over, or spin them around after they had careened off the road? On how many car trips had we shattered our windshields or bent a tie rod and had to hammer it straight with an axe? From past expeditions, we knew that all these things and more would happen as our snowmobile journey unfolded, but we were still clinging to the hope that our modern, car-like machines would power us over anything with minimal effort. We had our field clothes on, but we did not yet have a field mentality. The steep chute was going to change that very quickly.

I yelled, "I'll try first with a single sled," gunned my machine trying to get maximum momentum, hit the hidden stump, bounced left, lost speed, and got only halfway up the chute before my track started spraying loose snow grains and I came to a stop. There was no turning around on the steep hill, so we disconnected the sled, man-hauled it back down the trail, then backed the snowmobile down in reverse gear. Reconnecting the two, on my second try I went to the left. Same story. By then I was bathed in sweat and breathing hard from exertion. We dragged my snowmobile and sleds out of the way and then Jon tried the chute towing the big covered sled. The outcome was the same, but this time in backing down we managed to tip both the sled and snowmobile onto their sides. All hands turned out to right them. Before Jon's second attempt, we tried stomping a less-steep trail off to the left of the original trail. Wading through the thigh-deep snow to pack it down was exhausting, and of little value, as this attempt ended like the previous three.

Wrestling with snowmobiles and sleds below Rosebud Summit. *H. Huntington.*

By this time we had been at it for about two hours. We were all tired, frustrated, and I think all of us were wondering how, if we could not get up Rosebud, were we going to get up Eagle Summit or any number of other hills between Fairbanks and Hudson Bay.

Then in a very matter-of-fact way we all seemed to realize at about the same time that there was a job to be done and that doing it was the only way we were going to get up that hill and onward to Hudson Bay. The big parkas came off, the work gloves came out, and the aluminum shovels were taken off the sleds. We began to build a road by shoveling snow from the side of the trail into the trench the trail had become. As some of us shoveled, others packed. Someone got out a saw and cut the offending stump as low as possible. We moved the broken snowmobile out of the right-of-way so that our approach was straighter. We backed the snowmobiles down the trail to get a longer approach, and we positioned people alongside the steepest part of the chute so they would be ready to push if the driver showed signs of bogging down. All this took about an hour of hard work, but by then we had stopped worrying

One sled at a time, we blast up the chute. Dick Flaherty stands ready to push if needed.
H. Huntington.

Descending toward Birch Creek from Rosebud Summit. Eagle Summit is on the distant horizon. *H. Huntington.*

about the passing of time. We had all the time in the world. We could camp there and try tomorrow if it took that long. When we tried again, the first driver went right up, then the next and the next. Each of us made the trip twice, hauling one sled at a time, dropping the first at the summit of Rosebud and heading down to get the second. About four hours after arriving at the chute, everybody and all the equipment was at the top. It was windy and cold up there, especially since we had all worked up a sweat, but it felt good to be chilled by the wind. As it froze the sweat on my face, I felt somehow lighter, like I had left a lot of city baggage behind at the bottom of the chute, baggage I would not need for a couple of months. We were under way.

The long descent from Rosebud Summit to Birch Creek was unremarkable. The covered sled kept flipping over in the wind but with our newfound work ethic, we dealt with the problem quickly and easily. On Birch Creek near the Steese Highway we met up with the friends who would take Dave and Dick back to Fairbanks. After a quick goodbye, Dan, Glen, Jon, Henry, and I drove up the trail a few miles and camped in the last clump of spruce trees below Eagle Summit.

All through the night, I could hear the wind howling above the trees. Visions of mushers and dogs trapped by blowing snow punctuated my sleep. I awoke edgy and nervous but the night wind had disappeared, replaced by a still and sunny day, gleaming white. The race markers, festooned with frost feathers from the night winds, were so close together that you could almost touch the next one from the last. And as if that were not guidance enough, the tracks from the fifty mushers who had passed this way a couple of weeks before were still clear and easy to follow. We were not going to get lost in a blizzard. The snow was firm and hard. Pulling both sleds, I headed up the hill, finding I had ample power and traction. We were not going to get stuck either. Jon, pulling his heavier sleds, was right on my tail. In less time than it had taken us to get the shovels out of the sled the previous day, all five of us were on Eagle Summit.

While Jon and Glen dug out the rough-lock chains for the descent, I walked over the divide and down the far side. At this scene of so many mushing epics I expected a snow-covered cliff, but instead

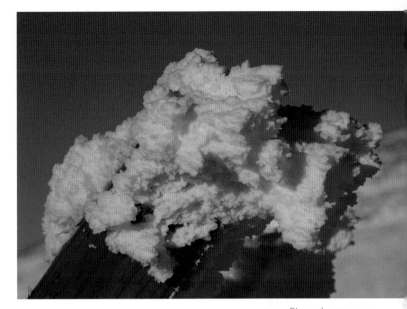

Rime plumes on a Yukon Quest trail marker.
H. Huntington.

found a drift with a modest cornice followed by a steep hill with a good run-out. It looked easy. Back on the summit, they had finished with the sleds, so I took off. I was down the hill in two minutes. In five more minutes I was back on the top with the set of chains, which were then installed on Jon's sleds. In less than an hour, we were all down. It had taken us an hour and a half in total to get over the dreaded Eagle Summit. Had we not wrestled with Rosebud the day before, we might have felt cocky. Instead, we felt relieved.

As we worked our way down Birch Creek and across the Yukon Flats over the next week, Rosebud and Eagle Summits lingered in our minds. Our appreciation for the dog mushers who race over these heights grew. After all, there were five of us and we had used teamwork and powerful machines to get over the hills. The mushers make their ascents solo. While we went over both summits in daylight, having slept well in between, the mushers are seriously sleep-deprived by the time they reach those points in the race, and they typically cross one or both summits in the dark. How they manage to get down Rosebud at all without serious accident and injury was a mystery to us. Those mushers are definitely made of tough stuff.

Later in the trip, we happened to meet up with William Kleedehn. He was leading the first leg of the inaugural running of the Dagoo 340, a sled-dog race from Eagle Plains on the Dempster Highway to Old Crow and back. We

William Kleedehn, Yukon Quest musher, in Old Crow.

had all read about this colorful character, a favorite with the press. Kleedehn, originally from Germany, had run the Yukon Quest ten times since 1990, placing second or third several times, and narrowly missing the win on at least one occasion. A big, robust man, Kleedehn had lost a leg in a motorcycle accident some years before, a handicap that is hard to detect when he is mushing or hiking. The overwhelming impression I had upon meeting him was, "Here is a guy as tough as the North." His massive and thickly veined hands looked like they stay warm even in the most biting cold without gloves, and his weather-beaten face looked like it had stared-down many a blizzard. He spoke with authority about mushing and life on the trail. I had read that he was a clever and wily racer, and I had a strong sense that in all other things he was a man who abhorred cant and pretense.

I asked him about Eagle and Rosebud Summits. A smile crossed his face. "Yes," he said with a mild accent, "Rosebud is the more difficult of the two." He knew of famous mushers, some who had won the Iditarod, who would not run the Quest trail race because of Rosebud. Too much hung in the balance for these "professionals." They might put together eight days of totally immaculate runs on the Quest, only to have it slip away due to an accident or a dog problem on Rosebud. They would not risk it.

I asked if he had had any memorable runs over Rosebud. Another smile crossed his face. He asked in a soft voice tinged with humor if I understood how the brake worked on a dog sled. It is a light aluminum contraption with springs and a couple of small carbide spikes mounted on the back of the sled, designed to be pushed like a pedal to slow the sled just enough to make the dogs stream out in a line. Not like the real brakes on car or snowmobile. His eyes lit up. "On Rosebud, one puts the brake down, then just holds on as the sled careens down a narrow steep tunnel of light from your headlamp. The sled whips around and ricochets off trees and overflow ice. The dogs run like crazy to stay ahead of the sled. It's wild!"

I wanted to ask Kleedehn more questions, but it was time for him to harness his dogs and get ready to start the second leg of the race. We said goodbye and wished him luck.

Why careen down an icy trail in the dark, risking injury? What's the attraction? The British mountain climber George Mallory's glib answer about Mt. Everest, "Because it is there," might serve. It's a challenge, a test of man and dog. Northerners admire tough, and winning the Quest is one definitive way to show that you are the toughest of the tough. But I stumbled on a deeper reason some years before our trip, one lazy summer day on the south bank of the Yukon River.

On that outing we had run my motorboat up the river from Circle toward Eagle, Alaska. My kids were young and they would get restless if we traveled too long, so we stopped at Biederman's cabin on the south bank across from the Kandik River. It was stiflingly hot and the old log cabin was dark and cool inside, a perfect refuge from the sun, the glare on the water, the clouds of mosquitoes, and the still thick air. Near the cabin was a log cache up on poles

Charlie Biederman with his mail sled, leaving Eagle for Circle about 1936. *Louise Biederman, Courtesy Eagle Historical Society & Museums.*

that had colorful fleece dog booties spilling out of a hole in the side, a vivid reminder that this was a checkpoint for the Yukon Quest race. Next to the cabin, hanging from a big birch tree was a rope swing, and there were many other signs that kids had spent a lot time here. As we explored the interior, old dishes, newspapers, books, and other relics spoke of a time when this was a full-time home.

Ed and Bella Biederman had lived in the cabin. Ed was a musher who had come to Alaska before the 1898 Gold Rush and soon found employment delivering mail along the Yukon by boat in summer and by dog sled in winter. His route ran from Eagle to Circle, about 160 miles each way. The family lived in Eagle some of the time, but spent summers at their cabin across from the Kandik River, fishing, putting up fish for dogs, and boarding dogs for other mushers. Ed's son, Charlie (1919–1995), started helping his dad deliver the mail by dog sled at an early age. The run took about a week each way, but with the cabin about halfway in between, they would get a nice break at home once each trip. When frostbite crippled Ed in 1935, Charlie took over the route. He kept the mail run until 1938, when a local bush pilot underbid him on the contract.

Sifting through the cabin's relics, I thought about what the Biedermans had done. Year after year without fanfare Ed and Charlie had made the heroic look normal. Through cold snaps of −60°F and blizzards that drifted in the trail, they dealt with overflow ice and open water every day. Without headlights, without satellite phones or GPS, and without modern clothing, they demonstrated their mettle, not by a single run over a Rosebud or Eagle Summit, but by repeated runs carrying the U.S. mail. In January 1995, Charlie Biederman traveled to Washington, D.C., to donate his father's twelve-foot hickory sled to the National Postal Museum, where it is now displayed. He died one month later.

While my kids amused themselves with some toys they had found in the cabin, I thought about how many times Bella must have worried about where her men were when they did not show up at the cabin on time, and her relief when they did. I thought about the tough runs in the cold and the dark and the glorious runs in the sun with snow sparkling on the river bluffs, when mushing up the river behind a strong team of dogs must have been the best job in the world. Connecting to this storied past was what sent modern mushers careening down Rosebud on a wildly bucking sled, and it was why we were here, too.

03

PORCUPINE HOSPITALITY

From Eagle Summit we continued down Birch Creek to the village of Circle, where the steep mountain terrain gives way to forested flats laced with lakes and creeks. At Circle we bought gas and left the Quest trail. From here, our path lay down the mighty Yukon River to Fort Yukon. There was no trail, so we made our way downriver picking out our own safe path. Two and a half days later we arrived at Fort Yukon, where we received a warm welcome. In addition to talking with most of the kids at the school, we were invited to the cabin of Earl Cadzow, a local resident, for salmon salad sandwiches on white bread. Earl then showed us the sights, including the grave of Archdeacon Stuck, a pioneering Episcopal minister and the first person to ascend Mt. McKinley. Next, the Alexander family came by and offered to let us use their cabin twenty miles up the Porcupine River. Finally, several citizens, recognizing that we were incapable of finding our way out of town with just verbal descriptions, guided us to the trail that ran up the Porcupine River to Old Crow. This was our first taste of northern hospitality, but hardly our last. Throughout the trip we found ourselves welcomed, aided, and entertained wherever we went, but perhaps nowhere more so than in Old Crow, a crossroads of northern history and cultures despite its having no actual road.

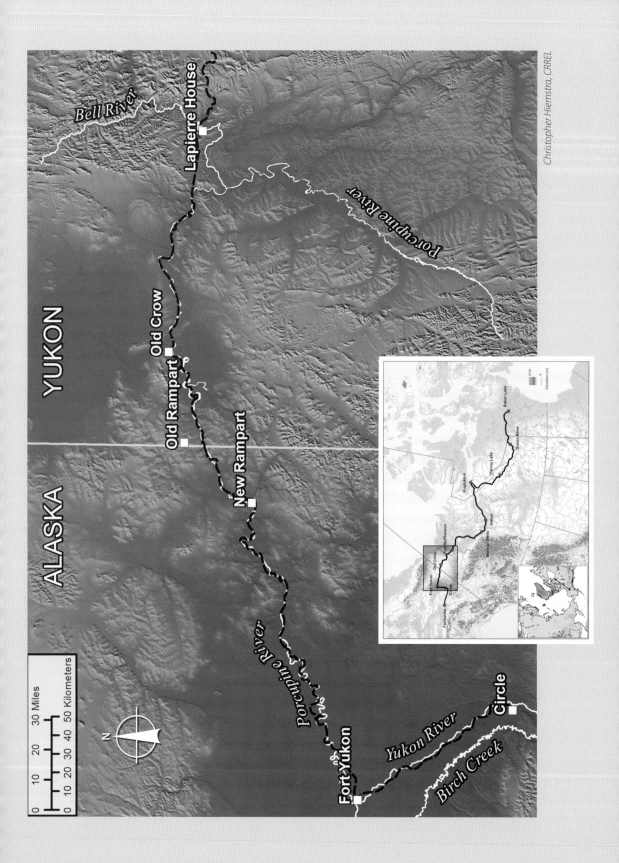

DAN'S SNOWMOBILE wasn't going anywhere. The clutch was toast. We would have to tow it into Old Crow, where we might have a chance of fixing it. Thus began another lesson in northern hospitality.

Skidoo snowmobile clutches have two plastic pucks that engage when the engine speed hits a predetermined level. Why the pucks aren't steel or something equally strong is unclear to me, but they are not. If the clutch manages to spin without engaging, frictional heat can build up, melting or deforming the pucks and rendering the clutch useless, which pretty much renders the machine useless, too. The pucks can only be replaced at the factory...not a useful option if you are on the Porcupine River, fifty miles out from Old Crow, which doesn't have a snowmobile repair shop anyway, let alone a factory repair service.

As soon as Jon diagnosed the clutch problem, we started rearranging our belongings to free up a sled, onto which we loaded the broken seven-hundred-pound machine. We then hitched this behind Jon's snowmobile and distributed Jon's other sled, plus the two sleds Dan had been pulling, between Henry, Glen, and me. The result was an odd-looking convoy of two snowmobiles nose-to-tail and three snowmobiles each pulling triple sleds that stretched a full forty feet behind.

Even as the sled reorganization was in progress, I was on the satellite phone trying to locate another clutch. The nearest Skidoo dealers were in Whitehorse, Fairbanks, Anchorage, and Hay River, all hundreds of miles from Old Crow. None had a new clutch in stock, and even if they had, getting it to Old Crow, serviced by only a few flights a week, posed problems. The best I could do was to find a guy in Whitehorse who thought he might have a used clutch in his bone yard, but wasn't sure. Calls to the Skidoo factory toll-free number never got past a soothing computerized voice that put me on an expensive satellite phone hold. A week and a half into the trip and we were looking at a week of waiting, a potentially catastrophic delay. Frustrated, but with no place left to call, I punched off the phone and put it away.

The triple sled loads towed surprisingly easily on the soft snow of the river. Jon pulled out cautiously at first but soon found that he could travel as fast as

the rest of us. With twin white rooster tails of snow spraying past him, Dan sat on his snowmobile smoking a pipe and gazing around, enjoying the view and the freedom of being a passenger rather than a driver. Realizing that he didn't need to hold the handlebars, he got out his movie camera and began filming the procession as it wound along the broad curves of the river.

Twilight was just starting to fall when our parade came into Old Crow. If our arrival in Fort Yukon had been widely noted, our appearance in Old Crow with triple sleds and a crippled snowmobile should have been even harder to miss, but the town was strangely quiet. We parked our rigs by the two-story Royal Canadian Mounted Police building virtually unnoticed. As the

Dan's snowmobile getting towed (below), which required three other machines to pull three sleds each (above).
H. Huntington.

FINDING THE ARCTIC

twin flags of Canada and Yukon Territory flapped overhead in a light evening breeze, I grabbed our passports and reported to the RCMP, which in this small village doubles as Customs and Immigration. The constable recorded our entry into Canada and directed me to the community hall, where

Calling for parts.
H. Huntington.

the entire town was gathered for a potlatch, a traditional Native community feast. I hustled over to the hall to find the school principal with whom we had arranged our stay. Jon and Henry wandered off looking for a snowmobile clutch while Glen and Dan stayed to make sure our rigs were safe.

My entry into the tribal hall was anything but low key. Whatever had been taking place in the hall as I entered stopped abruptly the moment I walked through the door. The room went dead silent, and more than a hundred heads swiveled my way. It must have been my outfit. I was still wearing my traveling parka, with its showy wolf and wolverine ruff. On my head was an equally conspicuous beaver fur hat, well frosted from the trail, and on my feet a pair of white bulbous bunny boots and red gaiters. My beard was iced and my cheeks were red and chapped from the wind. Clearly I had not arrived in Old Crow on the airplane, which anyway wasn't due for several more days.

With everyone watching, I stammered out as gracious a "howdy" as I could, and then said, "I am with a group of snowmobilers. We have come from Fairbanks, and tomorrow we are going to work with the kids in the school." Whatever I said must have been sufficient, because most of the people returned to eating and talking.

As I circled the hall greeting people, several elders came up and introduced themselves. I was made to feel at home. The potlatch was in full swing and the aromas of moose and caribou stew after ten days of one-pot meals was

heavenly. There were platters of meats and bowls full of fried potatoes, freshly baked rolls, and a big bucket of ice cream. They told me to sit down, thaw out, and to eat, but I quickly explained I had four hungry companions and asked if I could go get them. "Of course," was the reply.

In the time it had taken me to register with the RCMP, find the tribal hall, and get invited to dinner, Jon had met several townspeople, been directed to the local guy most likely to have a used clutch, struck a deal for the clutch, pulled it off the old machine, and was in the act of installing it on Dan's broken machine as I walked up. Moreover, the man who sold the clutch to Jon was helping to install it. Fifteen minutes later Dan's machine was running on its own. We ferried the machines and sleds to the school, then all five of us walked back to join the potlatch.

The party had a dual purpose. In part it was to celebrate the life of a man from the village who had recently died, and in part it was a feast for the dog mushers (including Kleedehn) who had arrived in town just ahead of us. Halfway through the Dagoo 340 sled-dog race, they would spend the night in Old Crow then head back out on the trail the next day. Of the ten mushers in the race, two were local. To us, the biggest surprise was finding an old friend, Solomon Carriere, among the mushers. We knew Solomon as one of the best marathon canoe racers in the world, having won two prestigious events in the United States, the seventy-mile General Clinton Canoe Regatta on New York's Finger Lakes, and the 120-mile Au Sable River Canoe Marathon in Michigan. In 1998 Dan and I had paddled against him in a five-hundred-mile marathon from Skagway to Dawson, losing badly while Sol and his partner won. Three years later Dan paddled with Sol to victory in the same race. We had not known that Sol was a competitive dog musher, but it should not have been a surprise, as he hailed from Cumberland House in Saskatchewan, a historic community dating back to the eighteenth-century fur-trade era. From Cumberland House, trade goods had moved overland to and from the Churchill

The people of Old Crow rely on caribou for subsistence.

River and Hudson Bay, and by water across Lake Winnipeg and then overland to the Great Lakes. Sol himself was descended from the Métis voyageurs who paddled the freight canoes on these routes. Perhaps it wasn't so surprising after all that he had gotten into competitive mushing, given that most of the old voyageurs had also run freight in the winter using dogs.

That night as we fell asleep in the gym at the Chief Zzeh Gittlit School, a sense of history and well-being settled over all of us. Our broken snowmobile was fixed, we had eaten well, and we had been warmly welcomed in this remote village.

The next day went by in a flash. We taught the kids at the school about climate change, fueled up our thirsty snowmobiles for the next leg of our journey, and watched as the dog mushers pulled out on the return leg of their race. About three hundred people live in Old Crow, clustered in a collection of colorful log and plywood houses on the north bank of the Porcupine River. The village occupies a narrow fringe of spruce forest between the river and a range of bare tundra hills, the Old Crow Range, to the north. Beyond the hills lies the Old Crow Flats, a vast region of lakes and rich wetland. The base of the hills is cut in several places by narrow ravines, also forested, and a few people live in houses tucked away in these little cozy canyons. Despite its small size, like all northern communities, Old Crow is a busy place, with people coming and going on four-wheelers, kids playing, dogs barking, and heavy equipment working. The local store and post office had a constant stream of traffic, even though there had been no new mail or supplies in several days. People were out driving or walking dogs on the river, or just enjoying the sunshine.

With the exception of a handful of non-Natives, most of Old Crow's residents are Vuntut Gwich'in, the People of the Lakes. They come by this name because traditionally they trapped muskrats and fished in the Old Crow Flats. When Chief Zzeh Gittlit, whose name means Crow May I Walk, died in the 1870s, the people started calling the gathering area on the north bank of the Porcupine River after him. Old Crow was just a place name until the 1920s, however. The original trading posts in this region were downriver at Fort Yukon, established in 1847, later at Old Rampart (1867), and eventually at New Rampart (1891).

The traders had to keep relocating their posts eastward as they discovered they were across the U.S.–Canada boundary. But even when they set up shop well inside Canada at New Rampart, the post did not last long. The Hudson's Bay Company operated New Rampart for just four years before abandoning it in 1894 because it was not commercially viable. Daniel Cadzow, no relation to our friend in Fort Yukon, re-established the trading post in 1904 and ran it until his death in 1929, but a number of factors were working against long-term success. First, the nearby border restricted hunting, fishing, and trapping by the Canadians. Second, a smallpox outbreak in 1911–1912 left a lingering sense among the Vuntut Gwich'in that New Rampart was an unhealthy place (see "Quarantine Island" opposite page). Finally, Old Crow was closer to traditional hunting, fishing, and travel routes. With the establishment of a store at Old Crow in the late 1920s, the final nail was driven into the coffin of New Rampart, which by the 1930s had only a few families still living there and today is a ghost town.

We left Old Crow headed to Fort McPherson the following day, but not without experiencing local hospitality a couple more times. Perhaps word of our stellar navigational skills had preceded us because both interventions were intended to keep us from getting lost. From Old Crow our way was east up

I KNEW THE ISLAND HAD BAD KARMA, even before I knew why. We had been up on the bluff exploring the restored buildings at New Rampart but now it was getting dark. We needed a place to stay, and the wind was rising, so it had to be a sheltered spot. I told the others I would check the large island we could see down below. I dropped down the

Nurse Harry Anthony inoculating the Linklater family of New Rampart in 1911. *International Boundary Survey Commission.*

bluffs, got on my snowmobile, and drove across the island—probably too fast. On the far side I went flying off a blind cut bank. The machine hit deep snow below the six-foot drop, nearly stopped dead, and I was flung forward hard against the handlebars. I sprained both wrists and broke the throttle. This island was a bad place. We would not camp here. I limped back to the others and we camped in small creek called Shanaghàn Kòhnjik (Old Woman Creek) across from the island. A year later, I saw a picture of the same island taken in 1911, when it was called Edmond's Island and it was covered with white tents and sick people. My bad feeling about the place was confirmed.

In 1910, a joint U.S.–Canadian crew came to New Rampart as part of the International Boundary Survey of 1909–1912. The crew was to survey, clear brush, and erect monuments along the 141st parallel, which marks the boundary between Canada and Alaska in this area. Some of the surveyors wintered over at the trading post, and the real work began in the summer of 1911. Dr. Gilbert Smith was assigned to the expedition as doctor. In July of 1911 he discovered a young girl with what he diagnosed as smallpox and a strict quarantine was imposed. Everyone was inoculated, Native cabins were burned, and the sick were exiled to the island, where a clinic was built. The healthy were placed in a detention camp behind the trading post so any epidemic could not spread through the territory. By mid-winter more than ninety people had been diagnosed with the disease, although records suggest there was only one outright death—which raises the question of whether it really was smallpox. The Vuntut Gwich'in believed the surveyors had brought the illness, whatever it was, and bad memories of the place contributed to their slow migration away from New Rampart upriver to Old Crow. ∎

Edmond's (now Willow) Island quarantine camp in 1911. *International Boundary Survey Commission.*

Remains of the Hudson's Bay Company trading post at Old Rampart.

the Porcupine River, then overland to the Bell River and Lapierre House. This route dates back more than 150 years, to a time when the North West and Hudson's Bay Companies reigned supreme. The section of trail between the two rivers is still referred to as a portage (locally pronounced "pour-TAHJ" after the original French term for carrying loads overland between bodies of water).

We didn't know exactly where this portage started, so I asked around Old Crow. Our first benefactor Peter Josie was passing on a ratty old Elan snowmobile and stopped to chat. Soon he and I had the map spread out on the ripped-up seat of his machine. With a gnarled finger he traced the way to the start of the portage, and even graciously offered us the use of his nearby trapping cabin. Our second benefactor Danny Kassi worked at the school and had spent several hours with us there. Danny got on Google Earth and printed out a map of the Porcupine River above the village, which he marked up with detailed instructions. Still not convinced we could find the start of the trail, Danny decided he had best accompany us at least a few miles out of town so that he could go through the directions with us one last time. Armed with two maps and two very fine descriptions, we were fairly confident that we would at least find the start of the portage, though we did appreciate our hosts' concern.

Maps notwithstanding, the start of the portage was anything but obvious. The trail cut off from the Porcupine River into a ravine so narrow and overhung by snow-covered alders that it was hard to spot. After running up the ravine for a few hundred feet in a tunnel of shrubs, the trail then abruptly angled up a steep bank on the right and topped out in a black spruce forest. It was hard to imagine that every item on the shelves in the trading posts of Fort

Daniel Cadzow's house at New Rampart in 1918. *Courtesy of the Yukon Archives-Tidd Collection-Photo YA7627.*

The same building under renovation in 2007. *J. Holmgren.*

The cut line marking the U.S.–Canada boundary meets the Porcupine River at New Rampart.
H. Huntington.

Yukon, Old Rampart, New Rampart, and Old Crow had at one time come over this route. A tin kettle that started its journey in England on a British ship, then been off-loaded in Montreal, New York, or perhaps York Factory on Hudson Bay, would have been carried through this ravine on a human back, after having been paddled in a canoe for three thousand miles. Every pelt brought into these remote trading posts and bartered for kettles, gunpowder, blankets, calico, or needles would have headed to England the same way.

The engine of this transportation system was the collective strength in the legs, arms, and backs of the voyageurs. Mostly of French Canadian descent, usually Métis (from another French term, meaning of mixed blood) with a smattering of Indian, Scots, English, and other races, these famed wilderness canoe-men opened the North with paddle and tumpline. They were all compact men, less than five foot five, incredibly strong, and inured to a level of hardship that today we would find difficult to believe. They were also flamboyant and emotional, and

Claude Tidd (right) and an unidentified RCMP officer flank a border monument along the cut line near New Rampart House in 1918. *Courtesy of the Yukon Archives Tidd Collection, photo YA7064.*

more often than not died young and were buried in the silent boreal forest far from home. For eighteen hours a day, these voyageurs squatted in birch bark canoes that ranged from twenty-four feet long *(canot du nord)* to thirty-six feet *(canot de maître)*, packed with several tons of cargo in ninety-pound bales. Paddling forty-five strokes a minute all day long, softly singing ditties in time to the stroke, they endured sun, rain, wind, injury, and imminent risk of drowning. At night, they camped under their overturned canoes, sleeping cold and wet, or in clouds of mosquitoes, their only luxury in camp their pipes and tobacco. They could run just about any river rapid they encountered, including some small waterfalls, and they did so because the alternative was a hernia-inducing portage of the cargo and canoe around the obstacle. When switching from one river drainage

Peter Josie (left) points out the start of the portage to the Bell River.
H. Huntington.

to another, however, the portages were inescapable, so on these hikes they performed prodigious feats of strength. Each voyageur was expected to load one ninety-pound bale in the small of his back, support it with a tumpline, then one of his mates would load a second bale between his shoulder blades. Straining under the load, they would head off in a crouch along the muddy and slippery portage trail, knees pumping, arms swinging. It was brutal work, and it killed a goodly number of the voyageurs despite their toughness, but the trade goods moved west and the furs moved east year after year, while the effort and struggle made the owners in England richer.

The portages, and the deeds of the voyageurs on the portages, were the stuff of legend. A voyageur could earn a Spanish silver dollar if he took three bales on a portage, a staggering load of 270 pounds, yet carrying this much was commonplace. There are reliable records of voyageurs carrying an unbelievable double load (540 pounds) on a portage. The trails ranged from a few hundred feet to several miles in length, with one of the longest and most difficult being the nearly eleven-mile Methye Portage between the Great Lakes drainage

Slightly idealized image of a voyageur canoe bearing two passengers, painted by Frances Anne (Beechey) Hopkins (1838–1918). *Courtesy National Archives Canada.*

Voyageurs shoot the rapids in a big *canot de maître* in another Hopkins painting. *Courtesy National Archives Canada.*

and the Mackenzie River. To get all the cargo across, the men had to make multiple trips. The canoes had to come over too and they weighed hundreds of pounds but were also fragile and could not tolerate rough handling. It was a tough life, but the voyageurs reveled in their hardships with the same

A scrub spruce flat near the confluence of the Bell and Water Rivers, site of the historic Lapierre House.

H. Huntington.

sort of pride champion athletes exhibit today. Neither wealth nor luxury rewarded their efforts, but an abiding sense that they were supermen, accomplishing what normal mortals could not, kept these men going.

Our trip over the portage ended when we dropped down off of a scrub spruce flat onto the Bell River where it met the Waters River. This is the site of Lapierre House, whose very name conjures up visions of flamboyant but tough voyageurs wearing gaily colored bandanas, their paddles flashing in the sunlight. We had asked people in Old Crow if there was anything remaining of the famous trading post and how to find it. Danny Kassi, who has a keen interest in history, described where he thought the buildings had been, but he was unsure what, if anything, was left. The recent history of Lapierre House is confusing. Photographs taken in 1920 suggest the house was falling down, yet written accounts indicate that several Vuntut Gwich'in families lived there until the mid-1930s. The Jackson Brothers are also known to have operated a store there between 1925 and 1935, and they must have had radio communication with Fort McPherson during the manhunt for the infamous Mad Trapper (see chapter 4).

Our search for the old buildings was short, as we needed to keep moving. Three of us waded and swam our way up through the deep snow on the riverbank and then post-holed about looking for signs that would tell us people had

Lapierre House already looking less than serviceable in 1920 (above), and a modern view of the building, looking toward the southwest, taken by Shirleen Smith, Vuntut Gwich'in First Nation (right). *Upper photo courtesy of the Yukon Archives-Tidd Collection-Photo YA7226. Lower photo courtesy of Shirleen Smith, Vuntut Gwich'in First Nation.*

once lived there. Other than some recent surveyor's flagging we couldn't find anything, and only later learned we had looked in the wrong place.

Henry, who had stayed down at the machines on the Bell River, yelled up to us on the bank, "Can you see the old trading post?"

"No," I answered. "Nothing here."

Yet even as we slid down the snow bank on our butts, I did sense something lingering, clinging to the place. How many weary and cold travelers had felt a warm welcome here at Lapierre House, just as we had in Old Crow? How many times had a musher come in here with a broken sled and found spare parts and willing hands to help fix it? In this corner of the Arctic northern hospitality was not only alive and well, it had permeated the land.

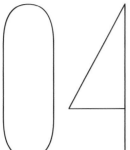

POIGNANT PASSING:

THE MAD TRAPPER OF RAT RIVER

From Lapierre House we worked up the La Chute River, climbing over the Richardson Mountains, the highest point on our trip. The mountains separate the Yukon and Mackenzie drainages, two of the largest watersheds in North America. From atop the divide, we descended to the Peel River and followed it to Fort McPherson. While traveling with Ernie Vittrekwa, an elder from Fort McPherson, we came upon the Porcupine caribou herd making its annual spring migration toward the Arctic Ocean. It is a ritual that has been repeated for more than seven thousand years. We were hardly the first people to cross the Richardson range in winter: the Vuntat Gwich'in have been doing so for hundreds of years. John Bell, who established a Hudson's Bay Company trading post at Fort McPherson in 1840, was probably the first non-Native to go over the imposing peaks. The most famous traverse by far, however, took place in 1932, when the Mad Trapper of Rat River made a desperate bid to evade capture by crossing the mountains in a blizzard. Millions heard his story because the advent of radio had brought the Arctic closer to the rest of the world. The arrival of aviation in the North ensured that he did not escape, an event that neatly marks the point in time when the old North began to buckle under the onslaught of modern technology.

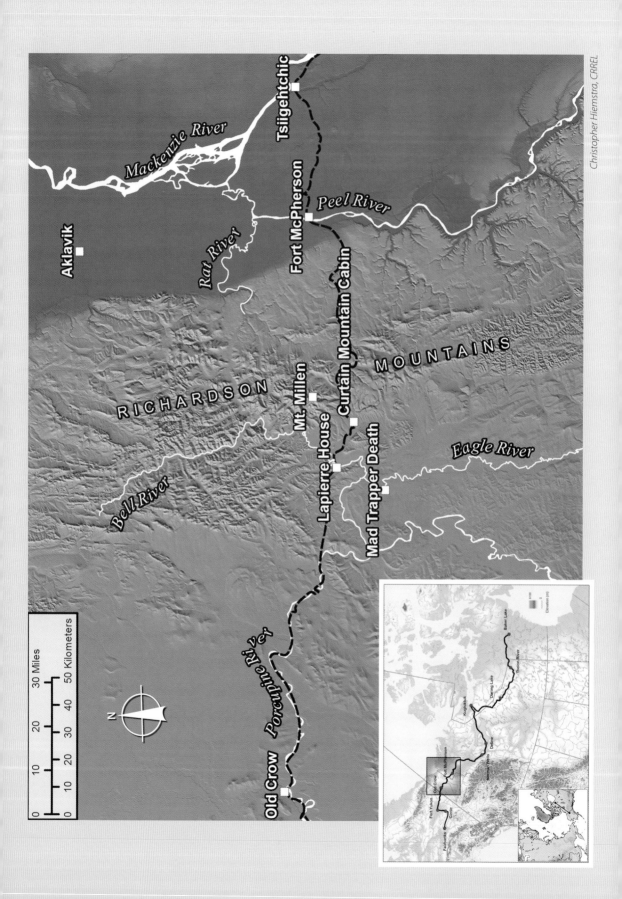

Christopher Hiemstra, CRREL

THE PICTURE IS UNREMARKABLE: an aerial photo of a snow-covered river crossed by caribou tracks. Spindly black spruce trees line the riverbanks. A couple of dark objects stand out against the snow, one in the middle of the river on a heavily used caribou trail. The dark objects might be caribou, but they are not. The one in the middle is Albert Johnson, the Mad Trapper of Rat River. The picture was taken at the exact moment his body was riddled by eight bullets. The other dark objects are his pursuers, five constables of the RCMP. For more than fifty days, over hundreds of miles of tundra and taiga, in bitter temperatures and blizzard winds, the Mounties had doggedly hunted Johnson, traveling by dog sled and snow shoe, wrapped in furs to stay warm. The remarkable thing about the picture is that it exists at all. It was taken from the cockpit of a Bellanca Pacemaker piloted by Wop May on February 17, 1932. A portion of the wing can be seen in the picture. May, a World War I flying ace and pioneer bush pilot, had been summoned by radio to assist in the manhunt. Without the radio the airplane would not have been in the hunt, and without the airplane the Mad Trapper would have gotten away, disappearing into the vast silence of the North.

The aerial photo marks almost precisely the moment when technology defeated time, distance, and weather, those three ancient protectors of arctic isolation and mystery. For thousands of years, this trio has kept the Arctic remote and austere. From the first Siberian hunters making tentative forays across the Bering Land Bridge thirteen thousand years ago, through Henry Hudson, cast adrift and fading into the mists of James Bay four hundred years ago, to Franklin disappearing with all hands in 1845, people venturing into the Arctic have been swallowed by the land. The three defenders of the arctic mystique had done a good job right up until the crackle of static and the drone of propellers arrived to challenge their power.

Of course pinpointing the change to a single moment is artificial, but as late as 1924 it had not yet taken place. In January of that year a United States Geological Survey expedition led by Philip S. Smith and J. B. Mertie, Jr. came to Alaska by steamer. The men traveled by horse-drawn sleds down the frozen

Eagle River scene photographed from Wop May's plane on February 17, 1932. The Mad Trapper (1) has just been killed by RCMP constables (2–6) after a grueling fifty-day manhunt. *W. S. Carter, RCMP, courtesy Glenbow Museum.*

Tanana River, arriving in the village of Tanana in the middle of winter. From there, they mushed supplies and canoes north into the Brooks Range where they settled in to await the coming of spring to begin their geologic mapping. Returning by canoe down the Killik River, they did not reach the arctic coast until late August and were lucky to catch a ride on a small schooner from Barrow to Nome. From there, they went overland and by river to Seward, where they finally sailed for Seattle in October, ten months after arriving in Alaska. Nine scant years later USGS geologists were flying into their Alaska field sites in a few hours.

Marconi built the first functional radio in 1886, and the Wright Brothers filed a patent for a workable flying machine in 1903. It took time before radios or planes were robust enough for arctic service, but Northerners recognized their value immediately. In one hour a plane could traverse more distance than a man could walk in a day. As soon as was practical, airplanes were equipped with skis, floats, or big tires, allowing them to land anywhere and in any season. Distances shrank. Similarly, outposts that formerly had contact with the outside world only a few times a year could now request supplies, deliver messages, or ask for medical assistance by radio. Communication times dropped from months to minutes. The radio altered the human landscape even more profoundly by bringing the outside world to the North in the form of daily news. No longer was it possible to miss world events such as the Lindbergh kidnapping or the start of a world war.

The Mad Trapper story begins in the summer of 1931, when a stocky blond man came into the Mackenzie River country via Fort McPherson. He said his name was Albert Johnson, and he was quiet and kept to himself. That was not unusual. It was the Great Depression and jobs were scarce. A lot of reticent and self-sufficient young men were drifting around the North living by hunting, fishing, and trapping. Johnson was noted, as strangers always are in small towns, by the clergy and the police, but his presence did not seem unusual.

In Fort McPherson, Johnson bought traps, a shotgun, and grub, loaded them in his canoe, then worked his way down the Peel and up the Rat River about ten miles, where he built an eight-by-ten-foot cabin for the winter. Building in typical northern fashion, he dug a hole several feet deep and then laid logs up around the hole. This design saves on the number of logs and makes for a squat little structure that holds heat well. It also serves as a pretty good fort in a shoot-out. He was the only white trapper in the area, but three Natives, William Vittrekwa, Jacob Drymeat, and William Nerysoo, were running traplines nearby.

The trouble began around Christmas 1931, when Nerysoo walked into the Arctic Red River trading post (now the hamlet of Tsiigehtchic) and reported to RCMP Constable Edgar Millen that Johnson was springing his traps and hanging them in trees or throwing them away. We will never know why Johnson did this, but we know it went against all trapline etiquette. In addition, it appeared that Johnson had failed to obtain a trapping permit. Millen responded by sending two constables to the trapper's cabin. Alfred King and Joe Bernard spent two and a half days mushing out to the cabin in −40°F weather. Upon arrival they noticed smoke coming from the chimney and snowshoes leaning against the wall, indicating Johnson was at home. King tried for over an hour to coax Johnson to let them in to talk. Though he caught a glimpse of the trapper through a small glass window set in the side of the cabin wall, Johnson said absolutely nothing during the encounter and never opened the door. In a world of Northern hospitality, this was weird.

Lacking a warrant, and sensing trouble, the two constables headed north toward Aklavik, the closest RCMP post, arriving a day and a half after their strange visit to the cabin. Four days had now elapsed since the start of their mission. In Aklavik, they picked up a warrant and were joined by Constable McDowell and Special Constable Sittichinli. The four were back on the trail heading south after spending less than twenty-four hours in the village. Mushing rapidly, they were at the trapper's cabin in thirty-six hours.

From their actions, we can surmise the Mounties were expecting trouble. Leaving the three other constables near the riverbank, King carefully approached the cabin door from the side away from the window. Keeping his side to the wall of the cabin, he reached out and rapped on the door. With an explosive bang, a bullet ripped through the door, passing into King's chest on the left side and exiting on the right. Despite the grievous wound, King was able, under covering fire from his companions, to crawl back to the riverbank. There his companions bundled him in the sled and started a desperate dash for Aklavik and the doctor. In a stinging blizzard, they covered the eighty miles in about twenty hours, arriving in time to keep King from bleeding to death.

The RCMP had a real problem on their hands. Their resources consisted of eleven men in Aklavik, three in Arctic Red River, and the Royal Canadian Corps of Signals detachment in Aklavik. The last, established in 1925, ran the radio station that linked the RCMP posts to the outside world. The constables could also enlist the aid of the local hunters and trappers, hardened men who knew the land, could track, and could function in the cold.

We can only surmise that Albert Johnson knew he had a problem, too. Without a radio, he had no way of knowing whether he had killed King, but he had to assume the worst. The weather, that ancient arctic protagonist, was against him. It was still cold, and his cabin would be the last shelter he would have if he fled. On the other hand, time and distance were working for him: he had days, rather than hours, to get ready before the Mounties would be back. He chose time over weather, prepared well, and stayed put.

Remains of the Mad Trapper's cabin a few days after the siege.
Courtesy Glenbow Museum.

The RCMP Aklavik detachment arranged by radio to meet the Arctic Red River detachment at the mouth of the Rat River. Two days later the parties rendezvoused as planned, bringing their combined force to eleven men and more than fifty dogs. They also had with them twenty pounds of dynamite. On the ninth of January, in −45°F weather, the policemen were in position by the cabin. Amazingly, the trapper was still there. Yelling to Johnson that King was alive failed to elicit any response other than a fusillade of bullets. As the short day wore on, the Mounties tried various ploys to dislodge the trapper. It soon became apparent that he had cut loopholes in the cabin walls and was firing from a pit in the cabin floor, protected from incoming bullets by the frozen dirt.

In the waning light, pressed by the cold and their dwindling supplies, the Mounties tried to force the issue using dynamite. They carefully thawed out the sticks (a ticklish business) and tried throwing them against the cabin walls. The blasts had little effect. Next they threw dynamite onto the roof of the cabin. The explosion blew a hole in the roof and knocked over the smokestack, but still failed to dislodge the Mad Trapper. In one final desperate attempt, they bound four sticks of dynamite together and heaved them onto the remainder of the roof. The explosion ripped the roof off the cabin and knocked out some of the wall logs, but failed to daze the unflappable Johnson. He shot out the flashlight of one of the men who stormed the cabin following the blast. A hasty retreat to the riverbank, out of range of the trapper's deadly fire, followed. Shivering in the dark near the banks of the river, the Mounties considered their options. There was talk of burning the cabin, but ultimately they decided they had to take the trapper alive. With supplies exhausted, and the trapper still holding them at bay, they had no choice but to head back to Aklavik.

The radio now began to play an even larger role in the saga. Long-wave broadcasts from Aklavik had flashed the news south of Constable King's shooting on January 6. This had piqued the interest of the news media and had been widely re-broadcast. Next came the report on January 11 that the trapper, dubbed the Mad Trapper by the press, had held out against a vastly superior force. His one-against-many struggle caught the sympathies of the Depression-era public. People started following the manhunt on nightly radio broadcasts. The drama served to boost the popularity of radio and increased the public's awareness of the Arctic. Everyone, it seemed, had a theory about who the Mad Trapper was and why he did what he did.

The increasingly frustrated Mounties in Aklavik did not have the leisure to speculate on the Mad Trapper's motives, but they were acutely aware that he was anything but mad. "On the contrary," wrote Inspector Eames, in charge of the manhunt, the trapper "showed himself to be an extremely shrewd and resolute man, capable of quick thought and action, a tough and desperate character." By January 16, the Mounties were back at the wrecked cabin, but the trapper was finally gone. New snow and drifting winds had obscured his tracks. He could have headed anywhere. The searchers, however, reasoned he would move up the Rat River toward the Richardson Mountains. For day after frigid day they found nothing and began to doubt they were even looking in the right direction, until January 28 when they picked up a faint trail on the overflow ice on a creek. They followed the signs until they petered out, then circling back and forth, they eventually picked the trail up again. With only about five hours of useable light per day, the tracking was painstakingly slow, but they were beginning to understand the Mad Trapper's methods. He was heading toward the Divide, the Richardson Mountains, but he was taking his time, sticking to the hard-packed snow on ridges and never crossing a creek unless it was on overflow ice. Like his pursuers, he was doing a lot of circling, but in his case, it was to circle back behind the Mounties to throw them off his trail. The cat and mouse game got more real on the twenty-ninth: the trackers saw a thin wisp of smoke rising over a narrow canyon off to one side of a ridge where they had picked up his trail. Carefully moving in closer, they could see a small fire and a tarpaulin, though not the trapper himself. It was dusk, so the Mounties quietly moved off to camp and prepare for an assault in the morning.

As light was breaking the next day, the four constables moved into position. Two of them, Riddell and Garland, dropped into the canyon below the trapper's camp and silently worked their way up the creek to within twenty yards of his tarpaulin. Once they were in position, Verville and Millen began descending to the canyon above the camp, but one of them slipped, making enough noise to alert the trapper. They heard Johnson lever a shell into the chamber of his Savage .30-30 and cough, yet at this point, he still had not been seen by any of his pursuers. Verville and Millen, trying to move into a position with an unobstructed firing line, crossed a small open patch between the spruce trees. Verville got across, but as Millen sprinted the short distance, the trapper fired, missing. Verville returned fire. Johnson, realizing he was vulnerable, leaped across his campfire and settled behind an overturned tree. As he did so, Garland fired from below him, which probably gave Johnson the first indication that he was surrounded. To the Mounties, it looked as if Garland's shot had hit home, because the trapper seemed to collapse behind the tree.

For two tense hours, there was no movement or sound. Calls for Johnson's surrender went unanswered. Perhaps he was dead . . . perhaps not. The Mounties could not see where he had settled, so they decided to move in closer. Riddell had just climbed back on the ridge above the canyon for a better view when he noticed something queer: it was the barrel of Johnson's rifle protruding through a bulwark of snow and root material. "Look out!" he yelled and dove for cover just as a shot rang out. Millen, further along the ridge, dropped to one knee and began firing at the mound. Johnson replied with three rapid shots, the third hitting Millen in the chest, spinning him around before he dropped. Under covering fire, Garland crawled to his comrade, tied his mukluk laces together, and used them to drag Millen to cover, but there was nothing else that could be done. He was dead, shot through the heart. The Mounties kept up sporadic fire at the mound until dark, then, recognizing the advantage lay with the trapper, withdrew to their camp.

HE ARRIVED IN THE NORTH under an assumed name. He kept to himself and he died before he could be asked about his history. His remains were buried in Aklavik in an unmarked grave. Since his death, the man who called himself Albert Johnson has been the subject of at least seven books, innumerable articles, and one Hollywood movie starring Charles Bronson and Lee Marvin. He is something of a cult hero. Invariably, people have asked, "Who was the Mad Trapper?" Author Dick North spent more than thirty years trying to answer that question.

These modern snowshoes are virtually identical to the ones used by the Mad Trapper during the manhunt.
Matthew Sturm.

Ultimately, he came to believe the trapper was a North Dakota bank robber named Johnny Johnson. Another writer, Mark Fremmerlid, suggests he was a Norwegian draft dodger named Sigvald Pederson Haaskjold.

In 2007 it seemed the mystery might be solved. The Mad Trapper's remains were exhumed for forensic investigation. In May 2009, the disappointing results were announced in a Discovery Channel program. Analysis of trace elements in the Mad Trapper's bones and tissues ruled out his having grown up in Canada, but left U.S. or Scandinavian origins in play. That meant both Johnny Johnson and Sigvald Haaskjold were still suspects, but so too were thousands of others. The show's producers were offering DNA kits to anyone with a relative that could have been the Mad Trapper.

Knowing the Mad Trapper's identity might help to explain why he did the things he did, but it would miss the most poignant part of the story. Regardless of who he was and where he was from, it is clear that the Mad Trapper came north to disappear. But he was already too late. The radio and airplane had arrived before him, compressing distance and time to the point where it was no longer possible to hide in the vast North.

In 2005 I was working in Barrow, Alaska, on a big sea ice research project. One day at lunch, the local whale biologist asked if I could take a few minutes to talk to a visitor. The man was well dressed, perhaps a little too fancy for Barrow with his Eddie Bauer clothes, but not unusual for town. He sat down and explained in a very reasonable way that he was an advance man for Paramount Pictures. They were planning to film a new version of *Moby Dick* using Barrow for some of the sea ice scenes. Julia Roberts would be in the movie. I was too distracted by my project to notice the obvious inconsistencies in his story (there are no women in *Moby Dick*; the ice in Barrow is nothing like the pack ice on the open ocean), so I listened to him and chatted for a few minutes about ice before I had to get back to work. A few days later, just as we were returning to shore, two Barrow policemen arrived in their GMC Blazers, lights flashing. They asked if I had been working with anyone in the film industry. I said no, but then remembered my encounter with the Paramount man at lunch. Barrow being a small place, the policemen found him easily later that day at one of the hotels.

It seems the Paramount man had jumped parole in California and was wanted on suspicion of murdering his wife in another state. Like the Mad Trapper, the man had come north to disappear. He too had done a few odd things that called attention to himself. But his chief error, the same one made by the Mad Trapper, was thinking the North had been shielded from the technologies penetrating the rest of the world. The Mad Trapper was snared by airplanes and radios. The Paramount man was undone by e-mail, fax, and telephone, but the result was the same. They shipped Mr. Paramount back to California in handcuffs. ▪

The Mad Trapper's guns and axe are now on display in the RCMP Historical Collections Unit in Regina, Canada. *Courtesy of the RCMP Historical Collections Unit, "Depot" Division, Regina, Canada.*

The next day Johnson was gone, having climbed the vertical cliff behind his camp in the dark. He had done this by chopping hand and footholds into the frozen snow with his axe. Once out of the canyon, the trapper had again taken to the hard-packed snow of the ridges, leaving no trail. After two weeks of constant backbreaking effort, the Mounties needed a rest and more supplies. The Mad Trapper must have been under even more stress because he could not easily hunt for food, nor build a large enough fire to dry out his clothing and sleeping bag. He was undoubtedly starving and cold. That he was still on the run was a testament to his toughness.

Had the foregoing events taken place in 1922 instead of 1932, the story might have ended at this point with the trapper disappearing forever into the mists of the North. But potent new forces were marshalling against him. A radio call had gone out for air support following Constable Millen's death, and within four days May was flying north in the Bellanca. On February 6, less than a week after the second shoot-out, May was actively shuttling supplies and personnel to the search scene, as well as looking for tracks from the air.

Furthermore, news of the manhunt had jumped the Richardson Mountains even faster than the superhuman Mad Trapper could travel. On January 21, radio station KNK in Fairbanks had broadcast a report that a manhunt was taking place on the east side of the mountains. It was heard on home radio sets by trappers living on the Porcupine, Bell, and Eagle Rivers. A posse formed at Lapierre House and was even then traveling over the Richardson Mountains to help in the search. The Mounties at the head of the Rat River were even using portable radios to talk to their base in Aklavik, coordinating their search efforts with those of the airplane and the other search parties, foreshadowing modern law enforcement practice.

Sometime between February 8 and 10, Johnson managed to cross the Richardson range somewhere north of the Stony Creek–La Chute Portage and south of the more famous Rat River Portage, possibly in the vicinity of Mt. Millen (so named decades later for the fallen constable). The terrain can rise up to six thousand feet high in this area, with treeline at two thousand feet. Gale force winds are the norm. Despite these terrible conditions, Johnson likely crossed over in a blizzard that grounded the airplane, thus escaping detection. On the twelfth of February, Peter Alexi, having mushed the 130 miles from Lapierre House over the Rat River Portage without a break, rendezvoused with the search party and told them the startling news that native hunters on the west side of the mountains had seen strange snowshoe tracks on the Bell River. These had passed within a mile and a half of Lapierre House. The Mad Trapper was over the Divide!

There are various theories about why he crossed. One is that he was headed for Alaska, where the RCMP would have no jurisdiction. Another is that he was forced over by his pursuers. In the two days before the desperate crossing, he had tried three times to circle around behind them on the upper reaches of the Barrier River, but each time he came out in front of his pursuers, the last time perhaps very close to them. The final theory is that he wanted to get into the Bell River's soft deep snow, which might tip the speed advantage from a dog team to a man on snowshoes. On February 13, May ferried four of the Mounties to Lapierre House, where they positively identified the unique tracks of Johnson's homemade snowshoes in the deep snow.

The chase now began again in deadly earnest. On February 14, May was able to follow the Mad Trapper's snowshoe trail from the air, tracking him down the Bell and up the Eagle River. By the fifteenth the four Mounties who had flown across the mountains were joined by eight more searchers who had mushed over the Rat River Portage. The combined party of twelve Mounties, with air support, started working their way up the winding Eagle River in pursuit. By the night of the sixteenth, with foggy weather keeping the Bellanca grounded, the Mounties knew they were closing in on Johnson, but they had no idea just how close they were. They camped that night on one side of an oxbow bend in the river, while Johnson was camped on the other side, the two parties separated by only a narrow neck of land. The crisis came the morning of February 17. Johnson, trying to move upriver, had run into two sets of ski tracks. These were probably left by local trappers not involved in the manhunt, but he could not know this. Thinking the Mounties were above him, the trapper switched directions and headed downriver, carrying his snowshoes and

Wop May's plane
in Aklavik, 1932.
*Courtesy of the
Glenbow Museum.*

walking on a hard-packed caribou trail in the middle of the river. Shortly thereafter he must have heard the dogs of the posse on the far side of the oxbow. Quite possibly he mistook the sound to be coming from behind him rather than ahead, reinforcing in his mind that he was cut-off upriver. He continued walking downstream.

Sergeant Hersey was the first to see Johnson, who appeared startled to discover the Mounties were ahead of him. As Hersey dropped to his knee to get into a position to shoot, the trapper jammed his feet into his snowshoes preparing to run through deep snow to the riverbank. Seeing Hersey about to shoot, the trapper instead whirled and snapped off a hasty shot. Again his marksmanship was astonishing. Hersey fell back, struck in the knee and elbow and chest by the single shot. Johnson continued toward the riverbank where the timber could provide cover, but with the other Mounties coming up fast, he had second thoughts and moved back toward where he had started, prepared to shoot it out on the spot. At this very moment, May flew over. The Mounties were able to quickly move into flanking positions on both riverbanks. When they got no response to their calls for surrender, they commenced firing. Without cover, outnumbered six to one, the Mad Trapper had no chance. He was hit seven times before being killed by an eighth bullet that severed his spinal column. Fifty-two days after it began, the chase was over.

But the work of the airplane was not. The Mounties bundled Sgt. Hersey into the plane, which landed in Aklavik within the hour (instead of the four days it would have taken by dog sled). The wounded policeman was operated on shortly thereafter, making a full recovery over the next few weeks. Johnson's body was taken by dogsled to Lapierre House, then flown the next day to Aklavik where he was examined and eventually interred. His death photographs show

a face distorted in a grimace of pain and hatred, the face scarred by frostbite. An autopsy revealed little other than that he was about forty years old, five feet nine inches tall, and 150 pounds. His possessions were inventoried,

A dog team and sled typical of gear the Mounties would have used while chasing the Mad Trapper. *Courtesy of the Glenbow Museum.*

and his heavy snowshoes, sawed-off shotgun, pistol, and Savage .30-30 rifle ultimately sent to the RCMP museum in Regina, Saskatchewan. He also had $2,410 in Canadian bills on his person, a considerable amount for a trapper during the Depression. The radio flashed the news to a listening world that the Mad Trapper was dead.

From the start, it was our intention to stand on the spot where the Mad Trapper had died, using Wop May's photo as a guide. However, our friends in Old Crow had urged us to avoid the lower Bell River, which we would have had to follow to get to the Eagle River. The Bell is known for bad overflow and is dangerous, so safety concerns trumped historical curiosity and we found ourselves traveling more than a dozen miles north of the shoot-out site. Nevertheless, we had not gone far from Old Crow before we began to experience the deep soft snow that the Mad Trapper might have been seeking on the west side of the Richardson Mountains. Just a few minutes of flailing around in it searching for Lapierre House left us breathless and sweating. We understood why Albert Johnson had quickly discarded the idea that he could sprint up the snow-covered bank of the Eagle River to escape the Mounties. Our occasional glimpses of the Richardson range ahead of us had revealed enormous white peaks towering over the dark spruce forests at their base. The view not

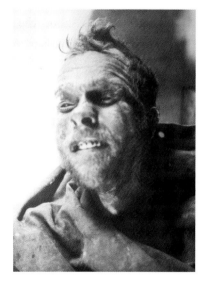

Albert Johnson death photo. *Courtesy of the Glenbow Museum.*

Soft snow in the trees is a sign there has been little or no wind during the winter.

only confirmed that the Mad Trapper was one tough traveler but also suggested that getting ourselves across the mountains with our heavy sled loads might be more difficult than we had anticipated.

Before leaving Fairbanks we had spoken with a musher with a lot of experience in the upper Porcupine country. He warned us that finding the trail up the La Chute River could be difficult, but recent snowmobile traffic had made it obvious where to go from Lapierre House. A narrow slot in the riverbank, just wide enough for a dog sled, ran through several hundred yards of dense overhanging alder before it emerged on a bench on the south side of the La Chute floodplain. The slot had been worn deep into the dirt of the bank by more than a hundred years of use. From the bench the way lay east toward Curtain Mountain, where we had been told there was a new shelter cabin. The thought of sleeping in a warm cabin motivated us to keep moving.

We were preparing dinner when Ernie Vittrekwa arrived at the cabin on his snowmobile. Ernie, an elder from Fort McPherson, was returning home from Old Crow. We had met briefly in Old Crow where I asked Ernie when he was headed back to Fort McPherson in the hope we might travel together. In the way of Natives from that area, noncommittal when it comes to uncertain winter weather, he had said vaguely, "Oh . . . maybe in a couple of days." When I asked what the trail was like, he answered, "It was okay." Ernie had traveled in one day what had taken us two.

Amazingly, thirty years earlier, Dan had met Ernie's father, William Vittrekwa, while seeking information about the Rat River Portage. At the time Dan was unaware that Vittrekwa Senior was one of the people who had had their traps sprung by the Mad Trapper and was a veteran of the famous manhunt. Ernie had spent a good portion of his youth in Aklavik where the Mad Trapper is buried, having been sent to the government boarding school there along with hundreds of other Native kids. It was an unhappy time for

Ernie and the others, forcibly compelled to leave home while very young. We talked of many things that night in the shelter cabin, but Ernie was too young to have known first-hand about the Mad Trapper, and apparently his father had not told him much about that historic event.

Curtain Mountain seen from the La Chute River trail.

We all arose the next morning to a clear but frigid −35°F day. Departing, we quickly ran into overflow ice on the La Chute trail. Once on a winter trip north of the Brooks Range I was traveling down a creek when I ran into some particularly nasty overflow. The first indication of trouble I had was that my snowmobile was propagating a bow wave under the ice ahead. I could see the ice rippling and heaving up, cracking out in radial lines more than thirty feet in front of my machine. It was beautiful to look at, but peculiar. It took a bit of time to grasp what was actually happening, since the mind wants to think of ice as a solid, not a liquid that can ripple and flow like water. Then it dawned on me that more than a foot of water was underlying the ice I was driving on and the only reason I wasn't stuck yet was that I was hydroplaning. Looking behind, I could see a swath of open water where I had passed, the surrounding ice still intact. It looked like an icebreaker had made a pass through pack

Frost flowers on the steaming overflow ice of the La Chute River. *H. Huntington.*

Ernie Vittrekwa.

Part of the Porcupine caribou herd.

ice. The ice this morning on the La Chute had the same look. It was steaming in the cold and noticeably wet in several places. Frost flowers, beautiful feathery growths of hoar frost, were everywhere. We got off our machines to reconnoiter, the ice fog enveloping us. The ice was definitely wet, but it didn't seem to be too dangerous, so off we went.

As we wound our way up the river on the ice, the surrounding forest became more and more sparse, the scenery steeper and more spectacular. Rounding a bend, we caught up with Ernie, who had started about twenty minutes ahead of us. He was standing next to his machine looking at a hill slope covered by thousands of caribou. We pulled alongside and watched for over an hour as bands of a dozen to several hundred caribou crossed the valley in front of us. Ernie said this was the first wave of the million-member Porcupine caribou herd on its annual migration to the arctic coast.

Before another hour had passed we topped out on the Divide, all too easily it seemed. It had taken less than three hours from the Curtain Mountain cabin, including caribou watching. The snowmobiles had little trouble pulling the double sleds. The trail on top was marked with rebar and yellow reflectors that could be followed in a blizzard.

We stopped to look around. The wind was blowing hard here, making the cold air biting, but we knew we would not be exposed for long and our clothing was excellent. The Mad Trapper, wearing ragged clothes and starving, had crossed within a dozen miles of here. In the clear air we could easily see that far. Seventy-six years earlier an intense arctic drama had been played

Somewhere in the distance the Mad Trapper crossed these rugged mountains. *H. Huntington (caribou and Richardson range).*

out here. We could span the years that separated us intellectually, but viscerally and emotionally, we could not even get close. We had had too much hot cocoa, oatmeal, and bacon for breakfast, and we had not worked hard enough in climbing up to the Divide. We were neither sweaty nor scared of being shot. There was no airplane flying overhead trying to spot us. The inexorable march of technology, of the aircraft and radio that had conspired to kill the Mad Trapper, of the GPS and Gore-Tex that now take the disorientation and chill out of blizzards, and of the high-powered snowmobile that has tamed long distances; all these had changed human interactions with this landscape forever. We put our hoods up and started down to Fort McPherson, where we arrived in time for good dinner and hot shower.

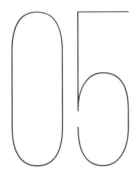

BIG MAC

After two days in Fort McPherson we headed east to Tsiigehtchic, formerly called Arctic Red River. The two communities are now connected by fifty miles of all-weather road, unusable by us since it had been plowed down to bare gravel. There was an old trail through the forest between the villages, nearly forgotten, but Ernie had drawn us a map of it before we parted. His map was uncannily accurate considering that he had not been over the route in decades. Our trouble wasn't with the map, but with the trail. It was unmarked, poorly brushed, and the deep snow had not seen a passage all winter. We made it to Tsiigehtchic, but at a price: one lost side mirror (swiped off by passing too close to a tree) and one burnt drive belt. We also pulled Dan's machine off a tree it had tried to climb, an acrobatic act that resulted in a cracked windshield, a missing kill switch, and a broken rib for Dan, although we did not find out about this last cost until later. After a day of repairs and regrouping in Tsiigehtchic we headed south on the mighty Mackenzie, one of the largest rivers in the world.

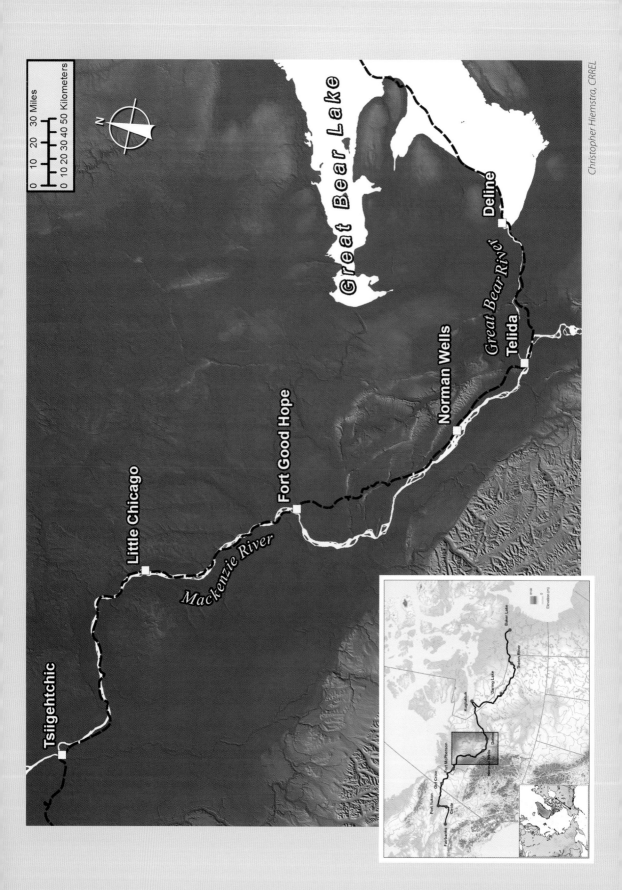

Great Bear Lake

Great Bear River

Deline

Telida

Norman Wells

Fort Good Hope

Mackenzie River

Little Chicago

Tsiigehtchic

0 10 20 30 Miles

0 10 20 30 40 50 Kilometers

N

Christopher Hiemstra, CRREL

EVERYONE WAS PISSED OFF AT ME, but for such an odd

reason. They were tired of being tilted. We were driving up the Mackenzie River, the Big Mac, on the shelf ice along the west side of the river. The shelf ice tilted east. On the river's east side it tilted west. We had been driving on the west side far too long and everyone was tired of leaning to the right to keep their snowmobiles from rolling over. They wanted to cross over so they could lean to the left for a while, just to balance out weary muscles, but there wasn't much I could do. Between the ice shelves was almost a mile of jumbled river ice. That alone might not have kept us from crossing over, but hidden amid the jumble were areas where the ice could be dangerously thin. You could drop through a hole out there and disappear forever. It wasn't worth it to cross, but abstract danger loses its potency in the face of continual discomfort. I could sense a mutiny coming soon.

Shelf ice forms in autumn when the water levels are still high but freezing temperatures prevail. The river freezes over, but even as it does, the water level drops, leaving an air gap below new ice. Eventually the center of this suspended

Shelf ice on the
Mackenzie River.
H. Huntington.

ice sheet breaks and is swept downstream by the current. The smooth narrow ice fringes along both shores, which are grounded on the riverbank, remain in place, though they tip downward toward the center of the river with a marked slope. On a small river, the ice shelves might be narrower than a sidewalk, but on the Mackenzie they are as wide as highways—tilted highways. The slope is unsettling, but wherever the central ice of the river is broken and jumbled, shelf ice is the only option for winter travel.

Only the day before in Tsiigehtchic one of the locals had made a pitch for us to fix the tilted trail problem by pioneering a flatter trail up the center of the river. My diary tells the story:

29 March 2007

We arrived in Tsiigehtchic about 8:00 PM, with twilight just falling. There, parked out front of the first house we came to, was a huge black Dodge pickup truck, brand new and shiny. The owner of the truck took our picture and let me inside to call Russell Andre. We had been told that Russell was the guy who knew the route up the Mackenzie River better than anyone else. We needed to talk to him. The truck owner's wife was inside the house, a grandmotherly woman who cooed and fussed over me when she realized how far I had come.

Russell's house was just up the road. It was the one with the kids playing on the trampoline in the front yard. I knocked and went inside. The house was modern, messy but not filthy, which was understandable considering that Russell was taking care of his four-month-old baby girl as well as several older kids. Inside, caribou jerky was drying on racks. A fifty-six-inch entertainment center against one wall was blaring out an ESPN show. Russell was young, maybe thirty-five, athletic looking, with raven black hair. He had been working during the winter as an environmental monitor on a gas and oil exploration project up the Mackenzie River near a place called Little Chicago. To get to work he had been commuting by snowmobile, ninety miles each way every two weeks. On his last trip home, he "blew his sled" (in this context, sled = snowmobile = snowmachine, though it definitely implies a snowmobile with higher performance than ours). Russell had to go to Inuvik to get a new sled before he could return to Little Chicago.

A young girl in Tsiigehtchic.
H. Huntington.

After explaining how to find and follow his trail, Russell started talking about how we should cut a new trail out in the middle of the river where it was flatter. He also suggested we cut across the big northern bow in the river by following one of the numerous seismic trails in the area, thereby shortening the distance we (and Russell) would have to cover to get to Little Chicago. Then he warned me about the thin ice in the middle of the river. I was new to the Mackenzie, but it seemed to me that there was an obvious contradiction here between wanting a flat trail and the danger of putting in such a trail. Also, we had had some experience trying to follow seismic and other non-trails. Just a few blown-down trees could cost as much time as the shortcut saved. I listened politely to Russell's suggestions, then returned to the topic of how to find his old trail along the river's edge. Russell, sensing we were unlikely to do anything bold out there, graciously drew a sketch map of the start of his trail. I left, wishing him success in getting a new sled. The kids were still jumping on the trampoline.

So there we were on the shelf ice, safe because we were not out in the middle of the river, but sore from being tilted.

The shelf ice did offer one benefit: it gave us a good view of the west riverbank we were hugging. Rising several hundred feet above our heads, the steep bluffs were covered by deciduous and evergreen trees. There was nothing exceptional about the bluffs except a strip at their base, devoid of vegetation, that continued along the bank as far as we could see. We drove for several hours before finally realizing what it represented. It was the high-water line of the river, and it was twenty-five feet above us. Far across the river we could see a companion bare strip above the shelf ice on the east side. The amount of water implied by the two strips was unbelievable: a sheet of water twenty-five feet high and at least four thousand feet wide, moving at about five miles per hour. A simple calculation suggested that more than a million cubic feet per second passed by here during high-water events.

We had read the statistics: At 697,000 square miles, the Mackenzie is the third largest drainage basin in the Western Hemisphere, exceeded only by the Mississippi and Amazon basins. Snaking more than 2,600 miles, it is the thirteenth longest river in the world, and it carries the discharge from three of the world's largest freshwater lakes—Great Bear, Great Slave, and Athabasca. But those were all just numbers. The high-water mark was tangible and real.

We were beginning to get a visceral sense that this river far surpassed in scale and power the other Arctic rivers of our acquaintance. That feeling was conveyed chiefly by the size of the bends. All creeks and rivers have bends, their size in some way scaled to the size of the stream. Small creeks bend back and forth over distances of tens or hundreds of feet. Larger rivers like the Tanana near Fairbanks wander back and forth over distances of a mile or perhaps a couple of miles. The first substantial bend in the Mackenzie we rounded upstream of Tsiigehtchic was more than ten miles long. It felt endless as we drove along on our little shelf of tilted ice. The sameness of the surrounding country enhanced the effect. Low forested land extended back from the river on each side for as far as we could see. Whenever we stopped, the surrounding country looked identical to the last stop.

I imagined that intrepid Scotsman, Alexander Mackenzie, must have been feeling the same sense of endlessness as he floated down the river in the summer of 1789. Mackenzie, at the time twenty-six years old, had set out from Fort Chipewyan on the south shore of Lake Athabasca traveling in four canoes with a party of five voyageurs, two of their wives, and a small group of Indians. His goal was the Pacific Ocean. His dream, to revolutionize the fur trade by

Driving on the frozen Mackenzie River. The treeline along the banks marks the high-water line.
H. Huntington.

HEAVY EQUIPMENT and pickup trucks that left their marks at Little Chicago could have come upriver on barges in the fall, but more likely they were driven up a unique winter road system. Constructed wholly of snow and ice each year, this four-hundred-mile network begins at the northern end of the all-season road at Wrigley and connects five remote Mackenzie River villages. In most places the winter road runs through a wide right-of-way cut through the taiga forest.

In December and January, as the snow cover begins to build up, workers from the Northwest Territories Department of Transportation roll, compact, and wet the snow until it forms a hard base that wheeled trucks and cars can drive on. Where there are lakes, the crews plow off the snow to

The ice-snow road between Tsiigehtchic and Norman Wells. *H. Huntington.*

promote natural thickening of the ice The weak links in this system are the

stream crossings. Any thawing and the creeks begin to open up, severing the road connection.

Over time, the NWT has been putting steel-grid bridges over the creeks to make the winter roads last longer. These bridges are particularly important for extending the life of the roads into spring, when the creeks can begin to break up before the tundra has started to thaw. Strangely, Alaska, despite similar winter conditions, does not build many winter roads.

The real "heavy lift" transportation capability for the NWT region, however, is on the river itself in summertime. Shallow-draft tugs ply the Mackenzie moving massive amounts of cargo and fuel on barges to supply the entire area up to the Arctic Ocean.

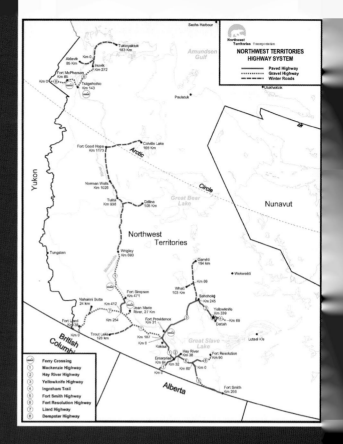

The winter road system of the Northwest Territories. *Courtesy Regional Superintendent at Department of Transportation, Government of Northwest Territories.*

A Mackenzie River shallow draft pusher tug owned by the Northern Transportation Company Ltd. *Jock McNiven, NTCL*

On the last day before the winter road closes not much snow or ice is left on the tundra.

connecting the North West Company's fur-trapping empire in the east with an ocean port on the west coast of the continent. Doing so was a matter of commercial survival for the upstart fur trading company, which was under considerable pressure from competition by the Hudson's Bay Company (HBC) and from the high costs of obtaining furs from the remote reaches of Canada.

Since the HBC's founding in 1670, fur traders had been spreading westward across Canada from Hudson Bay, seeking out productive fur-bearing lands. Denied access to the trapping grounds bordering Hudson Bay that had been reserved for HBC by royal decree, the North West Company began operations from a base in Montreal. Via the vast network of lakes and rivers that cover Canada, its traders had pushed west and north, eventually penetrating the Arctic, a huge end-run around the royal company. The lake and river route required North West Company agents to move goods and furs more than twice as far as their rivals, but the company was staffed by men of greater vigor and initiative than the more complacent servants of the HBC. Through heroic efforts, they had nearly succeeding in making the plan work. Still, time and distance were taking a toll, and unless something was done quite soon the North West Company might still fail.

Both companies' business was based on trading English manufactured goods, such as needles and blankets, for furs collected by Indians and a few white trappers. The best furs came from the frigid north, where animals grew luxuriant pelts for survival; hence, both companies were necessarily northern enterprises. They were also extractive enterprises that depleted resources in one area and had to continually expand into fresh territory. By Mackenzie's time, the trade was still lucrative but the handwriting was on the wall. The cost of obtaining the furs would soon eat into, if not wholly destroy, everyone's profits.

In his book *Voyages from Montreal on the River St. Laurence...*, Mackenzie himself described the problem: an order for manufactured goods would be placed in London in the fall of October 1796. They would be shipped four months later, arriving in Montreal in June 1797, too late to catch the canoe brigades that headed west earlier in the spring. Between June 1797 and the following spring, the goods would be made into trade items and bundled into ninety-pound bales. These would leave Montreal in May of 1798, headed west with the canoe brigades. The first part of the journey would be in thirty-six-foot freight canoes, each carrying seventy bales and powered by a dozen men. These voyageur crews, known as *les allants et venants* (the goers and comers), would paddle up the Saint Lawrence River, then up the Ottawa River, portage across to Lake Nipissing, and then run down into Georgian Bay on Lake Huron (a journey of hundreds of miles and thirty-six portages). From there, they would head to Sault Sainte Marie where they would pass into Lake Superior, the largest lake in the world. Facing 450 miles of open water, the crews would pray for calm conditions and make a dash for Grand Portage, Minnesota. Here the boatmen from Montreal would hand off the trade goods to *les hommes du nord*, the Northmen, who had wintered in the wild lands and had brought their fur pelts down to Lake Superior. These voyageurs paddled smaller, more maneuverable twenty-four-foot canoes and considered themselves a superior breed to their counterparts, the "pork-eaters," who wintered in and around Montreal.

The *allants et venants* would load the pelts into their battered canoes and head back to Montreal, while the *hommes du nord* would take the trade goods and head back into the taiga. Their return route lay through that maze of lakes that straddle the border between Minnesota and Canada now called the Boundary Waters, today part of Voyageur National Park and Quetico Provincial Park. From there they would work their way into Rainy Lake and finally down the Winnipeg River into Lake Winnipeg. From this immense lake, the routes diverged, with goods headed for the Mississippi drainage going south up the Red River, goods for the Rocky Mountains headed west up the Saskatchewan and its tributaries, and goods for the Arctic headed for Cumberland House and the Churchill River.

The voyageurs, those free spirits who paddled fifteen to eighteen hours a day for scant pay and little glory, powered the trade. Through their unmitigated toil they established a network of communication lines across vast prairies and boreal forests that ultimately led to the establishment of Canada as a country that spanned the continent. Still, by the time Mackenzie set

Marten is one of the furs that fueled the Hudson's Bay and North West companies.

out on his explorations, even the spirited voyageurs could no longer keep up with the growing strain of short summer paddling seasons and increasingly long paddling distances.

The key, at least to Mackenzie, John Jacob Astor, and a few other astute fur traders, lay in China. Some of the furs that arrived in London eventually made their way to China. Coveted by the Chinese, the furs were exchanged for silks and tea, generating even greater profit for the companies than furs sold directly in Europe. Mackenzie had the vision to see that if furs harvested in central Canada could be brought down to a Pacific port, it would shortcut the long overland route back through Montreal and Europe. Trade with China would be vastly easier, as would re-supply of the trading posts scattered throughout western Canada. The port would solidify a triangular trading system involving the New World, the Orient, and England, which would maintain control and reap the profits. Mackenzie's bosses in the North West Company agreed sufficiently to allow him to risk his life trying to find a route to the Pacific.

The entire venture appeared more feasible than it actually was because the maps available at the time placed the Pacific coast much closer to Fort Chipewyan on Lake Athabasca than it in reality it was. These maps were made by Mackenzie's predecessor and mentor Peter Pond, who had spent sixteen years in the Athabasca country. Initially, Pond had (correctly) mapped the waters flowing out of Lake Athabasca going northward into the polar sea, but with time as Pond's information—and his personal bias in favor of the existence of a Northwest Passage—increased, he changed the maps to show the great river of the north flowing west into Cook Inlet in Alaska. Armed with this latest map, and a sack of rubles to pay for passage across Russia and back to England, Mackenzie found himself drifting down the river that now bears his name.

The expedition made slow progress at first. The descent down the Slave River took just a few days, but there was still ice on Great Slave Lake, the tenth largest lake in the world. Winds had pushed the ice against the southern shore, so they worked their way across the lake through a series of islands, then along the north shore. Beset by ice, they were also attacked by clouds of mosquitoes, a pairing that seemed patently unfair. Passing the location of modern day Yellowknife, they inched their way west, eventually finding the outlet of the lake and the start of the Mackenzie River proper. Once on the big river, they moved at express speed, reaching the ocean near the present-day town of Tuktoyaktuk in two weeks. Along the way they passed, noted, and mapped all of the salient tributaries and features of the river, missing only a few such as the Peel River. Mackenzie's thoroughness belied his disappointment. He almost certainly realized early in the trip that the great river was unlikely to let out into the Pacific Ocean or Cook Inlet. At Camsell Bend, sixty-five river miles northwest of the modern town Fort Simpson, where the river makes a hard bend to the north, Mackenzie must have sensed he was unlikely to find the Pacific port he so ardently hoped for. Nonetheless, he recognized that there was value in charting the full course of the river and persevered.

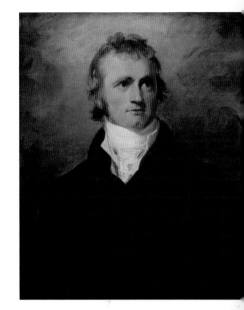

Alexander Mackenzie, painted by Thomas Lawrence, around ten years after his exploration of the river that bears his name. *Courtesy National Gallery of Canada (Mackenzie portrait).*

Through heavy wind and rain, his small party continued down the mighty river. It must have been on the minds of everyone that they would have to return home against the same strong current that was carrying them swiftly north. The mosquitoes continued to plague them as well. On July 5, Bear Rock came into view on the right-hand margin of the river. This rocky eminence lies just north of the confluence of the Mackenzie River and the Great Bear River, the clear-water discharge arising from Great Bear Lake. The Rock is a sacred place to Sahtu, who still live in Telida (formerly Fort Norman) and Deline. Mackenzie must have learned of the great lake from one of his Native guides because the Great Bear River appears on his map as the River of the

Great Lake. On the sixth of July he passed the future site of Norman Wells, today an oil and gas refinery town. The next day he flew down Sans Sault and Rampart rapids, the latter just upstream of the present-day town of Fort Good Hope. On July 8, he was near Thunder River, and by the ninth he had gone by Tsiigehtchic and passed Point Separation, where the river splits into numerous channels as it enters the great delta. If his journal is to be believed, it was not until this point that he began to harbor doubts that he was going to the Pacific Ocean.

At 68°N latitude Mackenzie finally wrote, "it is evident that these Waters must empty themselves into the Northern Ocean." Reality had hit, but the stubborn Scotsman would see the game out and follow the river to its end, wherever that might be. His men, on the other hand, were increasingly anxious to turn back, fearful they would not be able to make it to Fort Chipewyan before freeze-up. That would mean slow death by starvation. By being part-conciliatory and part-stern, and in part by appealing to their vanity, Mackenzie managed to wring from his crew an agreement to continue another seven days before turning around. It was enough. By the twelfth of July they began to see marine mammal remains in the abandoned encampments of Inuvialuit on the shore. By the fourteenth, they were camped on Garry Island in Mackenzie Bay. Though the water was still fresh with the river's vast discharge, there was a tide. They had reached the sea.

The return trip, about nine hundred miles against the current, must have been grim. About ten years ago, while preparing for a marathon canoe race, Dan and I had trained by paddling upstream on the Chena River. At times working as hard as we could, we would watch the bank go by in slow motion. In our case, after an hour or two of this intensive labor, we would spin the canoe around and sail on the current back down to where we had started, easily moving five times faster than our upriver travel. Mackenzie's men did not have this luxury. In the fast water of the rapids, they had to resort to lining—towing their boats with a line while wading in the river or sometimes walking on shore.

Mackenzie is rightly hailed as one of the great explorers of all time, his crowning achievement the discovery (at least by a Westerner) of the great river that bears his name. Nonetheless, as he and his crew toiled upstream, Mackenzie felt an acute sense of failure. On September 12, with ice forming on the lakes and rivers at night, the little party arrived back at Fort Chipewyan, having been gone 103 days. In a letter to his cousin Roderick, Mackenzie referred to the river he had just explored as the "River Disappointment," but he put a brave face on his results for the rest of the world. And the North West Company was quick to capitalize on the new geographical knowledge he had brought back from the North. By 1796 the company had established

Sunset behind Bear Rock.
J. Holmgren.

Oil and gas field rigs in Norman Wells.

a post on the upper Mackenzie. Three years later it had a post on Great Bear Lake near the present hamlet of Deline. In 1804, Fort of the Forks—now the town of Fort Simpson—was established at the junction of the Liard and Mackenzie Rivers. By 1805, Fort Good Hope was established and remains a major northern community. Within forty years of Mackenzie's dash down the river, the vast country it drained, with its rich and plentiful furs, came to be known as the "treasure house" for the North West Company, but by then the company had been taken over by its rival, the HBC. The need for a Pacific port remained, and Mackenzie would eventually find a route to the Pacific, but by that time the search had shifted south to the Columbia River, building on the reconnaissance of Lewis and Clarke.

Tilted shelf ice not withstanding, we made one of our longest daily runs that day on the Mackenzie—a full ninety miles—and arrived at Little Chicago as dusk was settling. The name is a corruption of a Gwich'in phrase meaning "where the geese nest," reflecting some nearby wetlands; it has nothing to do with the great U.S. city. From Russell Andre we knew that oil and gas exploration crews had been basing out of the place for the last few months, and I guess we also figured that with a name like Little Chicago there would be cabins and maybe even some folks living there. We joked that we would be able to order pizza, but we were sadly disappointed on all counts. No cabins, no ATCO trailers from the seismic crews, nothing but a big plowed-off area where lots of ATCOs and heavy equipment had been parked at one time. Now there were just a few empty pallets and an oil drum tipped on its side. Entering

FINDING THE ARCTIC

this area from the south was a bladed-off trail through the woods. The black spruce trees had been pushed out of the way by a big tractor and lay rolled up in piles along the side of the road. The snow on the trail was punched down and compressed by heavy steel tracks.

Superimposed on these were tire tracks of cars that had driven up from Fort Good Hope. Another broad snow road ran west from the big staging area across the mighty river and up the bank on the far side, disappearing into the endless spruce forest. Somewhere out there in the woods, the seismic crews had been roaming around, setting geophones and shaking the ground with big trucks to see if there were commercial quantities of oil and gas down below.

What would Mackenzie have thought? On his travels down the big river, he was thinking of furs and sailing ships. The roughnecks and cat skinners who had been at Little Chicago just a few days before were probably thinking about oil and sex. Times change, but maybe not that much.

FINDING THE DOUGLAS CABIN

*From Little Chicago it was seventy-eight miles to Fort Good Hope,
population 550. More than a billion barrels of oil are believed to lie
beneath the forested flats west of the river and, like elsewhere in
the North, finding a balance between economic development and
traditional values is proving difficult for the Dene and Gwich'in,
represented in town by the Yamoga Land and Xahweguweh
Financial Corporations. The town has seen other economic booms: it
was founded in 1805 as a trading post by the North West Company,
eager to capitalize on Alexander Mackenzie's discoveries. In 1859 a
Roman Catholic mission was established in town, its legacy a white
clapboard church, modest on the outside, but with a stunning interior
lovingly decorated by a succession of Oblate Fathers.*

*Leaving Fort Good Hope, we followed the winter road south. It
was due to close in two days because of warming temperatures and
much of the road had already been worn down to bare ground. Over
long stretches our only choice was to run on a narrow strip of dirty
snow on the side of the road. We arrived in Telida (formerly Fort
Norman) exhausted and covered with dirt. A day later we followed
the winter road to Deline, where we came face to face with one of
the sadder stories of the Arctic: radium mining for the atomic bomb,
done during and after World War Two with little regard for worker
safety, has been responsible for a high rate of cancer deaths in the
village. We also had the first sense that we were leaving the taiga
country through which we had been traveling since Fairbanks. Soon
we would enter Canadian Shield. The world seemed too much with
us in Deline, but as soon as we set out on Great Bear Lake we felt
freer and wilder. The Barrenlands were just ahead.*

Christopher Hiemstra, CRREL

WE WERE DEFINITELY NERVOUS as we looked out on the big lake. Great Bear is bigger than many states and out on the ice there would be nowhere to hide if the wind came up. Perhaps for that reason all hands pitched in with vigor when we stopped about twenty miles out of Deline to cut firewood. This was the last place we would be near shore. Snow off the lake had piled up against the forest edge and we sank up to our waists in deep drifts as we wallowed about cutting trees. Two of us hauled the dead spruce out onto the lake where it was easier to work, two cut the trees into firewood lengths, and Henry loaded the booty onto his sled. We left the site feeling a little more secure with enough wood to weather a storm of several days.

The nearest land was a faint blue line in the distance as we settled in for our first night on the lake, but despite our apprehensions there was hardly a breath of wind and we awoke to a still and crisp (−25°F) morning. The hard drifts and eroded snow dunes on the lake ice, however, attested to times when the place we were camped could be a white hell. Taking no chances, we had dug the tents in deeply, shoveling away the snow right down to the ice surface and then

Firewood for the Great Bear Lake crossing.
H. Huntington.

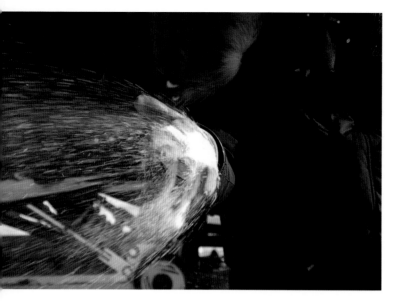

Saltating snow particles follow parabolic trajectories, seen here as the wind carries snow out of my hand. *H. Huntington.*

heaping mighty piles of snow on the tent valances to hold them down.

On the second day of the crossing the wind began to rise. Wind needs to exceed about twelve miles per hour before it can drift snow grains. Most of the day, the wind stayed below this critical threshold, but late in the day it crossed the line. Snow began to hiss along the surface, small snaking wisps curling and winding among the snow dunes. This transport of bounding and rebounding snow particles is called saltation. Individual grains caught by the wind follow steep parabolic trajectories that rise six to twelve inches above the snow surface. Once aloft, the grains accelerate as they are blown downwind, but eventually they descend and collide with the snow surface a few feet from where they started. The collision is important because each colliding grain ejects several new grains, which now enter the wind-stream. This cascading process not only sustains but actually increases the flux of grains with time and distance downwind.

The saltating layer rarely comes above a person's knees and in itself is not objectionable. The problem is that within a few hours some fraction of the hissing snow grains are pulverized. These lighter grains become airborne and will not settle back to the surface until the wind dies. Collectively, they are called the suspended load and they impart a hazy white cast to the air. Even with moderate wind, the hazy layer can extend thirty feet above the snow surface. When the wind is really screaming, the layer can spiral up several hundred feet. This day, the hazy layer was still pretty thin. Looking straight up, we could see blue sky and a bright sun above, but looking horizontally, there was a dead white pall to everything nearby and objects more than a couple of hundred feet away were indistinct. We knew if the wind speed continued to rise, this haze would become thicker and thicker until it would be impossible to see more than a few feet: the much-feared arctic blizzard. The full ensemble of hissing snow on the

Wind rising … it's starting to get ugly. *H. Huntington.*

dunes, white pall in the air, the inability to see anything at a distance, and the rising noise of the wind is what makes northern snow travelers nervous when the wind gets up.

Our route now took us near the Scented Grass Hills, a long mountainous peninsula that divides Keith and Smith Arms, two of the five arms that make up Great Bear Lake. They say the lake takes it name from the fact that its outline looks like a stretched bearskin. This bear, though, spans 180 miles from south to north and covers twelve thousand square miles. The name, which predates even Mackenzie's explorations, says something about the well honed topographic sense of the indigenous people who traveled this area before maps and satellites, for it wasn't until about the 1940s that anyone saw the bearskin outline in its entirety.

Our original intent had been to pass from Keith Arm to Smith Arm via a low valley that held two attractions. First, it ends in Douglas Bay, named after the explorer George Mellis Douglas, a consummate arctic traveler whom we all admired. Second, the 122nd meridian crosses the 66th parallel at the mouth of the valley. Back in the warm confines of our homes in Fairbanks, we had decided that we would bag this confluence during the traverse. An odd sport that did not exist until the advent of the GPS, confluence bagging consists of being the first to stand where whole number latitude lines cross whole number longitude lines. Most of these intersections fall on the world's oceans, but a few fall in remote but interesting locations like the west side of Great Bear Lake. We had rashly promised that we would bag confluences along the route and dedicate them to the school kids tracking the trip. So far, dense forest and lethargy had prevented any success.

On this day it was the wind that conspired to keep us from the confluence. Instead of veering toward the mouth of the valley, we headed toward the nearest land and a sheltered camping spot. Soon we were working through several lines of pressure ridges where the lake ice had been forced against the rocks of Etacho Point. Once called Gros Cap, Etacho Point is a broad foreland where sparse trees give way to tundra. Most of the point offers no protection from the wind, but we found a small pond set down below a ridge protected by spruce trees.

The plan for our third day on Great Bear was to make a big run—seventy miles—across one of the widest parts of the lake. In theory, we would end up at the easiest confluence to bag: 67°N, 120°W. This spot was out on the lake ice, with no trees, no steep terrain, and no excuses. How could we fail to bag this one? The first inkling of an answer came at breakfast. It was calm and sunny on the small pond, but we could hear the moan of the wind overhead and see the treetops swaying violently. The white haze of the previous day now extended higher. The sun was still out, but it appeared to be shining through ground glass. As we drove out of our sheltered spot, we realized that this might prove to be something of a breezy day. Out came our facemasks and nose coverings, as it was still quite cold. Driving back onto the lake had a risky feel. The ice, of course, was more than thick enough to support us, but by midday the nearest shelter would be more than thirty-five miles away. Moreover, we couldn't just bolt for the far shore. We had to make snow and ice measurements in several places during the seventy-mile crossing. This required stopping, digging snow pits, coring through the snow and weighing the cores, auguring a hole through the ice, and measuring snow depth every three feet along a 1,500-foot line. Henry was assigned this last job. He would start walking downwind with his probe, and when the rest of us were done with our measurements, Jon would go get him with a snowmobile. At the first measurement station, some ten miles out from Etacho Point, we could just barely see Henry through the blowing snow when he was at the end of his walk. At the second measurement station, he was obscured by the snow about halfway out the line, and by the third and last station, he disappeared less than a hundred feet from us.

As the day progressed the most worrisome thing was that the rising wind was sweeping increasingly large areas of the lake ice clear of snow. Driving along, we would peer down as we drove over a small patch of incredibly clear black ice. Pinhead- to fist-sized white bubbles could be seen suspended inside it and bubble trains looked like little constellations of spherical stars frozen into a black icy cosmos. Strange networks of cracks also permeated the top six inches. Deeper, the ice was virtually invisible, being both bubble- and crack-free. It was so clear, in fact, that at one point Dan expressed concern that the ice was only six inches thick, but our drill holes consistently showed five to seven feet of ice. The problem that worried us was that with the snow being swept from the ice, it might get hard to get traction.

Before the windstorm, rafted ice on Great Bear Lake. *H. Huntington.*

We began to weave about looking for tongues of snow to cross. The carbide cleats on the skis of our machines made an audible slicing sound as they left two parallel score marks etched into the black ice surface. As the day wore on and the wind continued to rise, the crossing from one snow tongue to another became longer, and our snowmobiles spun-out more frequently. We began to wonder if at some point we might run out of snow altogether. This would be double jeopardy, with no snow for traction, but also no snow to anchor the tents down if we had to camp. The only prudent course of action was to get across the lake as soon as possible. We altered course for Cape McDonnell, the nearest point of land about thirty miles ahead, and our next chance of bagging a confluence vanished with the scudding snow.

BLACK LAKE ICE

The autumn weather needs to be just right to make black ice. There can't be too much wind and the freezing water must be still and relatively free of dissolved air. It has to freeze slowly enough that the air can escape from solution without being trapped in the ice, and the ice has to get thick quickly enough so that it can hold up any snow that falls on it. If too much snow falls early in the season, its weight pushes the thin ice below the water level. Water then floods the base of the snow, where it refreezes, making a milky white basal layer called snow-ice.

Like most materials, ice expands at higher temperatures, contracts at colder ones. The daily and weekly cycles of winter weather will cause the upper part of the ice to expand and contract more than the deeper part, which is buffered from the big temperature swings. Cracks in the ice will generally be confined to an upper six- to twelve-inch layer. The result can be a little spooky, as the uncracked ice below is virtually invisible, making the ice appear to be only as thick as the cracked zone. There is something hypnotic about gazing through the cracked layer into the abyssal depths below.

The black ice on Great Bear Lake (with my boots for scale) was more than five feet thick.

Our landfall at Cape McDonnell was anything but auspicious. The Cape is low tundra. The GPS said we were ashore, but all we could see was more wind-blasted snow. Farther inland the tundra had been swept clean, leaving gravel, sand, and boulders, worse driving than the bare patches of ice. Deep inlets cut through the area, so even when we tried to run on the land, we kept coming back out on the ice. Fortunately, we had heard about a cabin on one of these inlets. We were unsure where it was and there had been some talk of open water near the cabin, but after about an hour of cautiously poking about, we found the place and quickly moved our gear inside out of the wind.

The bare ice patches get bigger; Glen dons his beaver mittens. *D. Solie.*

There is nothing as snug as a cabin when the wind is howling outside. Snow drifting in through the cracks between the logs just added to our feeling of security. We loaded up the wood stove and relaxed. Layers of icy pile and fleece were hung up to defrost and dry. It was Glen's birthday, which we celebrated with candles and a frozen cheesecake that we had brought from Fairbanks. Henry had purchased a toy snowmobile in the Northern Store in Deline that we gave to Glen as a present. The toy machine was a replica of an eight-hundred cc racing snowmobile, brilliant yellow, more racy and powerful than Glen's real machine. He loved it.

The wind was still howling the next morning and the world was hazy with blowing snow but we set out anyway. We quickly found ourselves abreast of the Narakay Islands, in Sahtu mythology a set of giant beaver lodges now solidified into rock. Legend has it that the world emerged from these lodges back in the mists of time. Trees, animals, the waters, even the Sahtu themselves came from here. Only the tops of the islands were visible, floating in the sky, their bases obscured by blowing snow. They looked ethereal and unreal. It was easy to believe we were near the center of the Earth.

Yet even before the Narakay Islands had disappeared, the unmistakable signs of civilization appeared before us. We came upon the end of the gravel

Glen gets a snowmobile for his birthday in the cabin near Cape McDonnell. *H. Huntington.*

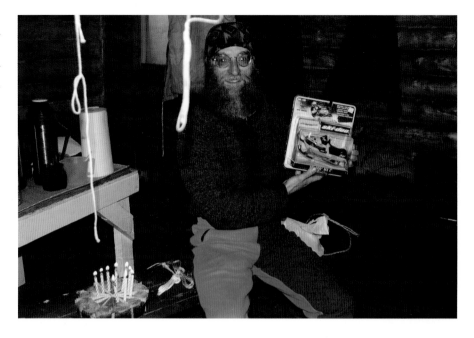

One of the Narakay Islands hovers above blowing snow out on Great Bear Lake. *H. Huntington.*

runway for Plummer's Great Bear Lake Lodge, the largest fishing lodge on the lake. Swept free of snow by the wind, the runway was long enough for a 737 jet to land. We followed along its full length and as we rounded its far end what appeared to be an abandoned town came into view. Dozens of white buildings with red roofs, fuel tanks, power lines, radio towers, snowed-in trucks, boats, barges, and heaped-up piles of caribou and moose antlers appeared. The wind was howling around the buildings, busily piling up drifts. Amid all this civilization, a stark contrast to the two hundred miles of wilderness we had just passed through, a line of nearly three-dozen eighteen-foot aluminum boats with new thirty-horsepower motors may have been the most impressive sign of the summer crowds. An industrial walk-in reefer told the tale: a lot of fish fillets went out of this lodge with the customers.

After half an hour of wandering around this ghost town and seeing the sights, hunger got the better of us and we began looking for a place out of the wind for lunch. One of the guest cabins was unlocked. Inside, we sat around a brown Formica kitchen table eating cold burritos and drinking hot tea. The room was modest, neat, and tidy. White terrycloth towels still hung on the rack in the bathroom, and the beds had pretty quilt-like coverlets and brass headstands. There was no heat, but out of the wind it was a fairly warm day. Perhaps this stop was not the *beau idéal* of a wilderness trip, but it was certainly good to get out of the wind. As a bonus, we caught a glimpse of ourselves in the bathroom mirror. Wow! We looked absurd wearing all that protective clothing on our heads and faces. Staring back from the mirror we saw an eccentric mix of neoprene masks, sunglasses, hearing protectors, neck gaiters, fur ruffs, mittens, goggles, and three-week-old facial hair.

We continued up the shore from Plummer's Lodge, dodging in and out of the forest as needed to avoid the buffeting winds near headlands. A small chain of ponds allowed us to circumvent one long peninsula where the wind looked particularly vicious. We wound from one pond to another, climbing slightly and then following a narrow valley bordered by a blocky granite cliff. Here we saw some of the first caribou tracks since the Richardson Mountains. In the trees the blowing snow was reduced to the point where we recognized

Industrial fishing in cold storage at Plummer's Lodge on Great Bear Lake. *H. Huntington.*

that it was actually quite a nice day. One pond led to another, then a small creek led back down toward Great Bear Lake. We corkscrewed down the stream, the soft snow flying from our machines, sun on our backs, sleds whipping around like crack-the-whip, just enough room between the shrubs and trees overhanging the creek to get by. And then we were there, spit out into the lake channel behind Ritch Island, the wind now blocked by the island, the magnificent sun-dappled channel running clear and straight six miles to the mouth of the Dease River, the extreme northern end of the lake. We had done it. We had crossed the seventh largest lake in the world.

The channel itself was a few hundred yards wide and the vanished Pleistocene ice sheet had scoured it hard. The bedrock ridges that edged the channel had been smoothed like loaves of bread. In places huge blocks of rock had been plucked out of the ridges by the southward flowing ice. Low outcrops on the shore of the channel were polished and striated. Scattered everywhere—on the shore, in the woods, on the outcrops—lay erratics, blocks of rock of all different sizes and kinds, transported here from hundreds of miles away by the Laurentide Ice Sheet. Among these were a few blocks of pink Precambrian granite, our first sighting of this signature stone of the Barrenlands.

Today the Dease River area is basically a wilderness, visited occasionally by trout fishermen, but at one time it was a vital link between the Barrenlands and the Mackenzie River system. The list of famous explorers who passed through the Dease crossroads, and in many cases wintered there awaiting the breakup of the ice on Great Bear Lake, is impressive: Sir John Franklin (1819–1822 and 1825–1827), Sir John Richardson (1827 and 1848), Peter Warren Dease and Thomas Simpson (1837), John Rae (1849), Vihljalmur Stefansson (1910), D. T. Hanbury (1902), George W. Melville (1908–1910), John Hornby (1908–1912), Douglas (1911), and Denny LaNauze (1915), in addition to all the unnamed trappers, traders, and Jesuit missionaries who passed that way. Before these white men showed up, Indians from the taiga used Dease Inlet and the Dease River as a natural corridor to the Barrenlands where they went to hunt caribou. Inuit from Coronation Gulf followed the same route south to hunt and gather wood from the forests. During the heyday of this crossroads, just before World War I, a number of white parties and extended Indian families spent their winters in this remote northern corner of Great Bear Lake.

Among these were Douglas, along with his brother Lionel, and a Swedish geologist named Sandberg. Douglas's early adult experiences were not in the frozen wastes of the North, but rather in the deserts of Mexico where he assisted his wealthy Uncle James in several mining ventures. But he had read about Samuel Hearne and his search for copper on the Coppermine River north of Great Bear Lake (see chapter 8). He may also have seen Richardson's account of these so-called mines in reports from the Franklin expedition of 1821. Uncle James agreed to finance a small yearlong expedition led by George Douglas to more thoroughly examine the copper deposits. The tale of that trip and the winter of 1911–1912 the party spent at Dease Inlet is elegantly told in Douglas's book *Lands Forlorn*.

On the surface, the venture appears to have been a sober, straightforward search for copper. Fifteen years earlier, gold had been discovered in the Klondike, not too far from Great Bear Lake, and huge profits were made. Five years after that, gold was found in the creeks near Fairbanks and on the storm-tossed beaches of Nome, and more men got rich. Even while Douglas was planning his expedition, the Guggenheim syndicate was taking a fortune in copper ore out of the Wrangell Mountains in southcentral Alaska. It was a time of great possibilities, with tycoons and industrialists making vast wealth. A lucky strike could set a man up for life.

George Mellis Douglas in the cabin at Hodgson's Point during the winter of 1911–1912. *G. M. Douglas, courtesy National Archives Canada.*

THE SHIELD AND THE CORDILLERAN

WITHOUT UNDERSTANDING the geology of arctic North America, there can be no understanding of its human history, patterns of settlement, oil and mineral development, or the track of our journey. Four billion years ago when the Earth was still very young, vast bodies of magma cooled and solidified deep within the land that is now central Canada. Pink and white feldspars interlocked with clear quartz and black hornblende forming the ancient granites that make up the Canadian Shield. With time, plate tectonics piled younger rocks against the western side of the Shield, forming the Cordilleran, an intense jumble of mountain ranges that parallel the Mackenzie River and extend all the way to the Pacific Coast. The western mountains look like rock waves breaking against an unmovable low reef, which is pretty much what they are.

Glacial erratics perch on bedrock smoothed by the Laurentide Ice Sheet near Dease Inlet.

Fast-forward to the Pleistocene ice age, beginning about 2.6 million years ago, which included at least five major periods of glaciation. High in the mountains on the east side of the Shield, year after year, more snow fell than melted each summer until small pocket glaciers coalesced into bigger piedmont glaciers, which then grew into a vast continent-sized ice sheet, the Laurentide. It extended from Baffin Island all the way to the Mackenzie River, covering almost the entire Shield. The ice gouged and ground the tough rocks, reaming out joint planes, eroding innumerable small lake basins, and excavating half a dozen enormous ones. In the Cordilleran, smaller glaciers carved out long straight U-shaped valleys between mountain peaks.

The interaction of rock and ice left two distinct hydrologic systems across arctic North America. Where the center of the Laurentide Ice Sheet had been, the crust of the Earth was depressed thousands of feet producing Hudson Bay and its lowlands. Farther west it left an uncountable number of lakes, large and small, and along the now-vanished margin of the ice sheet, enormous lake basins. These include the Great Lakes system that now feeds the Saint Lawrence River, and the other great lakes—Great Bear, Great Slave, and Athabasca—which feed the Mackenzie River flowing to the Arctic Ocean. Where the mountain

Cordilleran

Shield

Arc of Lakes

Chena River	Great Bear Lake	Lac de Gras
Birch Creek	*Dease River*	Alymer Lake
Yukon River	Lake Rouviere	Clinton-Colden Lake
Porcupine River	Dismal Lakes	Napatulik Lake
Bell River	Rockinghorse Lake	*Hanbury River*
La Chute River	Contwoyto Lake	*Thelon River*
Stony Creek	Yamba Lake	Beverly Lake
Peel River	Daring Lake	Aberdeen Lake
MacKenzie River		Shultz Lake

glaciers had been, long narrow fiords and finger lakes now feed the Yukon River, flowing west to the Bering Sea.

While our journey was technically

geologic heritage. During our trip in the Cordilleran we traveled almos exclusively on frozen rivers, while on the Shield we traveled mostly on fro

But a closer look at Douglas's writing, and his riveting black and white photographs, suggests a very different motive. He came for adventure and romance. The North was clean and invigorating: it had unlimited possibilities. A young man could test himself there, while at the same time escaping from a rigid and regimented society still emerging from the corset stays of the Victorian era. It was a place where economic depression and social barriers could be forgotten. If a fortune was made there, fine, but the real lure was freedom. Pierre Berton, the foremost chronicler of the Klondike gold rush, has concluded that the quest for self and experience, not gold, was what really brought more than thirty thousand young men and women north in 1898, and that lure was still potent in 1911.

To get to the Dease River, the Douglas party traveled by rail from Ontario to Edmonton, then overland to the Athabasca River. They raced down the river in canoes to catch up with the HBC brigade of scows heading for the northern trading posts with the annual consignment of trade goods and supplies. From Athabasca Landing, past Fort McMurray and down to Fort Smith on the Slave River, they paddled, poled, and pulled canoes, scows, and York boats. They saw the same great muddy rivers, wooded hills, and endless forests that had greeted Mackenzie 130 years earlier. The Douglas party was able to transfer to a paddle wheel steamer with a fancy dining salon for the long voyage down the Mackenzie River to Tulita. But once there, they were forced back into doing things the old way. It took Douglas and crew eight days to line their boat the *Jupiter* up the Bear River to Great Bear Lake, and another eight days to sail it to Dease Inlet. Caught in one storm, they were lucky to find an unnamed and uncharted bay (now called Jupiter Bay) where they were able to shelter from steep waves. After the storm, they sailed north again, halting briefly in fog near Etacho Point where we were wind-bound. There they met Joe Hodgson and his family camped on the beach. Joe was headed out to the Mackenzie after a winter of trapping on the Dease River. He was an old-timer, a former HBC man. He had built a rough cabin on the Dease River that he now "sold" to Douglas for some tobacco, bacon, and brandy. Hodgson headed south to Telida while Douglas and crew continued north. Faced with the same

seventy-mile open cross-
ing that we had attempted,
Douglas and crew also
opted to minimize the
distance and headed to the
nearest point on the northern shore, sailing directly
from Etacho Point to
Cape McDonnell. From
there, they sailed NNW,
passing very close to the
confluence that we had

The *Jupiter* tied up at Hodgson's Point on the Dease River in 1911. The bluff in the background helped us locate the old cabin in 2007. *George M. Douglas, courtesy National Archives Canada.*

failed to occupy. Skirting to the north of Ritch Island (then called the Big Island) with the wind now abaft the beam, the *Jupiter* virtually flew past the rocky, forested shore of Dease Inlet and into the Dease River. The exhilarating run ended only when the fifty-foot-long boat ground to a halt in the first riffle about six miles up the river. It was just below a horseshoe bend and across from a distinctive tan river bluff. Here Lionel Douglas built a sturdy cabin they occupied for the next year. From this snug base they pushed north toward the arctic coast on three separate occasions to map the geology of the Copper Mountains. They found no rich deposits, but they did find themselves in the thick of history, firsthand witnesses to some of the initial contacts between Westerners and the Inuit of Coronation Gulf (see chapter 7).

Prior to our departure, we had read all about the Douglas expedition and we had seen a few photographs of the cabin taken in 1912, but we were unable to ascertain in any detail where it was or whether it was still standing. We didn't even know on which side of the river to look, but we very much wanted to see the cabin if it was still there. Happy to be out of the wind and off the big lake, we headed up the Dease River. The sun was shining and we were flying up the river, with the snow spraying everywhere and furrow more than a foot deep in our wake. After days of rough traveling over hard snow, it was a tonic to swoop up this river at speed.

Lionel Douglas in front of the cabin he had just finished building in 1911. He was especially proud of its large fireplace (inset).
G. M. Douglas, courtesy National Archives Canada, provided by E. Mallory.

After passing several bends, our pace slowed slightly. I suppose each of us was looking for something that might flag where the Douglas cabin had been. A cut log, a lob tree, perhaps a familiar bluff. I was leading the group at the time and had just rounded a horseshoe bend when a tan dirt bluff on the right bank caught my eye. Something about it seemed familiar. I stopped and jumped off my snowmobile to look around and to tell the others that we might be getting close, but they weren't there. I turned around and backtracked a few hundred yards and saw that everyone had driven their machines up into the trees on the left bank of the river to a spot that looked like a nice place to camp. As I drove up the bank to join them, I saw Jon walking over to an old cabin. Its roof had fallen in and trees were growing up through the floor. With his keen eye and honed sense of where someone would build a cabin, Jon had unerringly found the place.

The Douglas cabin and the remains of its fireplace (inset) in 2007. *J. Holmgren.*

In the warm light of evening, we turned off our noisy machines and let the silence fill our ears. We gathered at what was once the front door, peered in through the broken and collapsed logs, noted the fine workmanship of the window and door frames, and above all, we admired the sandstone fireplace in the corner. Lionel Douglas had been inordinately proud of that fireplace, having made it larger than was customary to provide more heat. This was unmistakably the Douglas cabin. We set up our tents and cooked dinner, but our conversation was sparse. As the sun set in the west, hanging above the telltale bluff, it cast a golden light on the snow and made the spruce trees a rich dark green. This light, this view, all would have been familiar to Douglas, or to Franklin, or to a Native hunter traveling this route five hundred years ago. With little to say, we watched the sun set and let the timelessness of the place wash over us. If George and Lionel Douglas had come swinging down the river on snowshoes after a long day of hunting, it would not have surprised us much. And other than the strange black machines sitting in their yard, our being at the Hodgson's Point would not have been too much of a surprise to them either. Lots of travelers came by the point in the winter of 1911–1912. We would have offered them some hot tea to chase off the evening cold and swapped travelers' yarns long into the night.

of Great Bear is a second set of ruins, older by seventy-five years than the Douglas cabin, and of greater historical significance. It is the ruins of Fort Confidence, built in 1839 as a base of operations for the Hudson's Bay Company's first exploration of the Northwest Passage. Preferring to focus on commerce, the company had only grudgingly assisted other explorers in the past, including Franklin's expeditions of 1821 and 1825, and Admiral Sir George Back's 1833 trip down the Great Fish River (now Back's River). HBC's royal charter was up for renewal in 1838, however, and one of its clauses required the company to engage in scientific and geographic exploration. Sponsoring an expedition might win some needed government goodwill and, since several hundred miles of the northern coast of North America remained unexplored and unmapped, doing so might be profitable.

The company sent Thomas Simpson and Peter Warren Dease to do the job. Simpson was a younger cousin of George Simpson, then Governor-in-Chief of the HBC in Canada and an ambitious man who would prove to be a consummate traveler and explorer. Dease had been long in the country and was ready to retire. Yet despite their differences in age and attitude the two men made an effective team. Starting in June 1837 at Fort Chipewyan, they paddled their way down the Mackenzie River to the coast, then worked north and west all the way to Point Barrow, the northernmost tip of Alaska. Returning before freeze-up,

OLD FORT CONFIDENCE, GREAT BEAR LAKE.

they lined up the Bear River and sailed across the lake, arriving at Dease Inlet following a journey of more than four thousand miles. By late September they had built Fort Confidence, their base for the next two winters. From here, Simpson pioneered the route up the Dease River and over to the Dismal Lakes that was later used by Rae in 1848, Hanbury in 1902, Stefansson in 1910, Douglas in 1911, and by us in 2007. Simpson and Dease worked eastward along the arctic coast in the summer of 1838, passing more than a hundred miles beyond Franklin's farthest point. The next summer, they returned to the coast, exploring all they way east to King William Island and the Castor and Pollux River, effectively finishing the exploration of the Northwest Passage. They left Fort Confidence for the last time in September of 1839.

It was still standing in the summer of 1902 when Hanbury came through during his epic journey from Baker Lake to Great Bear Lake via the arctic coast. In his diary he wrote, "Old Fort Confidence was partly in ruins, but the chimneys still remained perfect."

By 1911, when the Douglas party made the twelve-mile excursion from their cabin at Hodgson's Point to the fort, all the logs had rotted away or burned but the chimneys were still standing. By 2007, two of the chimneys had fallen down but two were in surprisingly good shape. The forest had reclaimed much of the area where the

The chimneys of Fort Confidence in 1911. *G. M. Douglas, courtesy National Archives Canada.*

07

THE NORTHERN CROSS

We left the Douglas cabin in sunny weather, heading up the Dease River toward the Dismal Lakes. We knew that we would pass from taiga to the tundra of the Barrenlands during the day. The region where these two terrains come together has long been a meeting ground for three Northern cultures. Traditionally, the Sahtu have gone north from Great Bear Lake into this area in search of caribou, while the Inuit have come south in search of wood. Westerners have come to this crossroads, too, some hunting for adventure, others for souls. Results have been mixed.

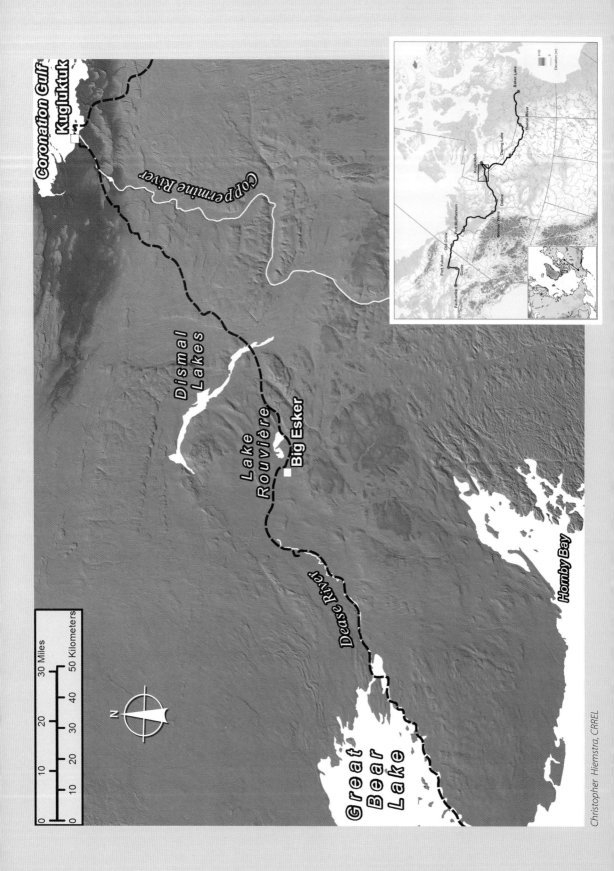

Christopher Hiemstra, CRREL

THE AXE MARKS on the stump were old. Could they be a century old? Perhaps. We were camped just inside a fold of the Big Esker south of Lake Rouvière. The lake was somewhere ahead, but where? Like so many before us who had tried to cross this transition zone between the vast boreal forests of the Mackenzie Basin and the stark Barrenlands of arctic Canada, we were confused, perhaps lost. The day had started pleasantly enough. We sailed up the river in soft snow, enjoying the scenery, stopping in the same places that Douglas had stopped to take pictures of rock outcrops. Later we would learn that we had matched several of his photos almost exactly.

Our plan was to run up the river fifteen miles and then head cross-country. From there we would cross Mountain Lake and then drop into the Dismal Lakes. The map showed most of the country bordering the river to be open tundra. It was a nice plan, but we realized it was deeply flawed the first time we tried coming off the river. The bank was about ten feet high, enough to block our view of the land adjacent to the river, but easily surmounted by the snowmobiles. No sooner had we gotten up the bank, though, than we found ourselves in a shrub jungle. On the terrace bordering the river willows grew in profusion, sticking up out of a snow cover that was punchy: hard in some places, soft and deep elsewhere, ideal for getting stuck. In the distance the shrubs were even thicker and despite the map indicating this was tundra, long narrow patches of spruce trees cut across the shrubby landscape. On past trips we had tried to traverse this sort of country and knew that with our heavy double sleds we were likely to spend hours stuck in bottomless snow mixed with willow. We descended back down to the river.

The river now headed in a northwesterly direction, unfortunately, away from where we needed to go. It also started winding around in oxbows and loops, forcing us to travel about two miles for every mile we made to the northwest. We had little choice but to follow the river, although it was taking a heavy toll on our limited gas supply, which, through miscalculation, was barely sufficient to carry us to Kugluktuk. We had to get off the river soon or we would be in serious trouble.

The best chance to do this came in another ten miles. A snow-filled stream entered the Dease River from the east, right where we needed to go. While the others took a tea break, I headed up this way without my sleds to see if it was a feasible route. A half mile on, the stream opened out into a lake that extended northeast for another half a mile. This was promising. I returned and got the others.

Not long after we had traversed the half-mile lake, we started getting into willows again. At first we could drive around or over them, but soon we descended into a broad valley where the fronds grew taller than a person. The snow underneath them was uneven and soft. Willow branches caught on our skis and scratched our windshields. We became separated, the visibility through the willows a mere dozen yards. Then, hidden right in the middle of the densest patch of willows, we came upon a trench about four feet deep, steep-sided and narrow. This trench, in summer a winding stream, was the reason for the willows. We were in a riparian zone. Some years back we had coined a more descriptive name for this type of feature: a tank trap. The willows surrounding the stream made it impossible to get up any speed while trying to drive across and the steep sides made it difficult to climb out of the trench on the far side without that momentum. Getting stuck in the bottom was unthinkable because the narrowness of the

A narrow section of the Dease River called The Gates (top) was also photographed in 1912 (bottom) by George Douglas. *H. Huntington; G. M. Douglas, courtesy National Archives Canada.*

FINDING THE ARCTIC

trench made maneuvering or turning virtually impossible. Usually we could find a favorable place to cross a tank trap, but the thick willows made navigating around this particular trap difficult.

I couldn't see the others, though I could hear their machines crashing through the brush some distance away. Everyone was looking for a spot to cross. I drove parallel to the trench until I saw what looked like a good place where I could ride a snow ramp down into the bottom, then follow a second ramp back out on the far side. I went down cautiously, but with enough momentum for the climb. Instead of smoothly accelerating out the other side there was a loud crack just as I reached the bottom of the trench and an area about the size of my snowmobile dropped two feet. My skis hooked under a lip of ice on the far side, and the machine stopped abruptly. I was thrown past the windshield, landing in thick snow under an overhanging bank. What I had just experienced is a common occurrence in the North, and occasionally dangerous. One of those deceptive ice bridges had formed in the fall when the water level was much higher—two feet higher to be precise. Later, snow had covered the ice. The weight and momentum of my machine had fractured this bridge, dropping me into the air pocket. I was unharmed, but I was truly and thoroughly stuck.

I knew the drill. I stripped off my parka and hat and got to work. By the time Dan found me I was soaked in sweat and exhausted. I had managed to unhook my sleds and drag them out of the trench. Then I turned my machine, with more heaving and dragging, and aimed it at the track I had descended. Next I tramped down the snow into a ramp that would take me out of the hole in the ice. With Dan tugging on the skis, and me pushing and driving at the same time, we got the machine out after another ten minutes of struggle. We reconnected the sleds and were finally ready to go. Glen had found a spot further up the creek where we were able to cross with ease, joining the others waiting on the far side. The willows were much smaller on this side and for a while the traveling was excellent.

Our trials were not over yet, however. After another ten miles, we could see a strange-looking ridge, about eighty feet high, ahead of us. It ran from

The top of the Big Esker: no place for sleds or snowmobile.

east to west and extended as far as we could see in both directions. Small patches of trees nestled into pockets along the sides of the ridge, and in places, a wall of boulders mantled its sides. Most troubling, it looked like a lot of bare gravel and rock was exposed on the crest, an impression that proved correct. There were a few gaps that seemed to cut through the ridge where we thought we might get across, but it was hard to tell if they cut all the way through. We worked in closer. The wind started to blow and wisps of snow hissed along the ground. The sweat in our clothes from our recent wrestling match with the willows froze solid.

The ridge was our first esker. The term derives from the Gaelic *eiscer*, meaning "ridge of gravel." These sinuous, narrow, steep-sided ridges are common in those parts of northern Europe and North America once covered by ice-age ice sheets. They are particularly prevalent where the ice sheets overrode hard, granitic bedrock, like the Barrenlands. Eskers range in height from ten to two hundred feet, and in length from a few hundred yards to tens of miles. There is general agreement that they form during the waning days of an ice sheet, when melting produces lots of run-off. This water flows along the surface of the ice in a blue channel until it finds a weak spot, where it drills down through hundreds of feet of ice to the bed of the glacier. The hole it makes—called a moulin, the French word for "mill"—is a frightening circular vertical shaft penetrating the dark depths of the glacier. Plunging into the hole in a spectacular swirling cascade, the water disappears with a thunderous roar. It is virtually impossible to stand next to one of these features without imagining what it would be like to fall in. A slip into the churning water, a rapid slide over a slick ice streambed while frantically, but futilely, trying to grab something, anything, to hold onto. After a spinning plummet into the blue bowels of the glacier, death would come quickly, either by injury or hypothermia, ending what otherwise would be a fascinating journey. The existence of eskers, however, tells us that the trip would most likely terminate in an ice subway tunnel with a river flowing through it. The gravel, sand, and rocks carried along by this torrent progressively fill such tunnels, leaving a ridge that maps out the vanished river's channel long after the ice is gone.

Our first attempt to cross the Big Esker failed. Climbing the steep side wasn't hard but the broad crest was scoured of snow and consisted of nothing but gravel and boulders. There was no way we could drag our heavy loads across that. We descended and continued east. And so it went for the remainder of the day. We would try to get across, fail, and be forced to work further east. Again we were not going in the direction we needed, adding to our worries about our gas supply.

And once again, the wind was making traveling unpleasant. By 7:00 PM we were done in and decided to camp. We began searching for a place out of the wind, which is how we found ourselves digging into a drift of snow below an offshoot of the esker ridge topped by old, gnarled trees.

Jon was the one who found the cut marks. Just above where we were digging, several trees below

Our camp nestled inside an arm of the Big Esker. The cut trees are just above the tents.

the ridge top had been cut down using an axe. The cuts were very old. The trees were just about the size one would cut for building a log cabin. We couldn't be absolutely sure, but it was possible that this was the work of Father Rouvière, a Catholic priest, who would have been cutting logs and hauling them to his cabin site on the north shore of Lake Rouvière in the winter of 1911–1912. He would not have known that his efforts to spend the winter on the lake, part of a larger plan to proselytize among the Inuit of Coronation Gulf, would lead directly to his death within a year. With the wind ruffling our fur collars, we stared down on this mute evidence of religious zeal. Our earlier frustration with willows, eskers, and declining fuel supplies was quickly forgotten as we thought about this young, starry-eyed priest, clad in his full-length black cassock and fur hat, chopping trees down in this remote spot so very long ago.

The bare outline of Father Jean-Baptiste Rouvière's story is simple enough. Born in 1881 in Mende, France, he was called to the church in 1903, becoming a priest in the order of the Oblate of Mary Immaculate, a brotherhood known as "the Missionaries of Provence." In these waning days of the Victorian era, there was still a strong sentiment that the White Man's burden was to bring civilization and religion (read: Christianity) to those of darker skin in the remote regions of the Earth. Never mind that the slums of London and New York City at the turn of the century were full of abjectly poor and desperate white people. Never mind, too, that in exchange for an unsought new religion, the Natives of the African and American continents also received whiskey and smallpox.

The stark country where Father Rouvière built the cabin he planned to use as a base for converting the Inuit of Coronation Gulf to the Catholic faith.

The Arctic represented the "hardest and most venturesome" mission field, and therefore the highest calling, according to Hudson Stuck, an Episcopal archdeacon who made his name along the Yukon between 1905 and 1920. It is no surprise that Rouvière gravitated to the North, nor that he found himself at Fort Good Hope

French missionary Jean-Baptiste Rouvière, visiting the Douglas cabin in spring 1912, was one of two Catholic priests murdered near Bloody Falls in 1913. *G. M. Douglas, courtesy National Archives Canada.*

in 1911. He must have aspired to be one of that group of men (and women) who at the time were termed "muscular Christians." These much-admired missionaries were of high moral standing and they had an iron-willed sense of religious duty, but in addition, they were good with a gun and knife. They could trap and hunt. They could mush and hike. Many of them, like Stuck, became celebrities, their lectures well attended, their books avidly read, their exploits celebrated. Rouvière, still quite green after spending his first four years in the Arctic in the relative comfort of missions co-located with HBC trading posts on the Mackenzie River, was not yet ready for the rigors of life along the arctic coast.

The priest's fate was effectively sealed, though, when his path crossed that of the waif of the North, that peripatetic traveler—some might say meddler—John Hornby (see chapter 12). Both men had come into the country at about the same time, but while the priest had remained in town, Hornby spent all his time living in the bush and learning how to hunt, trap, and survive. Between 1908 and 1911 Hornby lived on the northeastern shore of Great Bear Lake (now Hornby Bay). During his travels north of the big lake into the Barrenlands he had met some bands of Inuit from Coronation Gulf who came inland to hunt caribou. Following this meeting he sent a letter to Bishop Breynat in Fort Norman, alerting the Bishop to the possibility that the church might be able to convert these Natives by sending a good man up to the northeast end of Great Bear Lake. The letter fell on fertile ground because Breynat was already worried that Anglican missionaries would beat the Catholics to the arctic coast.

As for Hornby, there are good reasons to suspect his motives were not religious. First, he had been raised an Anglican, and the evidence suggests he had little or no religious convictions of his own. In fact, he was probably ambivalent about the presence of missionaries in what he thought of as "his country." Second, anyone the church sent up through Great Bear would need a guide, which would most likely be Hornby. The expedition that had brought Hornby to Great Bear was pulling out and Hornby needed another backer in order to buy the food and equipment that would allow him to remain in the country. Introductions were made and for the next year Rouvière and Hornby became partners of sorts.

Little time elapsed before Hornby showed his fickle nature. Right off the bat he disappeared from Fort Norman. The priest had to hitch a ride across Great Bear Lake by himself, arriving at Dease Inlet in mid-July. He was too late to accompany Douglas and his partner up the Dease River (they had left about two weeks before he arrived), so he idled away the time until Hornby finally caught up. The pair then worked their way up the river, crossed the Big Esker near where we were camped, and finally arrived at Lake Imaerinik (now called Lake Rouvière) in late August. After several days of aimless wandering about the tundra, the priest amazingly made contact with a band of Coronation Gulf Inuit who had come inland to hunt caribou. It was a strange meeting. Rouvière could speak none of their language, and the Inuit had seen few, if any, white men. What they made of the priest's crucifix, black habit, and his attempts to explain Christianity is hard to say. For the priest, the experience was beatific.

Rouvière quickly concluded that he would need to live near where these primitive people hunted and traveled if he was to minister to them, little realizing that they were nomadic. He decided to build a cabin on the northern shore of Lake Imaerinik, the last timber before the trees gave way to the

Barrenlands. After the initial phases of construction, Hornby lost interest in the enterprise and wandered back to Great Bear Lake. As autumn turned to winter, Rouvière finished the cabin, but about the same time the Inuit disappeared north, leaving the priest in magnificent isolation. When Hornby and Douglas returned to the lake to check on the priest in mid-October, Rouvière wisely agreed to return with them and spend the remainder of the winter at Dease Inlet.

During the winter of 1911–1912 the remote northeast corner of Great Bear Lake was a happy little outpost. With a devastating world war ahead of them all, and a stifling Victorian era behind them, its citizens were unusually carefree. Hornby and Rouvière spent considerable time visiting the Douglas cabin, where they played cards and chess, and discussed life. This was possibly the best winter of Rouvière's and Hornby's lives. But it was clear to Rouvière that if he was going to convert the Inuit, he could not remain near Great Bear Lake indefinitely. Hornby, vague in his plans as always, was an unreliable partner, so the priest journeyed the 350 miles back to Fort Norman to find more trustworthy help. The Bishop assigned him Father Guillaume LeRoux, another French Oblate—and a bad choice, it turned out, as LeRoux seems to have been short-tempered and arrogant.

The following summer Rouvière and LeRoux worked their way north, again crossing Great Bear Lake. In October they headed up the familiar Dease River route, past the Big Esker, then hiked overland to the arctic coast. There they found what they had come for. The Inuit were present in force: half a dozen families camped on the beach near the mouth of the Coppermine River, the site of the present-day hamlet Kugluktuk.

The priests had not made much progress in learning the Inuit language or culture, nor had they brought much food. The Inuit's supplies were not in much better shape and the presence of the priests must have strained the small community in several ways. The relationship between the natives and the priests nonetheless stayed cordial for the first five days, although the rituals the priests demonstrated must have seemed bizarre and alien to the Inuit. Then an altercation over a rifle between LeRoux and the man in whose igloo he was staying turned violent. The two fighters were quickly separated but it was clear that the conflict could have rapidly turned deadly. The priests were urged, in fact forced, to leave.

This they did, but it was a desperate move. Their cabin on the lake, that refuge and shelter in the trees, lay more than 150 miles away by an uncertain trail. The weather had turned wintry and snowy and the priests were still short of food. In addition, their sled was heavily loaded with gear but they had only a few dogs to haul it. The day after they left the arctic coast, two Inuit, Sinnisiak and Uluksuk, left the beach encampment, ostensibly to look inland for friends who had been out caribou hunting, but more likely to catch up with the struggling priests. At this point the story becomes murky. One version has Sinnisiak and Uluksuk falling in with the priests with the object of killing and robbing them. Another version has the desperate priests forcing the Eskimos to haul their heavy sled at gunpoint. Whatever the truth, it is undisputed that during a moment of inattention by the priests, Sinnisiak killed Father LeRoux by stabbing him in the back. He then grabbed LeRoux's rifle and used it to kill Father Rouvière. The frightened Inuit pair next gutted the two priests and ate their livers to ward off bad spirits. They then returned to the beach at Coronation Gulf. Their companions, hearing about the murder of the priests, returned to the bodies, recovered the dogs they had lent to the priests, and took clothing, books, and rifles. Silence descended over the tundra, as the winter snows covered the bodies.

The priests were not immediately missed. They had been expected to winter at Lake Imaerinik, so a full eight months elapsed before they were overdue. Eventually it became clear that they had disappeared and the RCMP was notified. It took three years to find and apprehend the murderers but they were finally brought to trial in keeping with the motto, "the Mounties always get their man."

An RCMP patrol under the stalwart Inspector Denny LaNauze followed the traditional route to the Barrenlands from Fort Norman across Great Bear Lake, up the Dease River, then to the arctic coast. A second patrol traveled by schooner and whaling ship around Alaska, past Point Barrow, then on to Herschel Island. Through careful and surprisingly culturally sensitive interviews with Inuit along the coast, LaNauze eventually pieced together the events surrounding the murder, found the killers, and had them transported to Calgary. First convicted of murder and sentenced to death, the duo was later re-tried and remanded to prison. After they had served only two years of loose incarceration, however, it became increasingly clear that these Stone Age hunters had little understanding of why their act was considered wrong and they were eventually repatriated to the arctic coast.

The wind picked up as the sun set. The light faded on the old axe marks. Our attention drifted off to tea, hot cocoa, dinner, and sleep. Our trail-numbed minds were unable to link these axe marks with any other event from our journey, but had we stopped to ponder why Father Rouvière was cutting trees in the late fall with such haste, we might have recognized that his fate was related to other events, some equally tragic, in a century-old competition between the Catholic and Anglican churches in the North. The fact of the matter was that Father Rouvière *had* to get to the Inuit of Coronation Gulf quickly or the Anglicans would have gotten there first. There had been a number of signs of this religious clash throughout our journey, but we failed to see the connections.

In Fort Yukon, Earl Cadzow, a natural booster of the town, had donned his dark green Carhartt parka, fur hat, and beaded fur overmitts, fired up his snowmobile, and led us to the grave of Archdeacon Stuck, who died of pneumonia on October 10, 1920. Stuck is buried in a grave marked by an eight-foot-high stone cross. Earl swept the snow off the bronze plaque at its base so we could read the inscription, "Well done good and faithful servant," written

Sinnisiak (top) and Uluksuk (bottom) as photographed by H. Wilkens on July 12, 1916. *Stefansson Collection on Polar Exploration, Rauner Library, Dartmouth College.*

in both English and Gwich'in. Stuck is famous for leading the first successful climb of Mt. McKinley, the highest mountain in Alaska at 20,320 feet, in 1913. He was also the author of five popular books on travel in the Arctic. His life's work, however, was the Episcopal Church (the American counterpart to the Anglican Church). Working out of Fort Yukon, he helped to establish a set of missions along the Yukon and Tanana Rivers as well as on the arctic coast. The missions included schools and hospitals that provided much-needed

succor and support during the terrible influenza epidemics that decimated Native communities between the late 1800s and World War I. These missions were strategically located to serve the people *and* to compete with the region's Catholic missions. In some cases both Catholic and Episcopal missions ended up in a single village far too small to support both.

Our second brush with missionaries and religion went unnoticed at the time. We had stopped to photograph the collapsed remnants of Old Rampart, the old HBC trading post halfway between Fort Yukon and Old Crow. On a hill overlooking the log ruins lies the grave of Reverend Vincent C. Sim, an Anglican missionary who proselytized along the length of the Yukon

A missionary should walk warily and circumspectly; before all else he should gain the confidence of the people, learn to speak their tongue, and understand the problems of their daily life.

— Diamond Jenness

H. Huntington

FINDING THE ARCTIC

ARCHDEACON STUCK DIES AT FORT YUKON

Missionary Was the First White Man to Ascend the Summit of Mount McKinley.

LONG LABORED IN ALASKA

Author Was Honored by Royal Geographic Society for His Achievements as Explorer.

The Rev. Hudson Stuck, Archdeacon of the Yukon, and the first white man to ascend the summit of Mount McKinley, died at Fort Yukon, Alaska, on Sunday. Word of his death was received yesterday by Dr. John Wood, Executive Secretary of the Protestant Episcopal Church.

The Archdeacon was born in England in 1863 and came to the United States in 1885. He was graduated from the theological department of the University of the South, Sewanee, Tenn. Before he went to Alaska he was Dean of St. Matthew's Cathedral in Dallas.

In 1905 Archdeacon Stuck resigned his post in Dallas after ten years' service and went to Alaska. He was associated with Bishop Rowe of Alaska, and wrote much about the Bishop and the land in which he was working. As Archdeacon of the Yukon he traveled thousands of miles by dogs and on foot and he helped build up a great church work in that country.

Word that he has succeeded in reaching the top of Mount McKinley came in a dispatch from Fairbanks, Alaska, on June 21, 1913. With a guide, Harry P. Karstens, Walter Harper and R. G. Tatum, a mission helper, the Archdeacon successfully accomplished the perilous trip, a trip that Dr. Cook claimed to have made and which others had tried and failed.

The Royal Geographical Society in March of last year awarded to Archdeacon Stuck the Back Grant in recognition of his travels in Alaska and his ascent of Mount McKinley. He was the author of "Ascent of Denali" (Mt. McKinley), and "Ten Thousand Miles with a Dog Sled."

The New York Times
Published: October 13, 1920
Copyright © The New York Times

between 1882 and 1885. Like so many of his flock, he finally succumbed to one of the serious epidemics that swept the country in the 1880s. His Indian-style grave, surrounded by a short white picket fence, overlooks the river in as beautiful but lonely a spot as can be imagined.

Our third brush with missionaries had been in Fort Good Hope, where we were given a tour of the Catholic church built in 1868 by Oblate priests. Both Fathers Rouvière and LeRoux had served there. It was early Sunday morning and the town was quiet and still asleep. We were anxious to get started for Telida about two hundred miles upriver, but our host, the principal at the school, insisted that we visit Our Lady of Good Hope before leaving. We wandered

The grave of Archdeacon Hudson Stuck in Fort Yukon (*H. Huntington*), and his obituary in the *New York Times*, October 10, 1920.

over to the church, not knowing what to expect. Sister Joan Liss graciously ushered us in.

The conventional white exterior of the church belied what was inside. The ceiling caught my eye first. It was intense blue and covered by a constellation of yellow stars, a facsimile of the boreal sky at twilight. Ornately carved and brightly painted pillars supported the ceiling. The altar was an intricate combination of woodwork, carving, and colorful paintings. On the walls folk-art murals depicted the Gospel. The overall effect of the bright colors and the profusion of unexpected artwork, painstakingly crafted over decades, was stunning. The most poignant painting, of an Oblate priest on his deathbed, was in the narthex. The priest, one of the artists who had worked on the church interior during decades of isolation and privation, was dying of consumption or malnutrition. He looked gaunt and homesick for the green fields of his native France. More than anything, the painting spoke of the price in human suffering of the effort to bring religion to the North.

None of these experiences came to mind as I drifted off to sleep at our camp on the Big Esker. It was only later, after the trip, that the axe marks began to haunt me and I dug into the history of religion in the North. The competition between the Catholics and Anglican/Episcopalians came as a surprise to me, but it was real. One eminent Canadian historian described how "fierce denominational rivalries were the order of the day...and sometimes led to feverish rushes to open new districts, like the race down the Mackenzie in 1858–59 between Archdeacon James Hunter (Anglican)...and Father Henri Grollier (Catholic)." An Episcopal history of Fort Yukon detailed the accomplishments of Episcopalian missionaries in the town between 1899 and 1990, never once mentioning that the Catholics had arrived there first in 1862 and had continued to visit the town for the next few decades. Similarly, Catholic histories were mute about the presence of the Anglicans, except when they occasionally complained about being stymied by their arrival before the priests. An account from Old Crow described how the petty rivalry between the two religious groups produced "tremendous confusion and turmoil among the Gwich'in."

By 1890 the score in Canada was Anglicans: ten missions and twelve staff, Catholics: eighteen missions and thirty-two staff. In central and northern Alaska the Catholics had sewn up the lower Yukon and Kuskokwim rivers with missions and had a strong presence on the Seward Peninsula, but the Episcopalians had secured the arctic coast and the central interior of the state. In the larger arctic towns (Fairbanks, Barrow, Yellowknife, etc.) both denominations were active. The competition in Alaska at one point became so fierce that a story, perhaps apocryphal, is told about how the U.S. secretary of the interior had to intervene and divide the Territory into religious spheres of influence to stop the discord.

The painted ceiling (left) and two pillars in Our Lady of Good Hope church in Fort Good Hope.

The ornate altar of Our Lady of Good Hope.

Being neither Catholic nor Episcopalian, I found that I had a strong negative reaction as I learned more about northern religious history. Life seemed too damned hard in the North, particularly between 1850 and World War I, to have to guess which path had the best chance of leading to God. How could these missionaries force such a choice on the Natives? Where was the spirit of cooperation one might expect from men of the cloth? Moreover, what right did those missionaries have to come in and replace Native beliefs with their own Christian creed? The entire history seemed the epitome of arrogance and presumption.

Then a knowledgeable friend suggested that I place the competition in a larger context. Ethnologists such as Knud Rasmussen and Diamond Jenness have vividly described how, prior to Western contact, the Inuit and Iñupiat were shackled by a system of superstitions largely based on fear. Because starvation, injury, and death were always just around the corner in their lives, Native cultures had developed elaborate but ineffectual systems of charms and talismans designed to ward off harm. A dark and frightening internal spiritual world had been created as a fitting counterpart to the physical world of privation and violence in which they had to live. Who was I to judge whether the arrival of Christianity was negative or positive?

And the story of Christianity in the North also encompasses the arrival of education and medicine. The first schools, the first hospitals, the first written languages, perhaps even the fish wheel, were all brought in along with the Bible by sincere and well-meaning missionaries. Perhaps more importantly, these clergy became allies of the Natives during a time of major social upheaval for these communities. Without missionaries, the inexorable changes sweeping the North might have been guided solely by whiskey dealers, avaricious traders, and corrupt government officials. As it was, by the time the pace of change had fully accelerated in the 1930s, the religious competition was largely settled and stabilized. Men like Dr. John Chapman and his son Henry had been ministers in Anvik for a combined total of sixty-one years, and Father Jette had lived most of his life in Fort Good Hope. They were part of the fabric of life and they were ideally placed to help navigate the profound modernization that was taking place.

Thousands of paper cranes hanging in the shrine were sent by the people of Hiroshima in sympathy for the cancer deaths that have occurred in Deline as a result of mining and loading unshielded uranium for the atomic bomb during the 1940s and 1950s.

Religious icons, framed black-and-white photographs of the Sahtu prophets, and other mementos fill an altar in the Deline shrine.

This positive side of religion in the North was on display in Deline. Traditional Chief Charlie Neyelle took Glen and me on a tour of the town. It was fun and he got to show off new buildings and construction projects, but near the end of the tour things got more serious. The Chief took us to a small cabin on the outskirts of the town, a place where he said people came for peace of mind. The white cross over the door announced that this was a Christian retreat. The cabin was peaceful, but displayed on the walls was ample evidence of pain, a stark reminder that life in the North remains more difficult and dangerous than in lower latitudes. There were framed pictures of young Sahtu who had died violent deaths, and pictures of youth

On the outskirts of Deline, Traditional Chief Charlie Neyelle showed us a building where people go for peace of mind.

who had committed suicide. There were crepe-draped pictures of smiling elders, now dead. A festoon of several thousand paper cranes, a gift from Hiroshima, Japan, reminded us that during World War II the Sahtu from Deline had mined the radium that went into the atomic bomb, but without proper radiation safeguards. Far too many cancer deaths had hit the community in the years after the war—so many that the people of Hiroshima, of all places, felt empathy for the Sahtu.

In one corner of the building, nestled in a shrine, were three battered black-and-white photographs of elderly Sahtu men. I asked the chief who they were. He answered solemnly that they were the three Sahtu Christian prophets, including the blind prophet Joseph Naedzo. As I studied the photographs and looked around the cabin I realized that over time this community had adopted, but also adapted, Christianity in ways that made it more relevant and responsive to their problems and needs. While the final accounting is not yet written, for better or for worse what I saw told me that the Northern Cross was here to stay.

08

KUGLUKTUK

Leaving Lake Rouvière, we headed north toward Kugluktuk on the Arctic Ocean. It was soon apparent that we did not have enough gas to make it. The deep snow and forced detours had taken a toll. We were going to have to do something: one idea was to siphon the gas out of three snowmobiles, put it into the other two, then send two people on to Kugluktuk to buy more gas and return. This plan's downsides were the 140-mile roundtrip and the fact that the three people left behind would be in about as bleak a spot as we had yet seen. Miraculously, before we had to execute that plan we came to a shelter cabin next to which was cached twenty-five gallons of gas in red plastic jugs, enough to see us all into Kugluktuk. We hesitated for about five seconds and then poured the gas into our machines. There was a name on the jugs, so we knew we could contact the owner in Kugluktuk, tell him what we had done, and run replacement gas back out to the cabin the next day. As it turned out, the owner preferred to have his gas in town and we were more than happy to pay for triple the amount we had used—arctic hospitality all around.

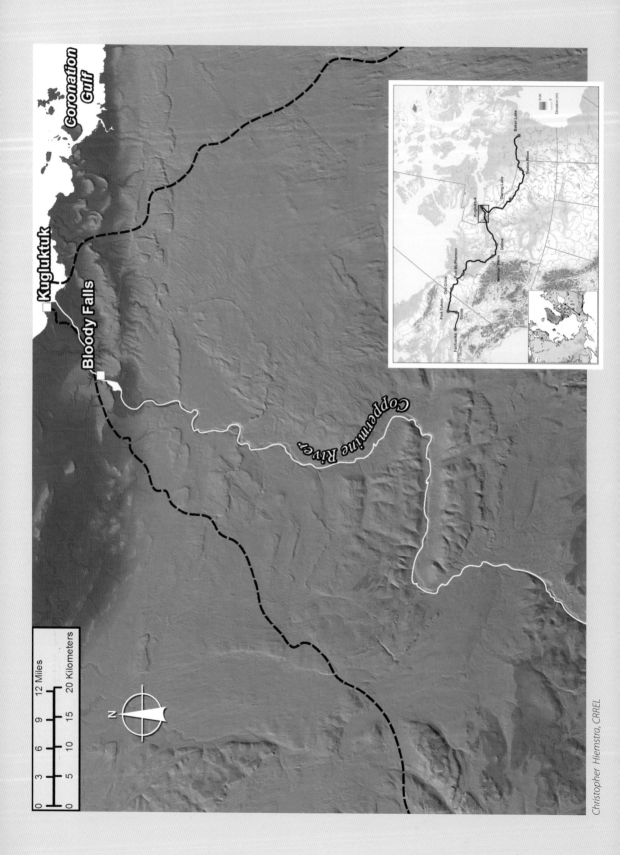

Coronation Gulf

Kugluktuk

Bloody Falls

Coppermine River

0   3   6   9   12 Miles
0   5   10 15 20 Kilometers

N

IT WAS IN THE BACK, near the snowmobile belts and the two-cycle oil, across from the snares and traps, just past a half dozen fox and ermine pelts. It was a snow knife. Nearby, Coleman lanterns and mantles and other miscellaneous camping gear were on display. Ninety-nine percent of the Kugluktuk Northern Store looked like any other supermarket stocked with food, drugs, and cleaning sundries, with a metallic gold ATM machine up front. But in this back corner were items that you would only find in the Arctic, including that knife.

The snow knife looked like a big butter knife with a long blaze-orange wooden handle. Its pistol grip made it possible to push the knife with the heel of the hand like a saw; room for a two-handed grip meant it could be wielded like a samurai sword. The handle was plain ugly and the butter-knife tip was certainly not very macho, but the blade seemed to be made of good steel, a point I would have opportunity to confirm later in the trip. A snow knife: I had always wanted one. No! I had always *needed* one. I bought it for fifty Canadian dollars and left with a smile on my face.

I used the snow knife the next day while making snow measurements. It was mostly a "tourist" day for all of us but Jon. He had to change the main engine seal on his snowmobile. It had been leaking oil since Great Bear Lake, leaving a dark brown stripe on the underside of his hood and threatening to cause his engine to seize-up. At each stop during our travels, Jon would open the hood, wipe up the oil, smile or frown depending on the amount, then ceremoniously burn the oily rag. We were all a little relieved that this particular malfunction had happened to Jon's machine so there could be no question of operator error or poor attention to maintenance on the part of those of us less mechanically inclined. Jon preferred to work alone on repairs, and the rest of us knew that we would only slow him down if we tried to help. Consequently, we planned other activities for the day.

Glen had decided to go off souvenir hunting in town. He had his eye on a soapstone polar bear carving. Dan, Henry, and I planned to go to Bloody Falls about ten miles up the Coppermine River. It is arguably one of the most

Glen bought a
soapstone carving
of a polar bear
in Kugluktuk.
H. Huntington.

famous sites in the Arctic. That intrepid Scottish traveler, Samuel Hearne (see chapter 11), had named the falls after witnessing a massacre of Inuit there in 1771. Close to a hundred Chipewyan and Cree Indians with whom Hearne was traveling had fallen on twenty sleeping Inuit who were camped at the falls to spear salmon.

For three years starting in 1769 Hearne traveled north and west from Fort Prince of Wales on Hudson Bay. The first white man to see this country, he had been sent by the HBC to survey the area and, if possible, locate the source of the native copper samples that Indians had been bringing into the fort for several decades. This was the same copper that inspired the Douglas expedition. The Indians with whom Hearne traveled had a different mission: murdering the Inuit who frequented the lower Coppermine River.

We had all read Hearne's account before our trip and to us the idea of a multiyear journey by Chipewyan Indians across thousands of miles of the Barrenlands to massacre hereditary enemies seemed unbelievable. Who would travel that far for the sole purpose of vindictive killing? But if bloodlust didn't wash as a logical reason for making the trip, what then was the real motivation? We had several spirited discussions on this topic, but it wasn't until after we visited the Sahtu in Deline that a clearer picture emerged. In Deline we met Leroy Andre, president of the Deline Land Corporation. In talking with him, it became clear that Native land claim settlements on the north side of Great Bear Lake were a sensitive and important topic. Did the Sahtu or the Inuit own these lands? Where was the boundary? He made a point of showing us Bloody Creek on a map, explaining that the name commemorates a place near Dease Inlet where the Inuit had massacred Sahtu some time in the distant past. Even in 2007 it seemed that relations between interior Indians and coastal Inuit could be touchy!

With this perspective, we realized that Hearne in 1771 had been caught up in a border skirmish that was part of a larger longstanding war for territorial control. The massacre was done with the clear intent of pushing the Inuit back north, thereby maintaining the bulk of the Barrenlands as Indian country. The prize in this territorial war was fish and caribou. Hearne was witness to a terrorist raid. From the Indians' perspective, leaving a number of dead Inuit on the Coppermine River would be exactly the way to send a chilling but clear message to cease and desist all incursions to the south.

Several facts support this view. First, the long route between Fort Prince of Wales on Hudson Bay and Bloody Falls was well known to the Cree and the Chipewyan who had named its many lakes and rivers. Established place-names enabled the Indians to plan a rendezvous several weeks and hundreds of miles ahead. Second, the Indians and Inuit relied on the same caribou and fish for survival, creating a natural source of conflict.

Vestiges of this territorial friction remain. When Native land claims in northern Canada were being settled in 1999, careful decisions had to be made as to where Inuit country (Nunavut) ended and Indian country began. The results of these political decisions continue to generate controversy and heat. Even today, real effort on the part of Indian and Inuit peoples is necessary to move beyond ancient racial antipathy. In Deline, when we told Leroy Andre of our planned route, he spoke with pride about a similar winter snowmobile trip he and several other men had taken to Kugluktuk in 2006, where they had been met with great hospitality by the Inuit. In 2008, the people of Deline made another "peace journey" and once again received a warm welcome, a sign that perhaps the powers of the Bloody Falls and Bloody Creek massacres are finally fading.

Driving up the Coppermine River, we saw a shoreline dotted with cabins—actually, in some cases, sizeable houses with large decks—used by the folks from Kugluktuk to get away from town. When we reached Bloody Falls, we could see where the river emerged from between dark brown diorite cliffs. The day was overcast and gray, which seemed fitting for this somber place. Just beyond the northernmost set of bluffs on the east side of the river was a beach, the site of the massacre. Hearne's account suggests that the killing took less than ten minutes, but there is some question as to where Hearne actually was during the event. His publisher, wishing to sell more books, had

Just beyond the brown diorite cliffs below Bloody Falls is the beach where twenty sleeping Inuit were massacred by Indians in 1771.

an editor add spicy details to the account while the book was in preparation. The resulting tale was so graphic (for the tastes of a 1790s audience) that skepticism as to whether the event had really occurred arose—that is, until John Franklin (the next Englishmen to come by Bloody Falls) found skulls and human bones exactly where Hearne had described the slaughter taking place.

So here it was just in front of us: a small beach under a dull winter sky 240 years later. I don't know about Henry or Dan, but I was having trouble conjuring up images of that long-ago massacre. The vacation homes, the hiking trail marked by interpretive signs, the ease with which we got there, made it all seem quite ordinary.

We parked the machines and climbed up the shoreline to where we had a better view. The dark brown diorite formed hexagonal columns with flat tops much like the Giant's Causeway in Ireland. Cavities and pits in the rock were filled with quartz crystals. For a stretch of about two hundred feet the river rushed down a steep incline, a flume of dark Prussian blue flecked with white foam, edged on both sides by bluish-white ice about three feet thick. The water's roar seemed alien in the otherwise frozen landscape. We looked at the river and quietly discussed whether it could be run in a modern canoe. Franklin had elected to portage it, we recalled. Later we learned that most modern canoe voyagers choose to portage as well. As we stood there, our thoughts once again returned to the massacre. The Cree and Chipewyan had crept over the hills on the far side from us, trying to surprise the sleeping Inuit. That was on a hot summer day. Today it was gray and cold. Then, more than a hundred people were here, today there were just three. The rocks, the river, the hills, seemed to be unchangeable under their winter blanket of snow; only we humans had changed. We set off to find a good place to dig a snow pit and take samples.

Normally in digging a snow pit I use a shovel to rough out the pit, then a spatula to square up a clean vertical face. This day I used my new snow knife. It did a good job, though not greatly different than the spatula. What was different was that working on the pit with the big knife felt more heroic. Despite the butter-knife tip, the blade definitely had a *feel*. When we had finished our work and I was about to put the knife away, it occurred to me that it just might be good for throwing. Now this urge may seem strange on the part of a sober fifty-year-old snow scientist, but some of my earlier history will put it in perspective. As a kid, my brothers and I were always interested in knife throwing. We played games like mumblety-peg. We aspired to be ninja assassins. At seventeen, when I moved into my first apartment, we got a heavy wooden cable spool for a table, but then discovered that if we left it up on end we could throw knives into it.

During geology field camp in the 1970s, I sharpened the pick on my hammer so that I could throw it hatchet-like at ponderosa pines. I still think the stainless steel throwing axe my son got for his thirteenth birthday is the coolest gift ever. For me, throwing a snow knife wasn't a long reach.

So I did. I threw my new knife at a drifted dome of snow. *Sprong.* The

Henry surveys Bloody Falls, which is really more of a rapids.

A knife-wielding scientist (the author) examines the snow near Bloody Falls.
H. Huntington.

knife went in and stuck, then sat there vibrating. It was beautiful! I pulled the knife out and tried again. *Sprong.* This was great. A new tool for snow pits, plus the biggest throwing knife I had ever had. The remainder of the trip, it became part of our science protocol to mark the spot before digging a snow pit by throwing the knife into the snow. *Sprong.*

At the time I knew nothing of the history of the snow knife. Had I, perhaps I would have been more respectful. This tool, along with the bone eyed-needle, the toggle-headed harpoon, and the stone oil lamp, had made it possible for people to live in one of the harshest environments in the world. Armed with nothing more than a snow knife, a patch of dense snow, and ingenuity, the Inuit had learned how to make a home wherever and whenever they needed. Today the true genius of the igloo is too often forgotten. Boy Scouts build igloos for fun during winter weekend camping trips. Survival and mountaineering schools teach igloo construction to thousands of people each year. But how many of those novice builders have any idea what makes the structure work so well?

Two unique properties of snow—thermal conductivity and sintering—are the secret to these brilliant buildings. Thermal conductivity is the technical term that describes how readily a material transmits heat. Snow is a terrible heat conductor, so it is every bit as good an insulator as fiberglass. It is not unusual in Alaska and arctic Canada to find the temperature at the base of the snow cover is 20°F to 30°F warmer than the top because of snow's low thermal conductivity. With igloo walls typically twelve to sixteen inches thick, it is no wonder that a stone lamp and half a dozen warm bodies can raise the inside temperature to tolerable levels no matter how cold it is outside.

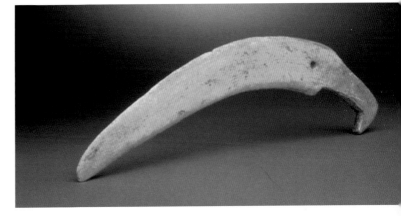

A nineteenth-century Iglulik Inuit bone snow knife from near Somerset Island, Batty Bay, Northwest Territories. *Courtesy Royal Ontario Museum.*

Sintering is a process that rapidly converts loose grains into a cohesive material at temperatures near, but still below, melting. Molecules within the material become highly mobile and migrate to the spots where the particles touch one another. These contact points soon grow into bonds and the entire mass is turned into a solid. Even when the air temperature is a bitter −40°F, snow is still quite close to its melting temperature and will readily sinter. As snow blocks are cut for an igloo, the knife leaves numerous small fractured grains on the block surfaces. When one block is stacked on another, the contacting surfaces sinter, essentially gluing the blocks together. Loose snow packed into the cracks between blocks also sinters, sealing the holes and further cementing the structure. Finally, the outer surface of an igloo is often smoothed and rubbed with mittens to promote a case-hardening that adds windproofing. A day or two after an igloo is built, the structure is strong enough to stand on.

The main use of a snow knife is to build an igloo. Historically, the knives were made from bone or ivory and date back thousands of years. These bone and ivory knives have a peculiar shape, more like a pruning saw than the knife I had purchased, although they are of comparable size with blades fifteen to twenty inches long. When we rendezvoused with Arvids and Chris halfway through the trip, they had modern metal snow knives (*panak* in the Inuvialuk language), which they had received after taking a survival course on the eastern shore of Hudson Bay. Interestingly, their modern knives mimicked the shape of the old bone knives, though made of modern materials. The ancient knives were probably not that strong. Numerous bone-knife fragments found in archaeological digs in eastern Greenland hint at a high breakage rate. To date, though, my attempts to borrow an ancient knife and test it by using it to make an igloo have been rebuffed by museums (for obvious reasons).

As soon as metal was available in the North American Arctic, the bone snow knife was discarded. At first, only small amounts of metal could be obtained, so the Inuit cleverly made knives with bits of metal inserted into a bone or wooden handle, like teeth in a jawbone. Later, as larger pieces of metal became available, full-metal snow knives were manufactured. Saw blades obtained from whalers from about the 1820s onward became an especially good source of metal for the knives. One particularly interesting specimen, found in eastern arctic Canada and now in a British museum, is a snow knife that was made from one the kitchen knives belonging to the ill-fated 1845 Franklin expedition fitted onto a long wooden handle. It looks functional and strong.

Strangely, while snow knives remain in use in arctic Canada, and still retain a distinctive design in each community, the knives seem to have disappeared from arctic Alaska. Numerous inquires in Barrow have failed to turn up a single modern snow knife. A few of the elders recall having seen knives used when they were younger, and prehistoric (perhaps several-hundred-year-old) bone knives have been unearthed at Nuvuk, the ancient predecessor of modern Barrow. Why the snow knife has disappeared in the Alaska Arctic remains a mystery.

Even where the knives are still in use, it is unclear how adept modern snow knife users are with this ancient tool. The early-twentieth-century explorer and anthropologist Knud Rasmussen was no stranger to the snow knife. In his thousands of miles of travel across the Arctic with the Inuit of western Greenland he probably built hundreds of igloos. I am sure he was pretty handy at it. On a trip near Baker Lake, however, he fell in with the inland (caribou-hunting) Inuit and was awed by their igloo-building skills. Whereas Rasmussen was used to building an igloo in about an hour with two people working, these masters-of-the-knife could build an igloo in a half hour working solo. The igloos I have built have usually taken several hours each and looked pretty bad when finished. True mastery in this ancient arctic skill has probably passed away for good in this modern era of heated homes and fast-traveling snowmobiles.

To be honest, though, the profound cultural heritage embodied in the snow knife was completely lost on me during the trip. I was just delighted I had a great big knife I could throw and use. Each time we stopped, out would come the knife from my back box, and then: *fffffttttttt—sprongggg!* I would throw the knife into a drift, grab my shovel, and get to work on the snow pit. Each big block of dense snow that I dug out of the pit, I would trim up and slice into shape, building a snow *inuksuk* next to the pit. In the evening, when I pitched my tent, I would cut blocks of snow with the knife and pile them up as a windbreak. The knife felt good. Cutting snow felt good.

But darker days were coming. Like a Greek tragedy, on the second to last day of the trip, I once again threw my knife into a drift, but instead of *sprong,* there was a loud *ping.* The blade was stuck in the snow, but the orange handle was sliding across the snow surface. The blade had snapped, and I was heartbroken. I had to do the snow pit using my old spatula. I had been demoted from a samurai snow warrior to short order cook. It was intolerable. I had to get another knife.

When we arrived in Baker Lake at the end of our trip, I went to the local stores, but unlike Kugluktuk, they did not sell snow knives. So I got the word out that I was looking to buy a knife if anyone in town made them. Word gets around fast in a town like Baker Lake and on our second day there a young woman of about thirty approached me. Her dad, who spoke no English, was with her. He had a knife to sell. It was heavily used, and the wood handle was cracked and repaired with duct tape, but to me it was perfect. This was a knife that already knew how to cut snow blocks for an igloo, a knife with history. With the daughter acting as interpreter, we agreed on a price of forty Canadian dollars. Then the old man asked me why I wanted the knife. I suppose I could have lied and said I was collecting them, but instead I told him the truth. I had broken mine. "How?" he asked. Sheepishly I told him about throwing the knife into the snow. His face broke into a huge toothless grin, the crow's feet next to his black eyes twinkling. For a brief moment, I saw the old man as young boy throwing *his* snow knife into the snow. His laugh told me he might have broken a few knives in his younger days. He asked to see the

SOMETIMES CALLED A STONE MAN, an *inuksuk* (pronounced: in-ook-SHOOK) is a figure made of stones, and anywhere from knee- to head-high. The Inuit people who lived and traveled in the Barrenlands of arctic Canada are thought to have built these stone markers to show travel routes, indicate direction and distance, or to identify important hunting or gathering places. An alternate origin theory has Martin Frobisher's men building a series of cairns in 1577 on a small island in Frobisher Bay, Nunavut, a practice that was then taken up by the locals. Whatever the origin of the figures, the word *inuksuk* means "to look like a person" and many *inuksuit* (plural) are built to look like human figures. For families and hunters traveling in this barren arctic landscape long ago, an *inuksuk* was a comforting sign that said, "people have passed here before" or, "you are on the right trail." Even today, people traveling out on the land will see a familiar *inuksuk* on a hilltop and know exactly where they are and which way to go. As we traveled east from Kugluktuk we began to see real *inuksuit* out on the land. The *inuksuk* is deeply rooted in Inuit culture and has become a symbol of safety, hope, and friendship. When the people of Nunavut were designing their new flag (pictured above) they chose the symbol of an *inuksuk* as their emblem.

Inukshuk. A. Huntington

broken knife. I took out the pieces and handed them to him. He felt the steel, flexed the blade and tapped on it with a hoary fingernail.

"This is good steel," he said. "You should fix this knife."

We shook hands and parted. That night, as I packed to go home, I carefully wrapped the old man's knife and my broken blade in padding and packed them away at the bottom of my duffle bag. There is more than carbon and iron in a blade. There are stories: of a long traverse, of an old man's life in Baker Lake, and of a tough and resilient culture that has figured out how to turn snow and cold from an enemy into friend. Inuit girls in southwest Alaska use ceremonial "story knives" to scratch designs in the mud while recounting traditional tales. I am sure these tales are wonderful, but I think the stories annealed into the steel and bone of real snow knives go even deeper. If we could know the stories embedded therein, how thrilling some of those tales might be. When I got home from our trip one of the first things I did was to weld my Kugluktuk knife back together and put a beautiful new wood handle on the Baker Lake knife.

Back home in Alaska, I put a new handle on the snow knife I bought from the old man in Baker Lake (left), welded the blade of the knife I bought in Kugluktuk, and built a new knife from a machete (right).

SEA ICE GOING, GOING, GONE

...on the arctic seacoast, although a glance at a map will show that most arctic villages not located on the big interior rivers are hugging the ocean. For thousands of years, coastal sea ice has provided a platform on which the Inuit and Iñupiat hunted for food: through the ice for fish and seals, on the ice for walrus, and in the ice leads for whales and beluga. Compared to uncertain caribou hunting, marine resources have always provided a reliable and rich source of protein. But as the ice pack has shrunk in recent decades, coastal ice across the Arctic keeps getting thinner, more unpredictable, and more dangerous to work on. In autumn and early winter the sea ice forms much later, allowing storm waves to hammer the coast. This makes boating more dangerous and accelerates coastal erosion that threatens to force whole villages to move inland.

The sea ice north of Barrow, Alaska, with an open water lead (gray fog on the horizon) in the distance. Sea ice conditions at Kugluktuk are similar.

Disappearing sea ice, that most dramatic and powerful emblem of global warming, is neither an abstract concept nor a distant harbinger of a changing planet for arctic coastal villages. It is a real ongoing transformation of their immediate environment, a profound alteration that village residents are experiencing every day.

The arctic ice pack began to shrink about thirty years ago, coinciding with the onset of global warming. These three decades have seen a net loss of ice equal to an area about the size of western Europe. Even more worrisome, the rate of ice decline has exceeded the predictions of virtually all computer models, indicating that we scientists do not fully understand the mechanisms driving the change.

In 2007, the summer extent of the arctic ice dropped to an all-time record low—the area of "missing" ice that summer could have covered half of the Lower Forty-eight United States—and the ice has not rebounded much since. If the current pace of shrinkage keeps up, the Arctic Ocean will be completely ice-free in summer within the next fifty years, perhaps even within the next twenty-five.

The ripple effects are likely to be profound. With the arctic sea ice gone, much shorter polar shipping routes between Europe and Asia will become practical, insurable, and heavily used. An oil and mineral-hungry world will also compete vigorously...

for the rich arctic reserves under the ocean or easily accessible from the newly ice-free shipping routes. Polar bears, which use the ice for hunting and resting, will struggle to adapt, and if they are to survive will have to spend more time on land. With more open water, the arctic weather is also likely to change—snow and rainfall amounts will increase, transmitting the impact of the diminishing sea ice to the land.

In October 1988 a few whales made news by getting trapped in the sea ice near Barrow, Alaska. In the past decade, I cannot remember the ice forming near Barrow before December. An uncertain future faces the subsistence hunters of the northern ice, while increased shipping, resource extraction, and industrialization is likely to transform the hazardous and lonely seas of the Arctic into something more like the heavily trafficked Baltic Sea.

Coastal erosion near Drew Point on the Arctic Coast of Alaska. *Courtesy of Chris Arp.*

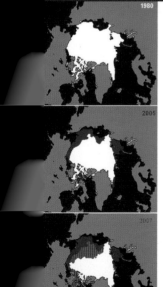

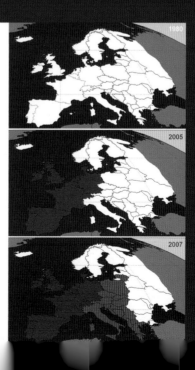

The loss of arctic sea ice (shown in red and purple on the left) is compared to equivalent areas in the United States (center) and Europe (right). *Figure courtesy of Don Perovich.*

09

THE STARVATION TRAIL

Kugluktuk was interesting but bewildering after the solitude of the trail. There were people to talk with to arrange for fuel and a place to stay, people to visit and to ask about soapstone carvings, officials to register with, school teachers and students to lecture to, and passersby on the street who asked where we were from. There were decisions to make, too many decisions. On the trail, the most momentous decision of the day often was what to have for dinner. We enjoyed the town but were soon ready to leave.

After visiting Bloody Falls we headed out into the Barrenlands once more. For a time we passed through a country of rock and snow. Then we drove across huge lakes with names hardly anyone has ever heard. When our trail intersected that of Sir John Franklin and his ill-fated 1821 expedition, we followed his route for two days. More than half of Franklin's men died, by starvation or murder, in that rocky country, but that was not to be our fate.

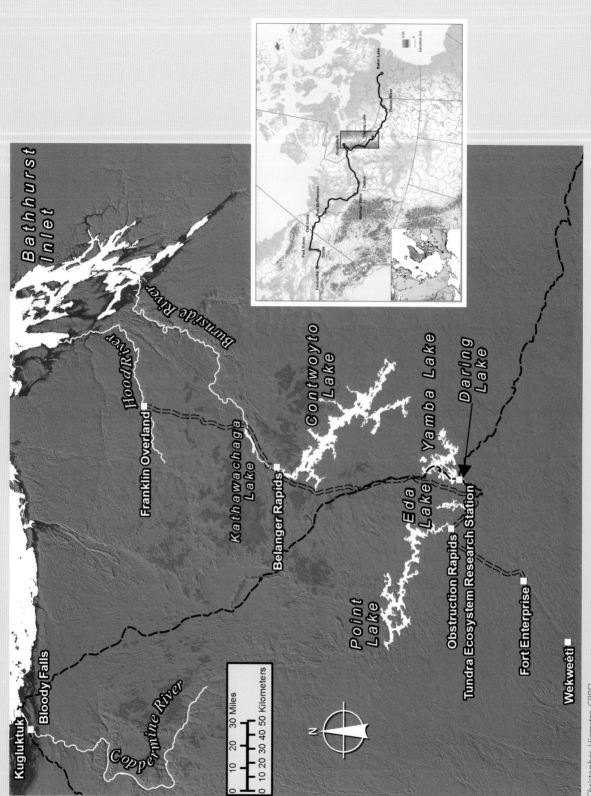

Christopher Hiemstra, CRREL

A BRASS COMPASS. A MAGNET. A dip needle. A large mercury-in-glass thermometer. Some decomposed books. We were not going to find them. We were not even going to try. But they were out here somewhere, cached under a rock, perhaps marked by a weathered cairn. They were stashed by Sir John Franklin's expedition on September 13, 1821, during the party's disastrous return march to Fort Enterprise after exploring the Northwest Passage. The brass compass, magnet, and glass thermometer might still be intact today. Just knowing that they were there was enough for us.

From Kugluktuk we had been following a snowmobile track we were told ran to the Lupine Gold Mine on Contwoyto Lake, but now we turned south to follow Franklin's "starvation trail." We wanted to see what the country looked like and get a little better understanding of one of the most infamous tragedies of Barrenlands exploration. It is not a natural route. It cuts across the grain of the land. It crosses rivers in illogical places and dead-ends at lakes. Since Franklin's passage, it has rarely, if ever, been used because it leads from nowhere to nowhere. We might well have been the first ones to be following this course on the ground since Franklin and his men limped by 186 years ago.

The contrasts could not have been greater. Franklin and his men were heading west to their home base. We were heading east. They were wishing winter would hold off and not catch them out on the tundra. We were hoping that winter would not end too soon. We were mechanized and fast. They had thrown away their last remaining canoe and had only their legs to carry them. Perhaps more important than anything else, we carried a handheld GPS unit and could locate ourselves precisely on accurate maps. They had no maps and only the crudest methods for navigation. Eleven out of the twenty men on Franklin's expedition would not make it back to the fort.

Sir John Franklin (1786–1847), British explorer, in a Louis Haghe lithograph of a portrait by Joseph Mathias Negelen. *Courtesy National Portrait Gallery, London.*

While planning our trip, I had carefully transferred Franklin's route to our maps, using his book and the journal of Dr. John Richardson, a surgeon and the expedition's naturalist, as guides. In 1820, starting from Great Slave Lake, Lieutenant John Franklin and his men had pushed north from Fort Providence, which is not far from the modern city of Yellowknife. They followed the Yellowknife River about 180 miles into the Barrenlands. By the shores of Winter Lake, on a small forested hill thirty miles from the modern Tlicho (Tåîchô) community of Wekweètì, they built Fort Enterprise, where they wintered. When the snow melted the following June, they started north again, portaging their canoes or dragging them over the still-frozen lakes, paddling when possible. Eventually they gained the south shore of Point Lake, one of the large headwater lakes of the Coppermine River. It stretches more than sixty miles, east to west. By July 2, 1821, they were out of the lakes and on the river proper, able to paddle continuously. Moving rapidly, they descended 250 miles to Bloody Falls in just thirteen days.

They passed the mouth of the Coppermine on July 20, within a stone's throw of the house where we stayed in Kugluktuk. Here they met the Coronation Gulf Inuit and traded for meat. Several Yellowknife Indians were traveling with Franklin at the time. While the Indians feared and loathed the Inuit, they also realized they needed to make peace. They asked Franklin to do his best to promote a rapprochement with their traditional enemies. This time there was no violence between Indian and Inuit.

In Coronation Gulf Franklin got on with his mission, which was to survey this sector of the Canadian Arctic, to ascertain if a Northwest Passage existed and could be transited by ships of the Royal Navy. With twenty men in two large birch-bark canoes, he headed east. For his French Canadian boatmen used to paddling lakes and rivers, this must have been terrifying. Instead of rocks, and rapids, there were salt water, tides, and curling waves. For Franklin and the other Royal Navy officers (Back, Hood, and Richardson), consummate sailors that they were, it must have felt like a return to sources. For the first time on the expedition they had more expertise than their men.

Skillfully they worked their way along the coast, exploring and mapping as they went, weathering several big storms. By August they had made their way into Bathurst Inlet, a fjordlike arm of the sea that extends more than ninety miles south into the Barrenlands. It is a maze of islands, complex headlands, and subsidiary inlets. It took weeks to explore. Franklin, anxious to make his mark on his first Arctic expedition, continued plugging away even after it was past time to turn back. His boatmen, well aware of what might happen if the season turned to winter prematurely, begged and pleaded with him to start home. Finally in late August he relented, but by now the canoes, fragile craft never meant for ocean waves, were shot. Fifteen timbers were broken in one, and on both numerous ribs were stove-in. The birch bark was in bad shape and might pull away from the frames with catastrophic results. These boats were unlikely to survive a return journey along the coast.

Franklin chose to return home overland. On August 26, 1821, the party started up the Hood River in their battered canoes. One by one, small events and bad decisions began to coalesce into a trap from which there would be no escape for half of the men. Within a day of starting up the river they came to Wilberforce Falls. Above the scenic two-hundred-foot falls the river was shoal and not easily navigated. They broke up their damaged boats to build two smaller canoes from the remains. Two days later, when the Hood River bent to the west, they started hiking south across the tundra. They cached many heavy items near where they had left the river but still each boatman had to carry ninety pounds of gear. The packs included relatively little food and they were reduced to subsisting mostly by hunting, with the very size of the group making it unlikely they would be able to find and kill enough game as they traveled. It was already autumn and the unpredictable caribou would be on the move. The danger signs were obvious, but they had no other options.

On September 1 it started to snow. Within a few days the temperature dropped below freezing and stayed there, but not before the men's gear was thoroughly soaked. Game became even scarcer and hunger began to sap the men's strength and will. They lived on *tripe de roche*—rock tripe, a black crusty lichen they were able to scrape off rocks. It filled their bellies but also produced

Lower Wilberforce Falls today (left) and sketched by Ensign George Back on Franklin's 1821 expedition. The red and yellow arrows indicate the location of the people in Back's engraving.

severe stomach cramps. The incessant wind made walking difficult, particularly for the men carrying the two canoes. One of the boats was irreparably damaged when the man carrying it was blown to the ground. They burned the remains, since wood was also was scarce out on the barrens. The small canoes had been serviceable for river crossings when lashed together, but with only one remaining, they would soon find such crossings to be perilous. As if all this were not enough, on September 10 they came upon the first of the large lakes that lay between them and Fort Enterprise.

It is difficult in this day of detailed maps and satellite images to understand what it must have been like to stand on a tundra hill and see a lake with no name stretching away over the horizon, knowing that to make the wrong choice in finding a way around it could mean death by starvation. Fifteen-mile-long Kathawachaga Lake was astride their route. Hearne had passed this lake and written of it, but his navigation was off and he placed the lake much farther west. Franklin, unaware that this was the same lake identified by

Hearne, and also unaware that Hearne's route south to Point Lake lay well to the west of them, decided to cross to the east side of the Burnside River where it flowed out of Kathawachaga Lake and work further south before heading west again. This was a big mistake. The caribou migration route was farther west, and there were less formidable rivers and lakes to cross in that region. The party might have still made it through had they made the correct choice here, but how could Franklin know?

Several more days walking and the party came down through the tundra hills on the east side of seventy-five-mile-long Contwoyto Lake. By now, Franklin should have realized that this was Cogead Lake in Hearne's book and that he needed to be west of it, but his writings do not indicate he realized this important fact until four days later. Now the party had to backtrack north until they reached the mouth of the lake, but this at least was better than traveling the extra seventy-five miles it would have taken to circumnavigate the lake. At the north end of the lake they cached a compass, dip needle, and other paraphernalia, recognizing that they needed to travel as lightly and rapidly as possible if they were to survive.

In trying to cross the swift outflow from the lake in their one remaining canoe, four men, including Franklin, were swept away. Only with the greatest of effort did the men get to the far shore, but not before one of the boatmen, Solomon Belanger, nearly perished from immersion and hypothermia. Franklin's journal was lost in the accident. Belanger (whose name now

Tripe de roche fed Franklin's party.

graces the rapids in which he almost died) was rescued, and the rest of the men were then successfully ferried across the river in the frail canoe.

Once across the lake they started south again, but the trap was now closing rapidly. On September 16, Franklin would later recall in his book, they "walked next day over a more level country, but it was strewn with large stones. These galled our feet a good deal. . . . We had not breakfast and but a scanty supper; we allayed the pangs of hunger by eating pieces of singed hide. Our appetites had become ravenous." On the nineteenth, Franklin recalled, "The men were very faint and marched with difficulty, having to oppose a fresh breeze, and to wade through snow two feet deep. The [last remaining] canoe was unfortunately broken by the fall of the person who had it in charge."

By September 21, the trap snapped shut. Franklin wrote, "The party were very feeble and the men much dispirited; we made slow progress, having to march over hilly and very rugged country. Just before noon the sun beamed through the haze for the first time in six days, and we obtained an observation in latitude 65° 7' 06"N. [From this] we discovered that we had kept eastward of the proper course.... We altered course immediately to the west-south-west."

Unfortunately, the Franklin party was now between two large lakes, Eda and Yamba. Their only alternative was to continue south until they could round the southern end of Eda Lake and turn west. While on this southerly leg, one final calamity hit. The broken canoe, which might have been repaired for an emergency river crossing, was abandoned by the men charged with carrying it. Nothing Franklin said could induce Peltier or Vaillant to carry it further, and since Royal Navy officers do not carry burdens like a canoe, the sole option was to leave it abandoned on the tundra. Discipline had broken down completely. The only reason the party remained intact was the boatmen did not know the way to the Fort Enterprise. Only the Royal Navy officers could navigate there.

After his altercation with Peltier and Vaillant, Franklin rejoined the main party to find that the men "had picked up some pieces of skin, and a few bones of deer that had been devoured by the wolves last spring. They had rendered the bones friable by burning, and eaten them as well as the skin; several of them had added their old shoes to the repast." It was from this event that Franklin later became famous in England as the man who ate his own shoes.

Luckily, when the party reached the southern end of Lake Eda the next day, they were able to kill five caribou. These they butchered and devoured on the spot. The

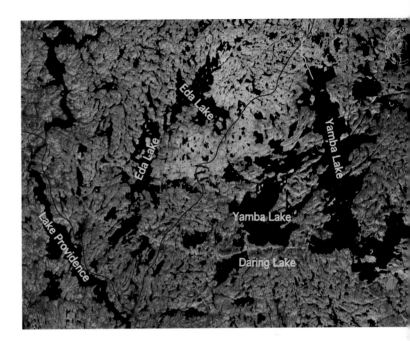

exhausted men petitioned Franklin for a rest day, starvation and exertion having taken too great a toll for them to continue without some recuperation. In their defense, these men were still carrying enormously heavy loads across rough ground, starving, and often wet and cold. Their British officers marched relatively lightly burdened in comparison. Franklin agreed to the rest stop, and the entire group thanked providence for the food. A long lake to the south that blocked their route was named Lake Providence in gratitude.

They followed Lake Providence west to where it ended and a large river exited the lake. It turned out to be the Coppermine River, which flows north here over continuous rapids into yet another large lake, Point Lake, where their journey had begun. They had come full circle and were nearly on their outbound route, except they were on the wrong side of the Coppermine River. Fort Enterprise was a now a scant forty miles away. Healthy, fully fed, and with a canoe to cross the river, the explorers could have made it to the fort in a single day. But, starving, wasted, and lacking any means of crossing the turbulent river, they were stuck. The loss of the two canoes was now catastrophic. It took a week of various stratagems and unsuccessful attempts before one of the hunters, St. Germain, succeeded in building a raft made from bundles of

Franklin's route (red line) went through an intricate landscape of large and small lakes gouged out of bedrock by the Laurentide Ice Sheet. Traveling in the autumn before the lakes froze, the party could be stopped by even a narrow neck of water. We turned off (yellow line) the historic route for better and safer travel on the ice of Yamba Lake.
Landsat image, NASA

willows. With it, he was able to ferry the group across the river one at a time. The rapids where they crossed are now known as Obstruction Rapids.

They were across the river and had a clear path to Fort Enterprise, but for some of the men it was too late. Within two days of crossing, Crédit and Vaillant could go no farther. They lay down in the snow to die. Junius, one of the Inuit guides, wandered off and was never seen again. Hood, a young Navy midshipman, unable to digest the rock tripe, weakened and could not travel any more. Richardson, the doctor-naturalist, along with Hepburn, one of those indefatigable British seamen who show up in so many of these exploration narratives, selflessly agreed to stay behind with Hood. The invalid seaman and his attendants set up camp in a grove of willows on the east side of what is now know as Starvation Lake. Franklin, recognizing that he could not delay the whole party for those who were faltering, agreed to the separation and planned to send aid back from the fort as soon as he could. The next morning, four more expedition members weakened to the point where they also could not go on. They stopped and camped in various willow thickets and sparse spruce groves, their probable fate death by starvation. The remainder of the ambulatory party, split yet again into an advance team led by Ensign George Back and a slower group led by Franklin, limped painfully on toward Fort Enterprise.

Death met both groups. Despite having set in place plans to have the fort re-supplied before his return, it was empty and abandoned. There was a good reason: it was a starvation autumn across all of the country north of Great Slave Lake. The re-supply party had failed in their mission, barely surviving themselves. They had to live on rock tripe for eleven days straight. The starving Franklin party moved into the cheerless and empty fort and slowly wasted away. Before relief finally arrived at the fort, Peltier, Samandre, and Beauparlant died of starvation, bringing the death toll to six out of twenty.

More was to come. Back at Starvation Lake, events took a macabre turn. As Hood lingered near death, tended by Richardson and Hepburn, Michel, one of the hunters who had turned back from the main party the previous day, arrived in camp acting quite strange. He brought the British sailors meat, which he said came from a wolf that had been gored to death by a caribou. The meat had an unusual color and taste. He asked for a hatchet as opposed to a knife when he said he was headed out hunting, and he was far more energetic than the starving British, who were living on *tripe de roche*. Michel was also heavily armed with two pistols, a bayonet, and several knives. He was vague about what had happened to Fontano, Belanger, and Perrault, the three companions who turned back with him, claiming they must have wandered off and perished. Richardson suspected murder and cannibalism, but he and Hepburn were too weak for open confrontation with the heavily armed Michel. Meanwhile, Hood continued to fade.

This tense stalemate held for days, until October 20. That morning, while Richardson and Hepburn were doing chores a short distance from the campsite, they heard the report of a pistol. Rushing back, they found Hood dead with a bullet through his brain. Michel, who had been with Hood just moments before, protested his innocence, but the wound indicated it could not have been suicide. Michel must have realized that until Hood died, Richardson and Hepburn would not travel to the fort and safety. Since Michel could not find the fort on his own, he hastened Hood's death. Richardson and Hepburn realized that they were next. Michel would kill them as soon as he was close to the fort. Richardson knew his only chance for survival was to kill Michel first. Three days later, as they marched toward the fort, he got his opportunity. Passing a lichen-covered rock, Michel claimed he was going to stop and gather some rock tripe. He would catch up with Richardson and Hepburn shortly. In all probability he was priming his pistols for the murders he was about to commit. Instead, just as Michel came even with the two British, but before he could draw his weapons, Richardson shot him dead.

Richardson and Hepburn's ordeal was not over. It took them six more days to reach Fort Enterprise, despite it being a scant forty miles away. The fort offered no succor. There they found Franklin and his remaining group starving. Not until nine long days later did a group of Indians arrive with supplies and slowly nurse the shattered and starving men back to health. The rescuers were Yellowknives under the leadership of Chief Akaitcho, alerted to the impending catastrophe

An inuksuk on a smooth rolling section of the Franklin trail.
H. Huntington.

by St. Germain, the hero of the river crossing at Obstruction Rapids. Sadly for so many of the men who explored Bathurst Inlet with Franklin, the aid came too late.

On our first day following Franklin's trail we traveled through the area he crossed on September 16, 1821. Like Franklin, we found this to be level, pleasant country. It looked like a rolling snow-covered prairie. The large stones that had "galled" the explorers' feet were buried under more than twenty inches of snow, which was a relief because hitting a rock with a snowmobile ski can destroy the suspension, taking the machine out completely of commission. What happens is the ski's carbide cleats hit the rock and dig in. The ski stops dead, but seven hundred pounds of engine and chassis continue moving forward. Something has to give and it is the trailing arm, a piece of the suspension that rides up and down with the ski. On a previous expedition, when we were hundreds of miles from any town, this exact scenario happened. We had to beat the buckled trailing arm straight with the back of an axe, then use hose clamps to reinforce it with a old axle shaft. The fix was ugly but worked for more than a hundred miles, although it probably would not have worked much farther.

Progress was good in that smooth rolling country, and as it got late we spied a rock bluff topped by a big snow cornice. At the base of such bluffs there is usually a level patch of snow that makes for excellent camping. We made a beeline for the spot, where it didn't take long to get the tents up and dinner going. Before sunset Dan climbed onto the bluff top above camp to film our activities. When he got back he reported that the bluff top had a heavy

FINDING THE ARCTIC

mantle of moraine boulders and, more troubling, that looking south the view resembled a rock quarry for as far as he could see.

Our second day on Franklin's trail was altogether different from the first. Dan had been absolutely right: we apparently managed to camp on a geologic boundary because from then on the rolling white prairie was gone. Ridges one hundred to two hundred feet high and few hundred feet apart crisscrossed the landscape. Small cliffs, glaciated bedrock bosses, and rocky bluffs with snow cornices replaced the rolling hills. There was no discernable order to these features and distributed over everything was the heaviest rock moraine

Our camp under the bluff, one day down the Franklin trail.

Colorful shavings mark our trail as tough sledding takes a toll on our equipment.
H. Huntington.

we had yet to travel through. In many places we had no choice but to drive over the rocks. It was also snowing and overcast, making the visibility poor.

Two more things made the navigation trying. The first was something we had noticed a few days earlier when we entered the Barrenlands. We found it difficult to tell the scale of rock features. Cliffs that appeared at first to be towering hundreds of feet above the valley floor shrank to thirty or even twenty feet high when we got close to them. We decided this illusion was caused by our being used to seeing similar types of rock structures in the mountains of Alaska and Colorado, but in the Barrenlands, the features were miniature. Even after this realization, we still tended to estimate distance and difficulty based on our over-estimation of size. The second problem was that there seemed to be no continuous drainages anywhere. We would drop into a valley, follow it for miles expecting it to become more distinct as we moved downstream, but instead it would end in a rocky dead end. Ridges did the same thing, petering out far sooner than we expected them to, or branching in odd ways. The moraine boulders and rock talus were just as thick in valley bottoms as on ridge tops and someone could have followed our route by tracing the slivers and corkscrews of black, red, green, and blue plastic we left behind as the sleds scraped over this abrasive ground.

The biggest excitement of the day came when I forgot one of the cardinal rules of traveling in a whiteout: fill your pocket with pebbles. When you come to what may be a snow slope you can throw a pebble ahead and see how

FINDING THE ARCTIC

steep it is. It is an effective procedure, although pretty comical to watch. In a solid whiteout, it is virtually impossible to tell a flat piece of snow from a cornice with a fifty-foot drop, so the lead driver stops and gets off the machine. Gingerly, he edges forward, sometimes even dropping to his hands and knees to crawl. If he still cannot tell what is ahead, he takes a pebble from his pocket and throws it out into the void. Every once in a while, the pebble disappears over an invisible white edge. Then the driver has to crawl forward a little more and try to see where the pebble went. Did it fall over a fifty-foot cliff, or did it drop over a six-inch lip? It usually takes more crawling and a few more pebbles before one can get a sense of what is ahead.

This morning I was careless. I had already negotiated a dozen snow slopes that I could barely see, and all had proved gentle. When I crossed yet another rocky ridge top with a snow slope on its south side, I drove forward and immediately realized I had made a bad mistake. I had just driven a seven-hundred-pound snowmobile towing two sleds weighing close to a thousand pounds each over a cornice. I was falling. I had just enough time while plummeting downward to push on the throttle. If I was lucky and the toe slope was gentle, I would need the snowmobile to be pulling hard as I landed so that my sleds would not push the machine and flip it over. If I was unlucky, this little adventure was going to end badly. Luck was with me and I landed in soft snow. With the track already revved up, I accelerated as soon as I hit, roaring away from the cornice in a cloud of snow dust. Looking back at the ridge I could now see my track coming over the lip. There was a ten-foot section where there was no track, then a deep furrow in the soft snow at the base leading to my machine. Just then Glen came barreling over the ridge toward the cornice. Because he could see me at the bottom, he must have figured the slope was OK, because over he went. He landed the drop well. Jon followed, then Dan, and finally Henry. We all gathered at the bottom and looked back at the cornice that could have been our ruin. At the very next patch of rocks, I filled my pockets with pebbles.

We weaved and dodged through moraine all day, traversing ground covered by Franklin between September 17 and September 21. We were aware that one slip in driving and we would be spending hours fixing broken snow-mobiles. Late in the day, I saw on the map that there was a way out. Yamba Lake was only five miles east of us, a frozen and smooth highway that would take us all the way to the Environment Canada research station at Daring Lake. Our trial by moraine was over. We knew we were wimps for taking the escape route, but we had seen what we wanted to see and we'd had enough. How did any of Franklin's starving, weary men make it through that terrible jumble of rock?

Over the years, there has been considerable criticism of Franklin and his leadership. Franklin's 1821 expedition was a disaster, but its death toll pales in comparison with what happened on his last expedition. In 1845–1848, during a final attempt to sail through the Northwest Passage, both of his ships were trapped in the ice and crushed. Eventually all 129 hands on that expedition perished. Mercifully, Franklin, an elderly fifty-nine years old when he left, died of natural causes before he could witness the wholesale death of his men. The last of Franklin's crew probably died of starvation while trying to sledge south to the Barrenlands and escape via Great Slave Lake. It was a forlorn hope for men unskilled in hunting and traveling. As in 1821, some of them were driven to cannibalism before they died of exposure, starvation, and scurvy. It took forty years and more than twenty-two search expeditions before the full story came to light. And that was only possible because the Inuit of the Canadian Arctic Archipelago remembered the fatal expedition and told searchers about the strange things they had seen: men hauling heavy useless long boats filled with silver plate, kitchen knives, and massive log books; starving men falling in their tracks and remaining unburied on the tundra. These stories have a dream-like, surreal quality. They speak of men so ill-equipped and ill-suited to the country that to the Inuit they must have looked like aliens from another planet.

The criticism leveled at Franklin is that he was so caught up in the rigid class and racial structures of the Victorian era that he was unable to accept the essential lessons of the land offered by his dark-skinned Inuit and Indian guides. Franklin never learned from them how to adapt to the North, and consequently he made the same fatal mistakes over and over. He never learned to hunt or fish. He traveled in parties that were too large to subsist off the land, and he consistently carried too much useless stuff but not enough food. He pushed his explorations too far into the ice, and too late in the season. He was also insensitive to the plight of his men, who were often burdened far more heavily than he and the other naval officers. But this comes as no surprise. Franklin and the other British sailors came from a society in which class and racial structure were so fundamental, so integral, that breaking out of these norms would have been virtually impossible at that time. While Franklin was struggling across the Barrenlands slavery still had forty-five years to run in the United States. How could Franklin listen to, or emulate, the Canadian boatmen, the Indians, or the Inuit? They were his inferiors.

It was also a matter of cultural differences in risk and reward, and those differences have not been completely erased even today. In March of 2005, I was working on a science project on the sea ice off Point Barrow, Alaska. The project was focused on measuring the effect of open water on the atmospheric chemistry of the coastal regions of the Arctic. For several weeks we had worked at the edge of an open lead. It was a spectacular and dangerous place because large pieces of ice kept breaking off the land-fast ice and drifting away. In the 1980s, thirty Native whalers from Barrow had drifted away with their snowmobiles and other gear when the ice they were on broke free.

Moraine boulders on the tundra. *D. Solie.*

In the old days, drifting away from the land-fast ice meant sure death, but in the modern event there was a rescue helicopter in Barrow, and the whalers had a beacon with them. Not only were they rescued, but so, too, was all of their gear. Nonetheless, the danger of working near the ice edge is deeply ingrained in the collective psyche of the people of Barrow.

For safety, we had hired one of the most skilled seal hunters in Barrow, Carl Kippe, as a guide. Ensuring the scientists' safety weighed heavily on Carl. He was always checking to make sure our snowmobiles were in good shape and, when they were parked, that they were poised for a quick getaway in case the ice started to crack. Several times he ordered us off the ice when things "just didn't feel right." My job was to be sure the science got done. It was inevitable that we would clash, and we did. It wasn't until near the end of the project that I really understood Carl's view. It crystallized for me one day when he said, "I don't understand how you scientists can risk your lives to collect numbers and samples." Earlier that same day, however, I had been with Carl when a seal surfaced in the open water of the lead. It was cold, maybe −20°F, and the lead was smoking and steaming with vapor. A strong current was pushing floes and ice pans along the ice edge at several miles per hour. These icebergs would emerge silently from the fog, drift by, then disappear without making a sound. Carl shot the seal and then took his little white skin boat to retrieve it. The boat looked like some sort of chopped off kayak made small enough to fit on a sled. It couldn't have been more than six feet long. Carl got in, still wearing his massive green parka and white snow pants, and paddled off. By the time he made it to the seal, it was hard to see him in the mist, and once he had the seal threaded on his towline, it was hard for him to regain the ice edge against the stiff current. Had he drifted away, or flipped the tiny boat, he would have died, for we had no means to rescue him. As I watched him bobbing about in the steaming black water of the lead I thought, *I don't understand how he can risk his life for a seal when he can buy meat in the local market.* We clearly had our cultural differences when it came to risk.

For Franklin, exploration was the path to fame and success in Victorian England. Death—his own or that of his men—was an acceptable risk, so he

FINDING THE ARCTIC

took it. If he had been a little more progressive, he might have accepted both the risk and the lessons the Native people could have taught him, thereby avoiding the catastrophes he suffered. In the history books he would now be a hero. For the Indians and Inuit with whom he came in contact, survival was success, and eating meant survival. Risking death while hunting was not only acceptable, it was expected, but risking death for some abstract concept such as the Northwest Passage was foolish. Sadly, on the starvation trail, they paid the price of Franklin's ambition.

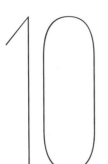

THE DIAMOND CONFLUENCE

From Yamba Lake we headed for the Daring Lake research station, where our two Canadian partners, Chris and Arvids, were waiting. Food and gas that we had preshipped before the trip was there, too. We packed up the snow samples we had collected so far to ship out by airplane, visited with some old friends doing research at the station, then after three days we headed east, now seven instead of five people.

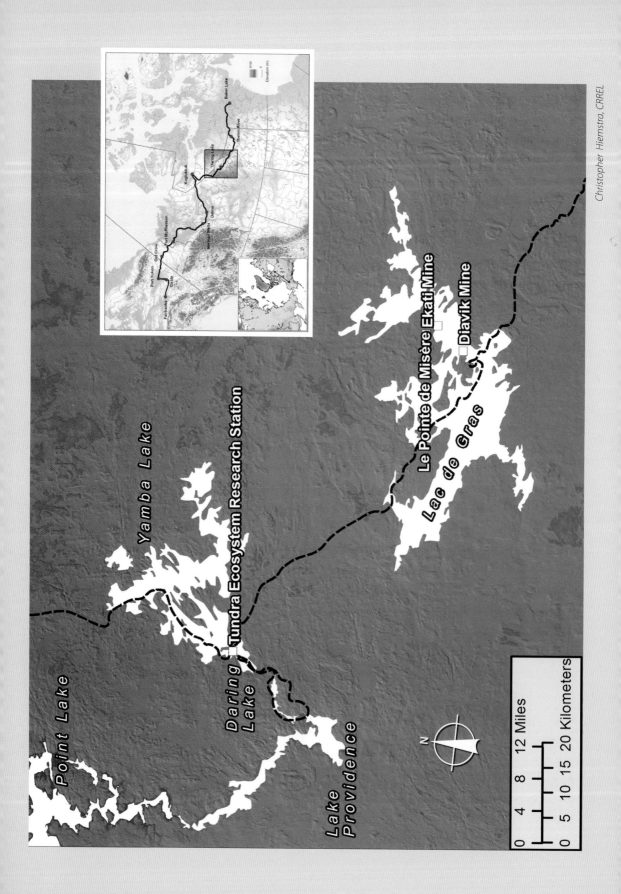

Christopher Hiemstra, CREL

ANOTHER "GREAT" ESKER stretched away to the east and west farther than I could see. It was a crisp sunny day and I had climbed to the top of it for some exercise. As I kicked steps in the drift snow along the side of the esker, my legs felt stiff and weaker than normal, a result of weeks of sitting and riding. On top, the esker looked like an elevated highway, fully two lanes wide, but paved with basketball-sized boulders and cobbles instead of blacktop. It would make for a bumpy car ride, but one with good views. I could see the esker curve gently around the shores of Yamba Lake, separating it from Daring Lake to the south. To the east, it disappeared over the horizon five miles away.

Should I walk along the esker to the east or the west? East seemed appropriate. That was the direction of the diamond mines. Twenty years ago, Chuck Fipke had worked his way eastward along this same esker, sampling minerals and desperately hoping for a sample that would tell him he was closing in on a diamond-bearing kimberlite pipe. His search had begun clear back at the Mackenzie River, now two weeks and five hundred miles behind us. Over a

The esker near the Tundra Ecosystem Research Station at Daring Lake.
H. Huntington.

period of ten years, as money allowed, he and his partners had followed the trail of the esker, slowly and methodically sampling beach sands and gravel bars, analyzing the samples for telltale signs that would announce that they were approaching the great diamond confluence. Like a giant vector, the esker had led them deep into the heart of the Barrenlands and to wealth beyond their wildest dreams.

To understand how an esker can lead to a diamond mine, one has to go back in time, first to an era that was warmer than today and then to one that was much colder. The warmer period, fifty million years ago, was a time of active volcanism across the Canadian Shield. The volcanic activity originated deep in the Earth, 150 miles below the surface. At that depth, the pressure of overlying rock can squeeze carbon atoms into tetrahedral packages that form the hardest known substance on the planet. From the equivalent of the charred remains of a campfire, diamonds are formed, but they will be forever inaccessible unless somehow they are delivered to the surface where they can be mined. That takes a specialized geologic express elevator known as a kimberlite pipe. A tube-shaped volcanic eruption of molten material travels up through the solid crust at speeds of nearly twenty-five miles an hour, melting the surrounding rock and ripping out hunks of this elevator shaft during its violent ascent. Diamonds, when present, get entrained in the eruption and borne up with other minerals. The upward journey is one of intense heat and violence. In most pipes, the rising diamonds are burnt, shocked, shattered, and otherwise ruined. Only when the rate of ascent is just right and the temperature moderate enough do gem-quality diamonds come to rest at or near the earth's surface. The alignment of all these necessary conditions is rare, and so too are profitable diamond mines.

The final stage of a kimberlite eruption, when the pipe breaks through to the surface, must be impressive (though no human has ever witnessed such an event since kimberlites have not formed for millions of years). Pieces of granite, chunks of mantle material, kimberlitic rock bearing diamonds, and all the wood and plant material covering the surface are blown sky-high in a plume of ejecta that eventually falls back into the crater produced by the eruption.

When the dust settles and the explosive action is complete, kimberlitic rock debris several hundred feet thick fills the crater. Even today, along with the rock in a kimberlite pipe there can be intact fragments of wood. In the Barrenlands, that wood came from ancient redwood trees similar to those found today along the Northern California coast.

Kimberlite from the Diavik Mine.

The pipe brings up other minerals along with diamonds: deep red garnets, glassy green chrome diopsides, and metallic black ilmenites. For years, diamond hunters knew that these other more common minerals held the key to finding diamond-bearing kimberlites, but they didn't know the code. From Siberia to South Africa, geologists collected the indicator minerals and puzzled over how they differed between diamond-bearing pipes and barren ones, but it wasn't until the 1970s, and the advent of the electron microprobe, that the code was worked out by geochemists in South Africa. Close to diamond-bearing kimberlite, the garnets would be high in chromium and low in calcium, while the iron in the ilmenites would not have been fully oxidized. The code, once it was worked out, was a closely held secret until the mid-1980s, when it finally leaked. Up until then, prospectors such as Fipke routinely collected samples and sieved them for the indicator minerals, but did not know how to use the information the microprobe told them. The code made the minerals into a trail of breadcrumbs that could, with care, be followed to the diamonds.

But the period of cold, snow, and ice that descended over the Barrenlands about ten million years ago made following that trail much harder. It produced the Laurentide Ice Sheet, which at its peak was several thousand feet thick and extended from the Mackenzie River east to the Atlantic Ocean, and

Red garnets, glassy green chrome diopsides, and black ilmenites found near Diavik Mine.

from the Arctic Ocean south to the Ohio River. The highest point of the Laurentide was in eastern Canada. From that distant ice divide, the ice flowed downhill, westward, scouring and plucking at the granite of the Barrenlands, gouging valleys and lake basins in some places, dropping vast fields of debris elsewhere. The kimberlite pipes were soft and easily eroded, so any surface clue to their presence was scattered. As the ice age ended, meltwater from the warming ice sheet poured through and under the ice, making the network of tunnels in which the eskers formed. The cruel joke played by the glaciers on the diamond hunters is that the breadcrumb trail is now smeared out hundreds of miles past where the minerals originated.

Fipke and his partners were patient. Starting near the Mackenzie River, summer after summer they worked their way east, sampling the eskers and adjacent lake shorelines, carting sack after sack of sand and gravel back to Kelowna, British Columbia, for sieving and microprobing. On one trip, Fipke scooped up a sample of purple-black sand from a wave-cut shoreline on a small pond north of Lac de Gras. A big esker ran just north of this lake, disappearing under its dark waters. On the same trip he also took a few samples just east of the forty-mile-long lake. The following winter, as he analyzed the samples in a locked windowless room, he realized that the breadcrumb trail had stopped. The lake sample had all the critical mineral indicators, but the sample taken east of the lake was barren. The kimberlite pipe was somewhere close to the small pond, but where?

By the summer of 1989, Fipke and crew knew two things: they were close, and they were almost out of money and time. They had yet to stake a single claim. As quietly as possible, they assembled a staking crew, thousands of claim stakes, helicopter fuel, tents, sleeping bags, and the other paraphernalia needed for a full-on staking campaign. There would be only one shot before word got out and the big boys—mining companies such as de Beers, Kennecott, Rio Tinto, and BHP—would descend on the area and stake everything in sight.

During the summer and extending into the stormy autumn, they worked like fiends. By October they had staked over 150 claims covering more than six hundred square miles of tundra and lake. In April they returned again and staked additional claims.

They had at least one good reason to think that their claims bracketed a diamondiferous kimberlite pipe. At the end of the April staking campaign, on the last day in the field, they had come upon a circular, cliff-line lake just west of Pointe de Misère, a peninsula sticking out into the northeast arm of Lac de Gras. This little forty-acre lake looked like it had been punched through the rock with a drill. Near the lake, when they scooped out a sample from the esker, a sparkling green chrome diopside the size of a pea appeared. Indicator minerals that large and pristine could only mean the pipe was nearby, most likely under the lake.

The diamond rush started in earnest in the summer of 1990. Despite the extreme measures the Fipke group had taken to try to keep their activities secret, word got out. While Fipke and his partners went looking for capital to develop the Pointe de Misère kimberlite, other big mining companies sent in teams and spent money like water in a staking frenzy. New companies and partnerships sprang up overnight, scrambled to find men, aircraft, and claim stakes, and tried to get into the game. Geology played little role in their activities. The plan was to get as close to the Fipke block of claims as possible and stake any open ground. And it wasn't a bad plan, either. In at least one case, the gamble paid off in a fantastic way when a small exploration company called Aber stumbled on the kimberlite pipe that ultimately became the Diavik Mine. More often, though, the staking frenzy merely relieved companies large and small of their money, transferring it neatly into the coffers of the aviation and logistical services businesses in Yellowknife.

By the end of the summer, Fipke and his partners had consummated a deal with BHP-Billiton, the Australian mining giant. In exchange for a fifty-one percent share of the claims, BHP would put up $500 million Canadian for mine development, and would pay forty-nine percent of any profits to Fipke and his associates. Fipke's personal share of the profits, about fifteen percent, is

Gas for the next leg waits at our Daring Lake camp at the foot of the Big Esker (above). Spot the sleds of the two Canadian members of the expedition, Chris and Arvids, who joined us at the Daring Lake research station (opposite page). *H. Huntington (sleds).*

worth more than a billion dollars today. Within five years, BHP had opened the Ekati Mine. Ironically, the kimberlite pipe under the circular lake near Pointe de Misère that started the rush had an insufficient concentration of diamonds to be viable, but six pipes about ten miles away, right in the middle of the Fipke claims, proved to be extremely lucrative.

The richest pipe, though, turned out to be just south of the Fipke claim block under the waters of Lac de Gras. It was found by Eira Thomas, daughter of the president of Aber Resources. Aeromagnetic surveys suggested the pipe was there; diagonal drilling from the shore proved it was a kimberlite pipe. An underground shaft and exploratory mine produced bulk samples that showed the pipe was exceptionally rich in gem-quality diamonds. This pipe became the Diavik Mine, and it was where we were headed next.

When I returned from my walk on the esker, the guys were busy checking our equipment. Arvids was filling sixty-three red plastic five-gallon jugs with fuel from the barrels of gas we had flown into the lake. Jon had his snowmobile in a shed where he was taking the engine apart again to see if he could fix the oil leak that was still plaguing the machine. Glen and Henry were trying to patch a hole worn through the bottom of the sled that carried our propane and cook stove, and Dan had gone off to see how ice fishing was done at Daring Lake. My walk on the esker, the respite from driving, the laid-back atmosphere at the research camp, were all a welcome change from the constant motion of the past month and the hectic preparations for the trip that had occupied most of the winter before we left.

Even arranging a tour of the Diavik mine had not been easy. Months before our trip, Chris had begun corresponding with his contacts at the mine, providing them with names, addresses, and social security numbers. A few weeks before we left on the trip, detailed forms were faxed to Alaska that we all had to sign. These were notable in one respect: we had to grant permission for a cavity search if required. The requirement made sense. We had heard that the entire production from the mine for several months could fit in a coffee can. The theft of even a handful of diamonds could be the difference between profit and loss at the mine.

Despite our diligence in filling out the forms, initially permission was not forthcoming. Apparently, the mine operators were wary of visitors. But Chris was persistent and things soon began to line up. Strangely, long after the rest of us had permission, Jon's approval remained stalled. We never knew the real reason for this, but we filled the vacuum with our own fantasies: his long patriarchal beard made him look like an anarchist. Or was it his stint operating a gold mine? Perhaps the operators feared he was too knowledgeable, too dangerous as an industrial spy. Eventually Jon's permission arrived, too.

Another imaginary scenario that surfaced during these preparations was that somehow we might actually leave the mine with a bag of contraband diamonds. I think every visitor to a diamond mine must have some version of this fantasy. Truth be told, I had kicked off the fantasizing before we left Fairbanks when I had sent Henry and Dan a short email about stealing diamonds. It was a way to relax in the midst of the frantic expedition preparations. How we would get these diamonds was not clear, but like Walter Mitty, we had a pretty good idea of how we would make our getaway. With a leather satchel full of diamonds tucked securely under the seat of a snowmobile, seven winter outlaws would escape by driving over the tundra on our black machines, tearing off in a blaze of snow dust, our superior driving skills foiling any attempts to stop or catch us. Of course, we would be wearing identical baggy white snow pants and parkas elegantly trimmed in fur.

Expectations were running high as we left Daring Lake for the run to Diavik. The mine was sixty miles to the east and we expected to make it in

Diavik fuel tanks on a hill beyond Jon's sled. Every drop of diesel used at the mine is trucked up ice roads from Yellowknife during a three-week period in winter.

a single day. The weather was splendid: sunny and cold with no wind. Diamond dust—minute ice crystals that condense directly from water vapor on cold, windless days—sparkled in the air, adding a magical touch to the scene. The tiny faceted crystals are so small they fall very slowly, floating down lazily and catching the sunlight. When diamond dust is present, the very air itself seems alive with a million brilliant sparks. Distant objects are blurred and seem to waver and change size and shape in weird ways.

As the miles ticked away, our anticipation rose. After a few hours, we came to a long hill at the bottom of which was the western arm of Lac de Gras. Dropping down the hill, we crossed onto the lake ice. Flatter and more featureless than the tundra, here the diamond-dusted landscape shimmered even more. Several times we stopped to make snow measurements. After a while, everyone started looking more to the left (north). Out there was the mine. What would it look like?

We were actually a little worried that we might miss the mine. You would think a huge open pit mine would be hard to hide out on the tundra, but weirdly, our information on its location was vague. The problem was the scale of the huge lake, and with diamond dust in the air, our visibility was limited to about three miles. Thankfully, about 3:00 PM, when the GPS indicated that we were still four miles from the waypoint I had placed as our best guess for the mine location, we saw a brownish dusty haze on the horizon. A few minutes later we began to make out manmade features: a smoke stack, a metal warehouse several stories high, then a long flat mesa made out of dirt and boulders.

We were just wondering how to get into the mine when we came to the ice road. This was a wholly different affair than the ice road between Fort Good Hope and Telida. The road surface was clear blue-black lake ice. The roadway was divided into two enormously wide lanes, the center marked by orange pylons. Three semis could easily have driven abreast in each lane, but no traffic was present because trucking had just been shut down for the season. After hundreds of miles of drifted and bumpy tundra snow, the road looked delightfully smooth, but as we tried to accelerate toward the mine, we spun out on the slick blue ice. We ended up driving on the narrow strip of snow that edged the main roadway. Still, it was good going and for the first time since Fairbanks we were able to speed along at forty to fifty miles per hour. The road made a huge S-shaped arc, first toward the smoke stack, then away. Just as it seemed as if we were going to bypass the mine entirely, we rounded a broad bend, and there right in the middle of the road was a drill rig. We stopped.

At a drill rig on the ice of Lac de Gras, the operator points out the way to the mine: "You can't miss it." H. Huntington.

It was a directional diamond drill. Two roughnecks in black coveralls wearing red hard hats were operating it. A diesel engine was belching blue smoke into the sky, and loud clanking sounds came from the business end of the drill. Pallets of propane and wooden boxes were piled around the rig on the ice. The roughnecks invited us into the back half of the rig, a caboose-like affair, where

THE COMBINED ANNUAL OUTPUT from the three producing diamond mines operating north of Yellowknife—the Ekati Mine (run by BHP), the Diavik Mine (run by Rio Tinto), and the Snap Lake Mine (run by De Beers Canada)— would fit in a couple of fifty-five gallon drums, easily flown to town on an airplane. But to fill those drums takes several thousand tanker-truck loads of fuel per year, not to mention tons of concrete and explosive prill. All told, it takes about six to ten thousand truckloads to supply these mines for the year. The 250 miles of unique ice roads those trucks travel (highlighted on the TV show *Ice Road Truckers*) are only suitable for use during sixty to eighty days in January through March, though, meaning deliveries have to be made at a rate of more than a hundred loads daily, regardless of weather.

This transportation system is already being pinched by climate change. Spring comes earlier each year, and winters are often not as cold as in the past, resulting in thinner ice. In 2006, spring came before the mine operators had time to push all of their critical loads up to the mines. To finish the re-supply, they had to switch from trucks to cargo planes and a huge Russian helicopter at an immense cost.

But climate warming can both *giveth* and *taketh away*. While the freeze-up and break-up of rivers and lakes underlying the Barrenlands ice roads may no longer be as

Bad day for an ice road trucker hauling fuel on the Mackenzie River ice crossing near Fort Providence. *Courtesy of DriveSteady.com.*

reliable, the sea ice in Gray's Bay on Coronation Gulf and in Bathurst Inlet is also freezing later in the season and melting sooner. All-weather roads from marine ports in these locations have been proposed and are under serious consideration. With a reasonably long ice-free season, fuel, heavy equipment, and other supplies could come north via sealift and be hauled south over much shorter distances (see "Sea Ice Going, Going, Gone" on page 150). So far, this option has not quite matured, and the ice roads from the south still work, but the decision point of change may come any time—in a year or in ten years.

Change is the only constant. With it comes both opportunity and displacement. All over the North, businesses face a complex calculus related to environmental change with options being computed, pondered, feared, wished for, and anticipated.

it was quieter. One of the roughnecks was logging rock cores that had been laid in a segmented wooden box. He explained there was a kimberlite pipe just west of us, one that had yet to be developed into a mine. They were drilling into it to see if the pipe had gem quality diamonds on its east side. Because most of the pipe was under the water of Lac de Gras, the exploratory drilling had to be done while the ice was thick enough to support the weight of the drill rig. The cores they had brought up consisted of a black, crumbly rock, almost like fractured coal. No diamonds sparkled in the black matrix . . . our first disappointment. We asked the drillers directions to the mine. As we exited the rig, one of the drillers said, "You can't miss it."

There it was again, the mantra we had heard virtually every time we asked for directions. From Fort Yukon to Deline, we had heard, "You can't miss it," then listened intently to the directions that followed, and still "missed it." But in all the previous cases we had been looking for trails only three or four feet wide in dense forest. This was an ice road two hundred feet wide, and we could see the mine up on the hill to the west of us. How could we miss it this time?

We roared off, following the road. At the first junction we turned right as instructed. We turned right again at the next, also as instructed, then followed the road for a mile until it started to narrow and peter out. The drifts along the side suggested it wasn't a major thoroughfare, or at least hadn't seen much recent use. Damn! We were on an unused ice road headed right back the way we had come. Had the roughneck said right then right, or right then left? Confidence sagging, I led the seven snowmobiles and fourteen-sled parade in a big U-turn. As I headed back I had to pass each of the guys one by one going the other way, and from each I got that "another fine mess" stare.

Finally we found the right ice road, sailed down it into a large parking area, and stopped. Two white crew-cab trucks sat there idling. Inside were our hosts for the mine tour. They wore hard hats and parkas with reflective tape. They had radios clipped to the lapels of their parkas. They were on the clock, connected, and on time—three things we hadn't been in weeks. After introductions all around, we parked our snowmobiles off the roadway, pulled out enough gear for the evening, and piled into the two pickup trucks. No worry of anything being stolen out here.

The first order of business was security. Ushered into a three-story glass building, we sat on black-vinyl-and-chrome seats waiting to be called. The sun streamed through the windows and the room felt uncomfortably warm. At the far end of the room there was an X-ray machine for baggage and a standard walk-through gate found in all airport security areas. One by one, we filed up to the security desk where two uniformed guards checked our names off a list and issued us a photo badge and a key to a dormitory room. We placed our parkas and overnight gear on the conveyor belt of the X-ray machine and then walked through the security gate. We figured they were screening for drugs and booze.

Next we were taken to a dormitory complex. From Barrow, to Prudhoe Bay, to Diavik, all northern industrial living quarters seem to be the same. They are prefabricated modular buildings lacking any homey touches, the antithesis of a log cabin. These prefab units can be stacked up and strung together like Lego blocks to accommodate as many workers as needed. At Diavik, the units were stacked three-high and stretched in multiple rows several hundred feet long. We lost count of the rows after we passed half a dozen hallways. We were told that the total dormitory complex capacity was over eight hundred, making this one of the larger villages we visited on the trip.

There is a strange emptiness to industrial dormitories. The corridors are narrow and lined with closely spaced doorways, each opening into a compact sleeping room. The corridor lighting is fluorescent and bright—too bright—and usually there are no windows, so there is no way to tell day from night, which is doubly confusing in a place where it can be dark all day or light all night. It is rare to see people in the corridors, but for good reason. At most mines and oilfields the workers pull long shifts, often twelve hours. Dormitory rooms are used for one purpose only, to sleep. As a result, except for a skeletal cleaning staff, the corridors are empty and signs on doors like "Quiet . . . Night worker" add to the empty feeling. Only during shift changes are the corridors briefly filled with sleepy people. The air in the dormitories is also invariably bone dry. Why this is the case, I do not know, but with a relative humidity of about zero percent, one night in the dorm and dehydration becomes a real problem.

After showers and phone calls home, we met our hosts for dinner in the cafeteria. The food was extravagant. There were three or four entrees, ice cream, four types of pie, salad, oranges, apples, bananas, and several choices of soft drinks and juice from a dispenser. Quite a change from the one-pot meals we had been eating for the past month. Through conversation at dinner we had our first unofficial chance to learn about the mine. It had blue and gold crews, each working two weeks on, then flying out on jets for two weeks off. Many of the workers lived in Edmonton, Hay River, Yellowknife, and other places far to the south. The pay was good but the hours were long and the schedule was stressful on relationships. We got the feeling that despite the good pay, burnout was high. At similar production facilities in northern Alaska, shift work has taken a heavy toll on marriages and divorce rates among the crews are several times higher than the norm. Drugs and alcohol could be real problems, too, hence the screening room we came through.

The next day our tour of the mine started with a thirty-minute computer-based orientation course and the distribution of safety gear. Armed with loaner steel-toed boots, orange visibility vests, hard hats, and safety glasses, we mugged for the camera. Arvids turned his helmet sideways, affecting an urban look, but Jon still came across like a patriarchal anarchist, just one with a hardhat. A white bus showed up: we got on board, and off we went.

Diamond mining is all about understanding kimberlite, and countless hours and lives have been spent in this pursuit. A kimberlite pipe has the shape of a giant carrot that tapers with depth. Ideally, to lower the cost of mining diamonds and increase the profit margin, one wants to dig only kimberlite and nothing else. But the only way to do this is to operate an underground mine, and that is very expensive. The other, cheaper, way is to dig down from the top, making a great hole, removing the kimberlite carrot and as little surrounding bedrock as possible. The miners call the surrounding rock "country rock" and even in the solid granite that surrounds the Diavik kimberlite pipe, the pit walls have to slope back from the carrot at a significant angle to avoid collapse. The deeper the open pit, the worse the dig-ratio of country rock to kimberlite. For a pit wall that slopes steeply at sixty degrees, for example, digging twice as deep into the kimberlite carrot requires removing eight times the volume of country rock. Eventually, the cost of digging the pit outweighs the value of the diamonds recovered.

Arctic science bandits model safety clothing at Diavik Mine. Clockwise from upper left: Jon, Chris, Arvids, Glen, and Henry. Dan is still picking a hardhat of the appropriate color.

At the Diavik mine, the cost of digging the pit was high from the start because the kimberlite pipe was actually under the water of the lake. Before the company could even start mining, they had to build a dike to hold back the lake water. As we looked down into the pit from an overlook on the dike, it was disconcerting to realize that miners, trucks, and loaders in the bottom of the pit were all several hundred feet below the surface of the lake. If the dike should break....

Later, the bus took us out to the spill pile we had seen from a distance. Huge load-haul dump trucks were toiling up out of the pit on the spiral road system, driving to the end of the flat-topped pile, then dumping their loads of tan and pink granite boulders. Our guides indicated that when the mine was played out they would have to do some reclamation and make the country look something like it did before. The spill piles looked a little like moraine material, so perhaps bulldozing them into less regular shapes would make them look like the handiwork of the Laurentide Ice Sheet, but the big open pit was going to be harder to hide.

Sadly, while the tour took us past the mill building, we weren't allowed in. Indeed, it dawned on us that while we were allowed to be near as much waste rock as we pleased, we were not going to be allowed near any kimberlite. Did they know about our diamond heist fantasy? It was evident that most miners never got near the kimberlite either, and the ones that did were watched closely by security. From the overlook we had seen drillers preparing shot holes in the kimberlite on the floor of the pit, but security was right there with them. Once blasted, the kimberlite was hauled out of the pit directly to the mill building, dumped on a conveyor belt, and brought inside, where there were a series of crusher mills and separators—though, of course, we didn't get to see these. The separators concentrated the diamonds, so somewhere in that big blue mill building, a wet, pulverized lag of kimberlite rich in diamonds was being bagged for shipment to Yellowknife for final sorting. We heard that in Yellowknife the sorting was done by a sealed optical scanner and the diamonds were dumped into a lockbox, for which only senior management had a key. None of the people we talked to at the mine had actually ever seen a Diavik diamond.

The final stop on the tour was the geology building, and here we got just a bit closer to the Fipke legend. Several young geologists were busy gearing up for exploration of nearby kimberlite pipes. They wore Filson vests and looked more like us than the rest of the miners. The office walls were covered with geologic cross sections of the local kimberlite pipes, and their shelves and cupboards were littered with rock samples and rolls of maps. Dust from blasting at the pit covered everything. The place had that healthy cluttered feel common to all working science offices. We had a chance to ask questions and even handle some samples of kimberlite. I noticed I wasn't the only one from our group who peered at the rock samples closely, half expecting to see a diamond trapped in the matrix. Mixed in with the rock samples were also some bits of wood, redwood remnants from the Diavik pit fifty million years old and looking like modern sticks of kindling.

Toward the end of the visit, I spied some vials of sieved sand samples on a windowsill. One vial contained dark red garnets, black chromites, and bright parrot green diopsides, the indicator minerals that had led to the treasure. The geologist spilled the vial out on his hand and the small grains sparkled in the light. They weren't diamonds, but they sure were pretty. I knew it was a brazen request but I asked if I could take the sample home. The geologist declined, as I knew he must, since microprobing these minerals might still yield useful information for a rival company. I had to be satisfied with a photograph of the glittering grains.

The tour over, we caught a ride to the dormitory, changed back into our field clothes, and walked back to the security center to turn in our badges and keys. Again the sun streamed in the glass windows of the center. We savored the warmth knowing we would soon be back out in the cold. Our ride arrived and took us back to where we had left our snowmobiles. We had only been

The open pit at Diavik Mine. *H. Huntington.*

gone a day, but it felt a little like we were reuniting with long-lost loved ones as we packed and got ready to leave. Other than a fine coating of blast dust, everything was as we had left it. We thanked our hosts with sincerity, for the interlude at the mine had been fascinating. Still, we were anxious to leave. Henry grabbed a souvenir rock from the roadway for his kids. The machines idled and belched blue two-cycle smoke as we adjusted zippers and goggles. I jumped on my machine and headed east across the lake. Watching in my rear-view mirror, I saw the mine get smaller and smaller. One by one, the headlights of six snowmobiles pulled out and swung in behind me. Ahead, there was nothing but snow-covered lake and tundra.

THE HIGH PRESSURE NEEDED TO TRANS-
FORM CARBON to diamonds occurs more than a hundred miles below the surface of the Earth. The rub is that in most places on Earth, at one hundred miles down the rock is molten and diamonds can't survive. Only in a few places on Earth, where the planet's crust is very old, is it thick enough to preserve diamonds. It is no coincidence that diamond mines are generally found in the same geologic provenances as ancient rocks.

The Barrenlands diamond mines in the Canadian Shield are no exception. About two hundred miles northwest of Yellowknife is the Acasta River, where in 1989 a sample of gneiss was collected that proved to be the oldest rock on earth. The zircons in this sample have been dated to about four billion years ago. There is something of a competition among archean geologists (those who study the earliest history of the earth) to find and date the oldest rocks, and other candidate samples have come from Australia and eastern Canada. But so far the Acasta gneiss has held off all contenders. For sixty-five dollars it is possible to buy a small pebble of the Acasta gneiss mounted in a plastic case. The nearest town to these ancient rocks is Gamètì, a Tlicho village about sixty miles away. It would be interesting to know what the people there think about folks spending a lot of money for old rocks.

世界最古の岩石
Oldest Rock on the Earth

アキャスタ片麻岩 39億6200万年前
Acasta Gneiss 3962 Ma
カナダ北西部 Slave province, NW Canada

［凡地学研究社寄贈］ R61547

A museum sample of Acasta gneiss, one of the oldest rocks in the world. *Courtesy of the Geological Survey of Japan–The National Institute of Advanced Science and Technology.*

11

BRAIDED STRANDS: THE FIRST INTERLOPER

From the diamond mines we worked east to Aylmer and Clinton-Colden Lakes, little-known lakes that combined stretch more than sixty miles. These would take us to the Hanbury River, which in turn flows into the Thelon, a highway through the wilderness heart of the Barrenlands. On the map I had inked in the routes of the many explorers who had passed through this region before us. The ink lines come together and crisscross, creating a web of history through which we passed. Our route twined and braided, both physically and symbolically, with these historic tracks, but especially with the tracks of two men, Hearne and Hornby. It was on this leg of the trip that their lives, exploits, and importance in arctic history came into sharper focus for us.

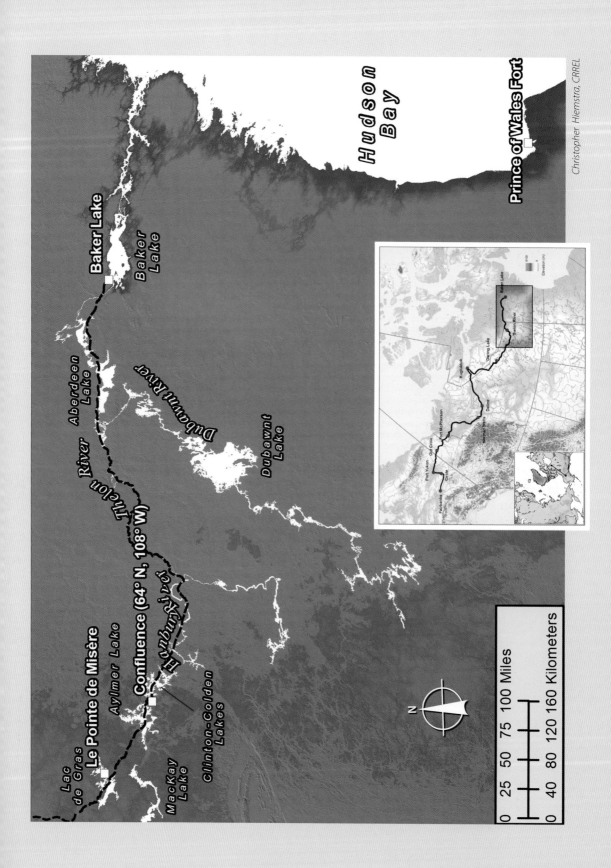

Hudson Bay

Prince of Wales Fort

Baker Lake

Baker Lake

Aberdeen Lake

Dubawnt River

Dubawnt Lake

Thelon River

Confluence (64° N, 108° W)

Hanbury River

Le Pointe de Misère

Aylmer Lake

Lac de Gras

MacKay Lake

Clinton-Colden Lakes

N

0   25   50   75   100 Miles
0   40   80   120   160 Kilometers

Christopher Hiemstra, CRREL

ARCHAEOLOGICAL REMAINS TELL US that aboriginal hunters came to Lac de Gras to kill caribou. Thousands of years before contact with the Western world these hunter-travelers passed over the black sand beaches that so excited the diamond prospectors, seeking the caribou that come each year to cross in the shallows where the Coppermine River spills out of the lake. In the shallow water swimming caribou can be speared. Had these now-vanished hunters seen a raw diamond they would not have bothered to pick it up, for you cannot eat a diamond.

The first written account from this area dates from 1771, when Samuel Hearne was traveling south with a band of Chipewyan Indians led by Matonabbee, the great Dene leader. They were retreating to timber before winter hit, having left Bloody Falls a month earlier. "We walked by the side of Large Whitestone Lake, which is about forty miles long from NE to SW," Hearne wrote on August 25. His feet were raw because the pace had been intense: thirty miles a day over rough country. His exact route is still debated, but almost certainly it passed within sight of Fipke's kimberlite pipe.

The next man to visit Lac de Gras and leave a written record was Warburton Pike, one of several eccentric British sportsmen who began visiting the Barrenlands around 1880 to hunt (see "Strange Wooly Attractors" on page 211). Pike traveled by foot and canoe. Working up though MacKay Lake at the end of September 1889 he arrived near the present site of the Diavik Mine. In his book he wrote, "[we] eventually made a wretchedly cold camp without a fire on a long promontory, to which we always after alluded as Le Point de Misère," naming the point that would figure so prominently in the diamond rush.

It is hard to imagine what aboriginal hunters, Hearne, or Pike would have thought if they were to wander

Samuel Hearne in 1796, twenty years after his epic journey. *Hudson's Bay Company Archives.*

Warburton Pike
(from his 1917 book
The Barren Ground
of Northern Canada.
New York: E. P.
Dutton.)

around this area today. They would be in danger of falling into one of several open pit mines, or worse, being run over by a truck. But had Hearne bumped into Pike, the latter's mode of travel, his clothing, his companions, and even his occupation would have seemed perfectly normal despite the lapse of 117 years. It is the next 117 years, the ones separating Pike from us, during which so much has changed: cars, airplanes, radio, satellites, the Internet, TV, GPS, and a whole host of technological advances that have altered the arctic world forever, far more than global warming has done to date. Two world wars, the splitting of the atom, and men on the moon separate us from Pike. The town of Yellowknife, not even an idea in 1880, has grown since his journey to more than twenty thousand inhabitants, and virtually all of them carry cell phones and use e-mail.

If Pike's visit marks when the pace of change began to accelerate, then Hearne's visit marks the start of those changes. He traveled through a world that was little altered for thousands of years and which knew nothing of the Western world's time- and mind-bending technological inventions. He brought little with him but his maps and journals, yet he began a process that links him directly to the diamond rush in the 1990s.

There were tentative contacts between Westerners and the inhabitants of arctic North America before Hearne. Around AD 1000, Vikings trying to get to Greenland were blown west to Newfoundland, Labrador, and Baffin Island, where they met, and fought with, local inhabitants. The Viking settlements did not last. Five hundred years later French and Portuguese fisherman began visiting the east coast of Canada largely to take advantage of the fishing on the Grand Banks, but they barely interacted with the locals. Starting in 1576, during a period of intense exploration and exploitation, Englishman Martin Frobisher visited Baffin Island several times to mine gold. The ore he brought home proved to be worthless, but Frobisher also returned with several Inuit, tales of rich furs, and his discovery of Hudson Strait, the entry to that vast inland sea, Hudson Bay. Violence marred his and many of these other initial Western-aboriginal interactions, but because each culture had something to gain, the exchanges continued.

The northern tip of Akpatok Island near Hudson Strait was probably seen by Frobisher on his voyages.

In 1610, Henry Hudson sailed the *Discovery* all the way up Hudson Strait into Hudson Bay. There his ship was trapped by sea ice, forcing the men to winter over. Supplies ran low and the men, fearing Hudson would want to linger for another year, mutinied. They set Hudson, his son, and seven others adrift in a boat never to be seen again. The mutineers, less four men murdered by the Inuit, survived to return to England, bringing with them priceless geographical knowledge that helped fuel two long-running exploratory thrusts, both with commercial overtones. The first was the search for the Northwest Passage, which continued unabated for three hundred more years in the belief that traversing arctic waters would lead to more efficient and lucrative trade with the Orient.

The second push was to tap the vast riches of the newly discovered arctic lands. The arctic fur trade began in 1668 when the *Nonsuch* wintered in James Bay and returned to England loaded with pelts. The following year King Charles II granted a charter to eighteen "adventurers" who put up money for a follow-on voyage and were granted exclusive rights to the trade and commerce in the lands adjacent to

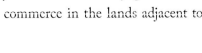

A romantic painting of Henry Hudson adrift in a small boat after his crew mutinied by John Collier (1850–1934). *Wikimedia.org.*

Hudson Bay. Thus the Hudson's Bay Company was born. Over the next two hundred years it thrived. Expanding operations, it established trading posts (called forts or factories) at several coastal locations including the Churchill River. The aboriginal population soon realized that by bringing furs to the factories they could obtain fabulous goods in exchange. The HBC traders were content to have the furs come to them, rarely venturing inland themselves.

Samuel Hearne joined the Company in 1766 as a seaman. He had served in the Royal Navy, where he saw duty in the English Channel and the Mediterranean Sea. It was during that time that he became inured to hardship and privation, a quality he would need in abundance on his Barrenland journeys. His first duty for the HBC was to sail a trading schooner up the west coast of Hudson Bay to start a bowhead whale fishery. The whale fishery was a commercial failure but provided an excellent arctic education for Hearne. From traveling companions he learned the rudiments of Inuktitut and Algonquian languages. Visiting scientists schooled him in zoology, astronomy, and natural history. Through sport and necessity he became a good walker and hunter. By 1769, the twenty-four-year-old Hearne was ready.

His assignment was to go west from Prince of Wales Fort and discover the source of the copper nuggets the Indians had been bringing in. The name of the purported source translated into English as Far-Off Metal River, and it was thought to be on some ocean to the west. Hearne was to map the route to the copper, claim all surrounding lands for England and the HBC, ascertain the feasibility of establishing a profitable trading post and mine in the region, and make scientific observations along the way. For a lone explorer, these goals were so ambitious as to be absurd, but neither Hearne nor his superiors at the fort knew this because they had no idea how far away the Far-Off Metal River was nor how inhospitable the Barrenlands could be. It took Hearne three attempts.

Hearne left on the first attempt in November in the care of Captain Chawchinahaw, a Dene of the Chipewyan tribe. It is likely that from the start Chawchinahaw had no intention of leading Hearne to the Far-Off Metal River, if he even knew where it was. Through privation and starvation, he hoped to force Hearne to abandon the quest early, yet still be able to claim his ample fee for being a guide. Discovering that the stubborn Hearne was unlikely to turn back, Chawchinahaw left Hearne and headed southwest into the taiga. Hungry and frustrated, Hearne and a few companions made their way slowly back home, hunting as they went. About a month after leaving, to his utter mortification, Hearne found himself back at the gates of Prince of Wales Fort. He was wiser in the ways of traveling but had acquired no additional knowledge about copper.

Sheefish or inconnu (*Stendous leucichthys* nelma [Pallas]) is probably Hearne's *"tickameeg."* This one was caught by net under lake ice in northwest Alaska, a method Hearne and Conne-e-quese would have used to catch fish in the eighteenth century.

He left almost immediately on his second attempt. This time his guide was Conne-e-quese, also Dene. On his first attempt Hearne had seen how essential women were to survival out on the land, and he had pleaded with the governor of the fort to allow him to take a Native woman with him to help haul loads and do essential camp work, but the request was denied in large measure due to sexual prudery. Hearne at this point chose to travel alone, the only Westerner in a band of three Dene families and two Cree Indians. This small party headed west in cold and snowy weather, but as the hunting proved more and more difficult, they finally had to settle down alongside a lake where their nets were able to catch a good supply of fish. They stayed until May. With the snow melting, the band started making its way northwest out into the Barrenlands. By July, with summer in full swing, they had migrated across the Dubawnt River and were somewhere near the headwaters of the Thelon River. Numerous other small bands of Dene had been coming into the area over a period of weeks, until at one point Hearne found himself in an encampment of more than six hundred people.

On August 12, Hearne's second attempt came to an end when his quadrant blew over in a gust of wind, shattering against the rocks. Without the quadrant to take astronomical readings for latitude and longitude, Hearne was just another hunter. He would not be able to discharge his exploration duties nor

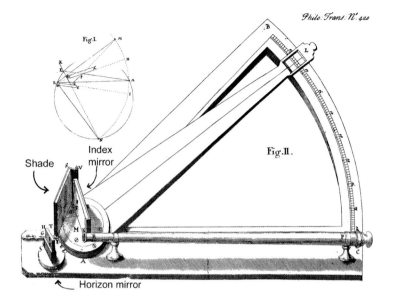

Fig.I.

Index mirror

Shade

Fig.II.

Horizon mirror

A Hadley's quadrant, similar in principle to a sextant, is used to measure the elevation of the sun and stars, allowing the determination of latitude and longitude. The model shown here would have been similar to the one used by Hearne. *Royal Society, London:* Philosophical Transactions of the Royal Society *(1731)*

report where he had been. For this reason alone he knew he had to return to the fort, but another compelling reason for doing so had been building. At the fort Conne-e-quese had presented himself as Hearne's protector, but out in the wilderness it was clear that Conne-e-quese was a leader of little consequence. Shortly after breaking his quadrant, Hearne and his two Cree companions were visited by a small group of Dene thugs and robbed of most of their gear. Conne-e-quese could do nothing to protect them. Without a strong sponsor, there was a widespread feeling throughout the gathered Dene bands that Hearne had no business being out on the Barrenlands.

Once again Hearne headed back to the fort, now six hundred miles away. Winter soon overtook him. The Dene with whom he traveled had already prepared winter clothing and snowshoes that they donned as the snow piled up. Hearne had collected furs for winter suits, but none of the Dene women would sew these for him, nor in the treeless wastes was there any material from which to make snowshoes. Post-holing through the snow and shivering, Hearne stumbled along falling further and further behind the party. Had fate not intervened, it is likely he would have died.

Salvation came in the form of Matonabbee, the great Dene leader. Out of the snow he appeared leading a small band toward the fort. Startled to find a white man so far out on the tundra, he gave Hearne a warm otter fur suit and told him of the nearest trees where there would be materials to make snowshoes. Then over the next week, he slowed the pace of his march so that Hearne would be able to catch up with him and they could travel together. A tall man and a natural leader, Matonabbee had lost his father when a baby and had been adopted by the governor of Prince of Wales Fort, living there for four years before being returned to the Dene. On reaching adulthood, he was sent twice by subsequent governors on HBC missions far to the west of the fort to negotiate peace treaties between the various tribes, diplomatic tasks he had carried out bravely and effectively. These treaties were needed to ensure that the Natives put their energies into procuring furs rather than war. Matonabbee was moderate in habits and manners, impressive in his strength and abilities out on the land. In short, a more noble and romantic figure emerging from the mists to rescue Hearne would be hard to imagine.

Something about the partnership of Hearne and Matonabbee is uncanny. In an era of little cultural mixing or understanding, both men had gone further than most in blending two cultures within themselves. They were both bilingual and both comfortable in Western and Native worlds. Knowingly or not, together they were the sharpened edge of the wedge of arctic change, and more than a hundred years before slavery was abolished in the United States they set an admirable pattern, still not fully realized today, of tolerance and cultural blending.

Within two weeks of returning to the fort, Hearne, led by Matonabbee, was ready to depart again. This time Hearne seems to have taken a country wife and almost certainly was adopted into the Chipewyan band led by Matonabbee. For the next two years he fully shared their life, starving with them when the hunting was bad, gorging when it was good. Freezing in the wind and snow, sweltering and cursing in the summer when the bugs were bad, his life was theirs.

There is a small subculture today fixated on tracing the route taken by Hearne and Matonabbee. They use Hearne's account and maps to try to ascertain the modern identity of the Thelewey-aza-yeth, Peshew, and Clowey Lakes he mentions, and they try to determine where the party crossed from the drainage of the Thelon to the Back River. Despite this intense and loving scrutiny, it is still unclear exactly where the explorers traveled. In broad outline we know they headed northwest from the fort making sure to stay well below treeline. By April they had traveled almost seven hundred miles and were nearly south of Great Slave Lake. Here, on another lake that the scholar W. A. Fuller has identified as the modern Spearfish Lake, they made an abrupt turn to the north, showing an impressive grasp of the lay of the land for this is a place where treeline dips far to the south, allowing rapid access to the tundra where traveling is easier.

At the beginning of May the band was just two days' march south of treeline, where they lingered as groups converged from various directions, swelling their numbers to more than two hundred. They built canoes and hewed thick planklike shields from logs. The canoes were for crossing Barrenland rivers that would soon be flowing fast with snowmelt runoff (as Franklin's troubled expedition discovered). The shields were more ominous; the Chipewyan were headed north for blood. From the beginning their intent had been to travel to Bloody Falls to kill Inuit. Guiding Hearne to the copper was an add-on that happened to coincide with their own interests. Horrified, Hearne made some mild remonstrations against the violent plan, but the only result was that he was accused of being a coward by some of the more hotheaded warriors. His position as an adopted son of the Chipewyan, the only white man for a thousand miles, was extremely precarious, so he wisely agreed to the plan and kept his misgivings to himself.

Canoes and shields complete, on May 20 the Chipewyan headed north, leaving the forest behind. After another week the group was at Whitefish Lake, not far to the east of Great Slave Lake. Here about sixty of the fittest warriors and a similar number of women set out, armed and ready for war. Matonabbee had selected the two of his seven wives who had no children to accompany him and Hearne, and the other warriors similarly lightened their loads and the size of their parties. With fish and game plentiful near the lake the others remained behind to wait.

The war party moved swiftly, covering ten to thirty miles a day. By the beginning of June they were traveling rapidly over the ice of *Thoy Kye Lyned*, or Aylmer Lake, where our track intertwined with theirs (see "Whiteout on Aylmer Lake" on page 206). By late June they were crossing the *Conge-catha-wha-chaga*, or Burnside River, where Franklin would later nearly come to grief.

The weather was abysmal with sleet and heavy snow despite it being the height of summer. Several of the warriors became discouraged and turned back. On July 14 the remaining war party finally reached the Coppermine River. Within a few days scouts sent north had spied Inuit fishing on the river below a set of rapids. The adventure now moved to its bloody climax. Nothing Hearne could do or say, if he said anything at all, was going to alter the course of events.

Treeline in the Barrenlands is not a line, but rather a patchy transition zone between taiga and tundra that can span several miles. This stretch near Lake Providence is typical of where Matonabbee and Hearne crossed farther to the east.

The outcome of the massacre at Bloody Falls was never in doubt. Sixty Chipewyan warriors fell upon twenty sleeping Inuit without warning. The Inuit had no time to arm themselves or fight back, and no chance to escape. A second group of Inuit camped on the east side of the river observed the massacre, escaping harm because the Chipewyan had no canoes to cross the swollen torrent. The warriors shot arrows at the Inuit across the river, but these fell harmlessly into the water. Finally they fired their rifles. The Inuit, having never seen rifles before, did not understand the danger. They stood transfixed until one of them was shot in the leg. Then they moved back out of harm's way. Satiated with the blood they had already spilled, the Chipewyan warriors moved off.

But what of the copper that had instigated Hearne's journey? The day following the massacre the war party traveled north to the Arctic Ocean, where Hearne erected a marker on the rocks above what would become the municipal water intake for the town of Kugluktuk, a site where Franklin's party would camp fifty years later. Two days after that, the war party was forty miles south of the coast traveling fast. Here they briefly stopped at the be so damned big? Not that we could see it. We couldn't see anything. We were in a whiteout. Describing what that is like in visual terms doesn't work: there is nothing to see. White clouds above, white snow below, blowing snow filling the space in between. No horizon, no shadows, no definition. Nothing.

You don't see a whiteout; you feel it. Like an out-of-body experience, you float in a white world. At times vertigo sweeps over you. Always, your eyes strain to see something . . . anything, and soon they do. They see black arcs, hills that aren't there, and other strange illusions. A caribou dropping can appear to be the size of a house right up until you pass it by and realize it would fit in the palm of your hand. Flat lakes are tipped to the right by a consistent ten-degree angle, or if you are Henry Huntington, tipped to the left.

So there we were, seven snowmobiles in a line floating in space, on a lake unknown to more than a handful of people but big enough to cover most of Connecticut. Hearne had been here once. It was cold with a sharp breeze, so my facemask was on, which had caused my glasses to fog up. Since there was nothing to see, I had given up trying to rub the frost off of them. The ear buds of my iPod, deep under my fur hat, were blaring out Jackson Brown's "Doctor My Eyes," which seemed somehow appropriate. In my rear-view mirrors I could see the others' headlights. I knew Jon and Dan were also wired for sound. I wondered what they were listening to.

At that moment all seven of us were engaged in an Act of Faith. We were betting our lives, or at least our immediate well being, that Nature was going to be well behaved, that everywhere the ice would be thick enough to support the weight of our machines. No thin spots, no places where methane gases rising from the lake bottom had eroded the ice but left the snow cover intact. We knew too well that more arctic snowmobilers die of drowning than of any

other cause. One terrifying story told in western Alaska is of two snowmobilers out on Golovin Bay driving home at night. All of a sudden beneath their machines, instead of white snow and ice, there was nothing but black water. Their only hope was to water skip— drive so fast that the machine planes over the water. One of them made it. The other was recovered days later, his boots thrust so hard into the foot holes in the cowling of his machine it was hard to break him loose for the undertaker.

As leader of our caravan, I was engaged in a second Act of Faith: trying to believe that the *sastrugi* (a Russian word for rhythmic snow dunes) were uniform and even. I feared that somewhere out there was an invisible sastruga twice the size of its neighbors. It is nerve-wracking knowing that at any moment you might be violently pitched off your machine by an unseen bump. Yet at the end of the trip, Chris told me he had checked his speedometer and discovered I drove faster over bumpy ground in whiteout than in good light. What he didn't know is that after the long session on Aylmer Lake there were grooves worn in the tops of my boots from jamming them into my snowmobile's foot holes.

The full absurdity of what we were doing became plain when we arrived at a pressure ridge. During a big windstorm on the larger lakes, the ice will

tectonics, one ten-mile-long section of the ice will plow into another, and where they collide, the ice buckles, thrusting up a ridge that can exceed ten feet in height. All seven of us stopped and peered at this one. Yes, it was a ridge, but how high was it? Was it rough or smooth? White against white, we could tell nothing other than that there was a ridge blocking our path. I got off my machine and tried peering from closer up. Still no clue. There was so little definition, I found it hard to walk. Was I going uphill? I dropped to my hands and knees and began crawling. Soon I had crawled up a snow ramp that rose smoothly about four feet. We could get across here. Had the whiteout cleared just then, a spectator coming upon us would have marveled at the sight: one grown man crawling slowly and painfully up a snow ramp any infant could have managed while six grown men watched him with rapt

Crossing an ice pressure ridge on Beverly Lake in slightly better conditions than described in the text. Chris is taking great care not to roll his machine while Glen (left) and Arvids watch.

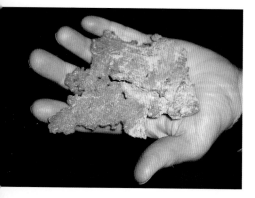

A piece of native copper, from the Santa Rita pit mine in New Mexico, is probably similar to the one found by Hearne.

so-called copper mines, the source of the samples that had been brought into Prince of Wales Fort a thousand miles away. It was a graben of dark brown volcanic rock, heavily picked over by Inuit and Dene. Four hours of searching by all hands resulted in the discovery of a single four-pound nugget that Hearne carried all the way back to London. As a rich source of copper the "mine" was an utter disappointment. No HBC vessels would be filling their holds with copper down at the coast. And even if the mine had been richer, transporting the copper would have been difficult because the Coppermine River was so full of shoals and rapids it was barely navigable by canoe. Standing there amid the dark volcanic rocks, Hearne must have realized that his quest was a failure from a commercial standpoint.

The great land—taiga.

Moving at a pace that is hard to believe, the warriors were back inland with their families and women eight days after leaving the coast. Reunited, the group continued south and by August 25 was near Lac de Gras and the future diamond mines, where our track again crossed theirs. By December they had reached Great Slave Lake, Hearne being the first Westerner to see the tenth largest lake in the world. Traveling south of the great lake, Hearne and Matonabbee spent the winter hunting. They began heading east in the spring, reaching Prince of Wales Fort on June 30, 1772, having covered close to five thousand miles.

It is easy to focus on the massacre and miss the key elements of change highlighted by Hearne's remarkable journey. The violence was sad and unfortunate, but violence is hardly unknown around the world today. Perhaps more striking to a modern sensibility is the fact that the land Hearne traveled through was nearly

FINDING THE ARCTIC

empty. The maximum number of people Hearne saw at one time was about six hundred Chipewyan. Few estimates of the indigenous arctic population at the time of his journey exist, but the inhabitants of the entire region could not have exceeded twenty thousand people—Yellowknife's population today.

Another striking feature of Hearne's narrative is the overwhelming presence of the land, which, with its animals, fishes, plants, and daily and seasonal cycles permeated everything the Dene did. If, to a New Yorker, bright lights, the ebb and flow of traffic, and concrete canyons are the hallmarks of the city, for Matonabbee and his band, the great arc of sky, the cycle of seasons, and the landscape of rocks and waterways was the fabric of their lives. Time after time in the narrative, we read about how the travelers endured rain, snow, or gale without teepee or tent. The connection between the people and the land was raw, unfiltered, and omnipresent.

The great land—tundra.

The last striking feature of the narrative is the inescapable connection between hunting, fishing, and staying alive. This immediacy is nearly impossible to understand today, when for us the connection is between work and money. If we have money we can get food, and government and nongovernmental social networks exist to ensure that even without money we probably won't starve. Several times in the narrative Hearne bemoans the wanton waste of the hunters, who during plentiful times would kill a dozen caribou and take only the tongues. But for Matonabbee and the others, these windfalls were so rare they needed to indulge themselves. They knew that sooner than they would like it would be back to business as usual, with unrelenting and often unrewarding hunting and gathering to stay alive.

I think back to a class trip I took in elementary school, to Independence Hall in Philadelphia. While Hearne was slogging through the snow with a small band of Chipewyan in 1771, there were already thirty-five thousand people living in Philadelphia. The elegant Hall had already been built, a beautiful brick and wood structure with comfortable rooms and sunlight streaming through its multi-pane glass windows. The hours of the day were marked by the chiming of bells. The delegates in the Hall wore brass-buckle shoes, white silk stockings, breeches, and ruffled shirts. They did not miss any meals and they thought in abstract terms about politics and government, democracy and freedom, writing elegant phrases with quills on parchment. News of their actions was spread on printed broadsheets carried across the ocean by sailing ships.

The gulf between that world and the Arctic of 1771 was enormous. Yet, at a far more basic level, new ideas, technologies, inventions, and diseases were starting to spread throughout the Arctic from Prince of Wales Fort on Hudson's Bay as well. These would change how people lived in the region forever. Hearne and Matonabbee were the first messengers. They traveled in a primitive and pristine world that was grand and violent. Time and distance ruled, and life was lived close to the edge of survival. Change was coming, and they were helping it to come. Still, what a privilege to have seen that world before the change arrived!

THERE IS A TUNNEL CUT into a hillside near Fox, Alaska. It was built in the early 1960s by the U.S. Army Corps of Engineers to study permafrost, something the Corps might need to know about if they were ever called upon to excavate frozen ground or tunnel into it to make a bomb shelter. The first fifty feet of the tunnel cuts through an ancient debris flow, a small landslide that occurred during the waning days of the last ice age. The frozen soil and rock debris is full of twelve-thousand-year-old bones. There are Pleistocene horse teeth, ponderous leg bones of wooly mammoth, and even the preserved remains of ancient beetles.

High up on the left wall of the tunnel, a large single horn of a steppe bison protrudes from the frozen silt. The horn is grayish-white and ribbed, splintered at the end where it must have hit something hard. Visitors love to look at this horn because it has an air of mystery about it. Is it still connected to a skull, or perhaps even a full skeleton, buried in the frozen wall? The horn is mute, giving away nothing. Visitors seem to know instinctively that this is the horn of an exotic animal, a prehistoric creature like nothing they have ever seen before. Still, perhaps they feel the stirrings of ancestral memory from a cold time before the dawn of the written word, when men chased creatures like this with spear and fire.

I had the same feeling the first time I saw a muskox. Actually, it was just the skull of a muskox and it was in a glass display case in a museum. Even through the glass, the skull had an antiquity that seemed to stir some primal memory. The next time, when I saw a real muskox, the effect was even stronger. It was a big bull. He was standing at the top of a small bluff on the west side of the Sagavanirktok River about five miles north of the Brooks Range. The sun had just set on a brisk September day. Dan and I had pulled our canoe up on a cobble beach on the east side of the river when we saw him, a dark silhouette against the green tundra. The bull stood by the bluff for a few seconds and then ambled away. If a dragon had been there instead, the impression it left would not have been any more intense. Had our run down the river rapids also managed to transport us backwards twelve thousand years? We stood frozen, staring at the space where the muskox had been.

The skull of a muskox seen in the Wildlife Office in Kugluktuk.

Helen Falls on the Hanbury River.
H. Huntington.

In 1924, John Hornby (see chapter 12) had the same reaction when he and his partner came upon a band of eleven muskoxen just below Helen Falls on the Hanbury River. Hornby had enticed his friend James Critchell-Bullock to accompany him on what may have been one of the worst expeditions ever into the Barrenlands. Nine months earlier they had paddled up Great Slave Lake, portaged miles across the tundra into Artillery Lake, paddled another forty miles up that lake, then worked north past the treeline. Their plan, if they had one at all, was to winter in that inhospitable realm to get a jump on the other trappers working in the area. Lacking any suitable trees for building a shelter, they dug into the base of a sandy esker and made their home in a dirt cave. The winter passed in grim fashion and when spring finally came they decided to escape by going east down the Hanbury and Thelon

Rivers to Baker Lake. They reached Helen Falls by mid-July and once again had to resort to portaging gear and canoes. Late one evening, as they were packing loads along the shoreline below the falls, Hornby clutched Critchell-Bullock's arm and hoarsely whispered "Musk-oxen, Bullock! Musk-oxen." About two hundred yards away, in a thicket of willows, the half-buffalo, half-goat-like creatures were grazing. Despite the fact that the men were starving, no thought of shooting the animals crossed their minds. For the two wasted wanderers it was a spiritual experience that made all of their trials and difficulties worthwhile.

They were seeing the last remnants of an extensive herd that once roamed the Barrenlands. The muskoxen's near-extinction had come about because they are so easy to kill. The animals' defensive response is to form a living circle and stay put. With females and young in the center, the big bulls face outward with their horns nearly touching. The circle may be an effective defense against toothed-predators such as wolves or bears, but against high-powered rifles it is suicidal. As a result, the magnetic attraction muskoxen seem to exert on people almost destroyed the species.

Between 1888 and 1909 there were at least seven expeditions into the Barrenlands by eccentric British and American gentlemen of independent means for the sole (or major) purpose of hunting muskoxen. At the same time, Natives armed with high-caliber rifles were hunting the animals for food. Under mounting pressure from sportsmen, Indians from the southern taiga, and Inuit hunters from the arctic coast, the muskoxen population crashed. It did not help that their rich fur and hides became valuable commodities as well. More than fifteen thousand hides were shipped from Canada to Europe between 1860 and 1916. Canada passed the Northwest Game Act in 1917, banning the hunting of muskoxen for their hides, but it is estimated that fewer than five hundred of the animals remained in the Barrenlands by 1924 when Hornby and Critchell-Bullock came upon that ragtag band. In the decades since, the muskoxen have recovered enough to allow for limited hunting once again. Today, several thousand muskoxen are thought to live in the Barrenlands, with another eight hundred along the lower Mackenzie River and on Alaska's North Slope. Further north on Victoria and Banks Islands, tens of thousands of muskoxen are thriving.

We had failed to see any of the creatures since entering their territory just north of Great Bear Lake, although in Kugluktuk signs of them were everywhere. We shared the Coppermine Inn with several wealthy hunters who were headed south the next day for a guided hunt. Wandering around town, we saw a long-haired, dark-colored hide draped over a porch railing, a massive head lying on a crate drifted with snow, and a skull in a glass case in the game warden's office.

During the run from Kugluktuk down to Daring Lake, and then over to the Diavik Mine, we kept a keen lookout for them, but saw neither tracks nor the animals themselves. After we left the mine, the weather turned overcast and gray with enough wind to produce a continuous low-grade whiteout for days. The endless pall was getting depressing, so to break the monotony I conceived of a harmless prank that revolved around our inability to bag even a single latitude/longitude confluence since the trip began. As we entered Thanakoie Narrows, which connects Aylmer and Clinton-Colden Lakes, I started altering course to the south, but in what I hoped would be imperceptible increments. Every few minutes I would look at the GPS and then bear right just a

Seen on the streets of Kugluktuk. *D. Solie.*

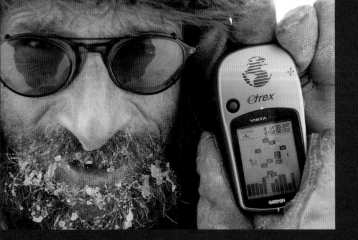

In my rearview mirrors I could see the others coming up fast. If I wanted to save the prank, I needed to take him into my confidence quickly.

"Yeah. We're almost at a confluence. I wanted to surprise everyone."

"Okay," he said.

That was it. We started out again before the others caught up and asked what was wrong.

We continued a few more miles, threading our way around rocks and boulders scattered across low hills. It was impossible to see where the tops of the hills ended and the sky began. The rocks just seemed to be suspended in gray space. I looked at my GPS: Less than half a mile.

Now, I would like to say that I pulled into the confluence, stopped, and showed everyone my GPS triumphantly, but that is not what happened. A peculiarity of navigating on a snowmobile using a GPS is that as one gets close to a programmed waypoint the navigation gets erratic and the GPS begins to display contradictory instructions: Bear right. No! Bear

little more—not so much that the line of six snowmobiles behind me would curve, but enough so that after about twenty minutes we were driving south rather than southeast. Soon we were headed right toward the confluence of 64° North, 108° West.

Just when it seemed I had managed the turn without any of the others noticing, Jon accelerated and pulled up even with me. He motioned me to stop.

"You know we are way off the route, right?" he asked.

ert. No! The point is behind you. Turn around. The result is that instead of making a gallant high-speed arrival at the point, I ended up corkscrewing around like a moth circling into a flame. Having seen this performance before, my companions immediately knew that we were arriving at some GPS waypoint, and the only logical one that could be out here was a confluence. With a last back-and-fill maneuver, I stopped and looked at my GPS: 64° 00.0′N, 108° 00.0′W. The others clustered around me and I held up the GPS for them to see.

Dan, however, had stopped about a few hundred feet from the rest of us and was getting out the movie camera. On a small hilltop about three hundred yards away was a cluster of dark brown, almost black, animals. Sixteen muskoxen were grazing on the top of a hill. Even at a distance, we could see their blue-black muzzles and blond-colored horns. The soft coats on their backs and the long hair on their chests were blowing in the stiff wind. They watched us warily with large black eyes. We were likely the only humans they had seen during the winter, or perhaps ever. They didn't circle up and they did not run. They just stood in a close group and stared at us with an unflinching gaze.

We gazed back at the muskoxen for a few minutes, then Dan, Glen, and Henry tried to move in closer for better pictures and the band stampeded off the top of the hill and disappeared from sight. Disappointed, we regrouped at the confluence, took a few photos, then headed back out into the gray gloom toward Baker Lake. As we worked our way down through rocky hills toward Clinton-Colden Lake, we passed the muskoxen one last time. They were running, probably to get away from our strange, noisy smoke-belching machines. Their dark fur was flying, their hooves kicking up snow that got picked up by the wind, the animals' dense compact bodies wheeling together in a synchronized motion with a certain familiarity I could not place.

The elusive
muskoxen.
H. Huntington.

12

BRAIDED STRANDS: THE LAST REFUGEE

Now we were on the same map sheet as Baker Lake and could see our final destination each time we checked our progress. The pace of the trip quickened. When I was in the U.S. Coast Guard, we called this "channel fever"—the desire for a trip to be over days before it actually was. Our route was down the Thelon River, which was easy traveling so our daily mileage increased. Chris had set up a gas cache at Hornby Point and we were bent on getting there as fast as possible. Our track had crisscrossed John Hornby's since leaving Telida on the Mackenzie River more than a thousand miles behind us. At Hornby Point the braiding would stop, for there Hornby's track ends in a lonely grave marked by a white wooden cross.

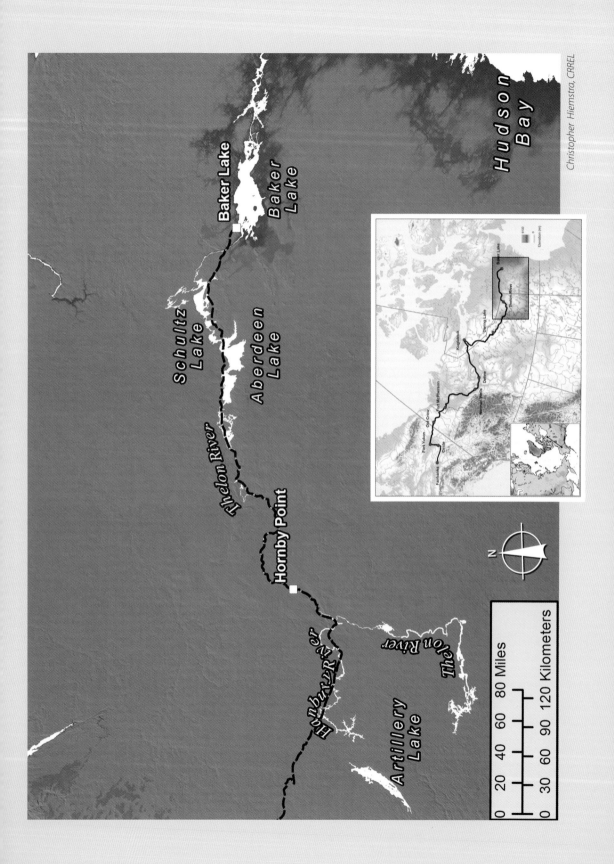

Christopher Hiemstra, CRREL

Hudson Bay

Baker Lake

Baker Lake

Schultz Lake

Aberdeen Lake

Thelon River

Hornby Point

Hanbury River

Thelon River

Artillery Lake

N

0   20   40   60   80 Miles
0   30   60   90   120 Kilometers

SOME WILDERNESS SPOTS are sacred: the Nanda Devi Sanctuary in Nepal, the slot canyons of the Escalante River in Utah, John Muir's hut in Yosemite Valley, and Dick Proenneke's cabin on upper Twin Lakes in southwestern Alaska. While doing an aerial reconnaissance of the glaciers in Lake Clark Park in 1987, I landed at Twin Lakes. Dick was already a famous wilderness hermit when I was introduced to him. He had lived there, miles from the nearest person, for more than two decades. His snug cabin, carved from local logs with exquisite craftsmanship, is the quintessential wilderness home. The low Dutch door of the cabin looks out on an immaculate brown sand beach that Dick would carve into patterns using a handmade wooden rake. He had befriended the local birds and squirrels. The Twin Lakes are a stunning turquoise color from the silty water flowing off of the glaciers in the mountains that tower over the lakes. Dick documented the building of his cabin in 1967 in a book called *One Man's Wilderness*. It has fueled the wilderness aspirations of literally thousands of people worldwide. Dick passed on peacefully in 2003, but the cabin is still there, maintained by the Park Service basically as a shrine.

Hornby Point is another sacred wilderness spot, also something of a shrine, but one with an altogether more somber feel. In the spring of 1927 John Hornby (47), his nephew Edgar Christian (18), and Harold Adlard (27) died there of starvation. They had traveled across the Barrenlands too slowly and missed the caribou. The two young men were new to the North, but Hornby should have known better. He had come into the country in 1904 as part of a group of muskox hunters. Those companions may have been after big game, but there can be no doubt that John Hornby came to the Arctic seeking wilderness and an escape from a too-civilized life in England.

The facts of Hornby's life are fairly easy to ascertain, but whether he was a hero or a fool is harder to determine. Much seems to hinge on who is telling the story, since Hornby himself never put pen to paper. Like many, when I first encountered him in the literature I thought him a fool, totally unprepared for the harsh Barrenlands, disorganized and a bungler, not worthy of the attention

John Hornby, date unknown, probably in Tulita (previously Fort Norman). *Courtesy Prince of Wales Northern Heritage Centre.*

history had bestowed on him. He was no wilderness icon like Proenneke, as some had made him. Now I think his fame may serve a useful purpose: like the Mad Trapper, Hornby's life and death marks the transition between the heroic human history of the Arctic we love to read about in books, and the modern Arctic we actually live in. We honored Hornby's memory by camping at Hornby Point, and by a little piece of bungling that he might have appreciated.

Hornby was born to wealth, the son a famous English cricket player. He could have surrendered himself to a life of leisure, of lawn parties and weekend socials, but some deep-seated need to escape drove him to Canada at age twenty-three. He landed in Edmonton, at that time the gateway to the North. The diminutive (five feet two inches) Hornby soon fell in with James Cosmo Melvill, another wealthy young Englishman who wanted to hunt muskoxen in the Barrenlands. Melvill had the resources to bankroll an expedition to Great Bear Lake and seems to have taken on Hornby because of the little man's reputation for toughness: he had once run the hundred miles from Edmonton to Athabasca Landing because the train wasn't running. Within a few short years of Hornby's entry into the North, it was said that he could out-walk, out-pack, and out-paddle anyone, even the Indians, though perhaps it was Hornby himself who spread this view.

With the Melvill party Hornby first came to the northeast corner of Great Bear Lake. For three years they hunted and explored, at one point penetrating to within forty miles of the Arctic Ocean, but close scrutiny of their sojourn suggests a certain aimlessness in their wanderings and gives the impression that the trip to Great Bear Lake was more an opportunity for freedom than for serious exploration. The clean cold air of the Barrenlands blowing down to the lake intoxicated the men. Hornby at this time became romantically involved with Arima,

Arima, Hornby and dogs at the cabin near Fort Confidence. *Courtesy of the Stefansson Collection on Polar Exploration, Dartmouth College.*

an Indian woman. It was by far the happiest period of his life.

The Melvill party came out to Telida from Great Bear Lake in the summer of 1911, just as the Douglas party was headed in (see chapter 6). Melvill went off to hunt elsewhere and Hornby, reluctant to leave his beloved Barrenlands, tried to insinuate his way into the Douglas expedition. George Douglas was having none of it. He found Hornby eccentric, peculiar, and evasive when it came to answering any direct question about the country. They sat up all night talking about the North while Hornby dipped his dirty fingers into the sugar bowl in the dining room of the steamer. Despite Douglas's initial dislike of the man, though, this meeting was the start of a two-decade-long friendship. The next day the Douglas party struck out for Dease Inlet without Hornby, but Hornby was soon able to join them as Father Rouvière's wilderness guide.

When the Douglas party quit the North the following summer, the idyllic little community at one end of the big lake began to unravel. The impatient and ill-tempered Father LeRoux, who had joined Father Rouvière, managed to drive a wedge between Hornby and Arima, ending their relationship. The priests were dead within a few more months, murdered by Coronation Gulf Inuit, and by late 1913 Hornby was seriously ill. Sick and disenchanted he came out to Tulita just in time to learn that Great Britain was at war.

He enlisted in the Alberta Dragoons and by April 1915 he was in France, where he fought in the second Battle of Ypres. Later he became a second lieutenant. He seems to have volunteered for dangerous missions. In June 1916 he was wounded in the back and neck during action, some say by machine-gun fire. The circumstances remain murky, but he was awarded the Military Cross, indicating he was real hero. Despite the medal, for Hornby the war was over. He was shipped to a London hospital to recuperate from his wounds. These slowly healed, but his mind did not. Suffering from what today would be called post-traumatic stress disorder, he eventually took leave and then, without permission, decamped back to Canada. Shattered in mind and body, his instincts guided him back to Edmonton. Though he was technically AWOL, in an institutional act of kindness the Army honorably discharged the broken warrior in 1916.

The following year he was back at Dease Inlet on the north end of Great Bear Lake, the scene of his happiest years, but of course, everything had changed. Arima was with another man; newcomers were occupying the Douglas cabin, the priests were murdered, and the cabin he had helped to build on Lake Rouvière had been vandalized and burned. Hornby retreated back to his old cabin on Caribou (now Hornby) Bay. There food was scarce and the Indians starving. Then he accidentally crippled himself with an axe. It was a bad winter.

His next two winters were even worse. His initial intent seems to have been to stay on Artillery Lake well out in the Barrenlands, but poor planning left him at Fort Reliance in the thin taiga forests at the end of the Great Slave Lake, a place where the caribou were known to be scarce. Again he wintered in a tiny, squalid cabin. It was almost as if he was seeking out starvation this time. As his biographer George Whalley has written, "Hardship and starvation seemed to take on a positive value for [Hornby]." At one point during the winter, thinking his death imminent, Hornby built a coffin, placed it in the cabin, and lay down in it to die. The local Indians found him and nursed him back to health.

One might think Hornby would have been ready to give up on the North after three grim and disastrous winters in a row, but instead it called to him ever more strongly. In Edmonton Hornby met James Critchell-Bullock, another war veteran, and embarked on one of his strangest adventures yet.

Critchell-Bullock, casting about for what to do after the war, was impressed by the older man's northern exploits, which by then had received a fair degree of attention in the press. Together they came up with the idea of a joint scientific and cinematography expedition to the Barrenlands, though in Hornby's jumbled mind it was to be more of a commercial venture: they would establish themselves farther out on the tundra than any other trappers had ever done and thereby make a killing trapping white foxes. In the summer of 1924 the pair headed out in the company of several other trappers. Even before leaving civilization, Critchell-Bullock began to be frustrated by Hornby's capricious and sometimes odd ways, and things only got worse as they worked their way to the end of Great Slave Lake. For example, Hornby refused to take along a man that Critchell-Bullock had hired because "he had brown rather than blue eyes."

James C. Critchell-Bullock. *The frontispiece from Waldron, Malcolm. 1931.* Snow Man: John Hornby in the Barren Lands. *New York: Kodansha International.*

While the other trappers built cabins in the small patches of timber along forty-mile-long Artillery Lake, Critchell-Bullock and Hornby pushed north from the lake out into the Barrenlands. There were no trees and relatively few shrubs, but abundant wind. On the lee side of a big esker they dug a seven-by-ten-foot trench, roofed it with what few sticks they could scrounge, covered the trench with more sticks, canvas, and dirt, and moved in.

Thus began an eight-month period of living like troglodytes. Life in the trench was gruesome and became more so during the long course of the winter. Sand and dirt would trickle down from the roof getting into everything, and the stove on the lee side of the esker would not draw properly, so it filled the place with smoke. Worse, they had only a limited number of candles, never enough to dispel the gloom and dark. With time, as the snow built up outside, the ridgepole showed signs of failing, so more props were introduced, further

An esker near the headwaters of the Hanbury River is about the size of the one Hornby and Critchell-Bullock made their home for the winter. *H. Huntington.*

constraining movement in the already small living space. By the end of the winter there were more than a dozen props in and around their beds and cook stove.

There was the inevitable friction between the two men during the winter: call it cabin fever. Critchell-Bullock was fastidious; Hornby could skin a wolf on his bed and not mind the blood, entrails, and mess. Restless as always, at one point during the winter Hornby mushed back to Great Slave Lake where he started a rumor that Critchell-Bullock had gone insane and wanted to murder him. Perhaps a misguided practical joke, the rumor traveled all the way back to Fort Resolution and prompted a late-winter visit to the esker cave by the RCMP. At the cave, the Mounties were puzzled to find Critchell-Bullock apparently quite sane and Hornby somewhat cracked, but then the small man was always that way. At another time during the winter, Hornby seems to have had a heart attack. Critchell-Bullock found him unconscious in the snow and revived him. Hornby then recovered enough to go out for a sub-zero run the next morning. But together they persevered and survived with the diminutive Hornby always doing more than his share of the backbreaking labor associated with trapping and living in the Barrenlands.

They could have returned home by the way they came, but instead they decided to head east, get into the drainage of the Hanbury River and follow it and the Thelon River to Hudson Bay. This would be a seven-hundred-mile trip, almost three times as long as returning via Great Slave Lake. It was an odd and foolish decision that nearly cost them their lives, but also brought them to their brief encounter with the fabled muskoxen (see "Strange Wooly

Attractors" on page 211). They compounded their problems by carrying out the plan, in typically inept fashion, without reference to David Hanbury's 1904 book *Sport and Travel in the Northland of Canada*, which described their intended route in detail.

After leaving their esker cave in the spring with a sled loaded down by two canoes, four hundred fox and wolf pelts, and camping gear, they were pinned down by late-season blizzards. Eventually they found themselves on an arm of a large lake—today Critchell-Bullock Arm of Smart Lake—connecting to the Hanbury River. Whereas David Hanbury had found the river easy to descend with short portages around the few rapids, Hornby and Critchell-Bullock found a swollen river that they had to face in overloaded and damaged canoes. Each portage took eight trips to move all of their heavy kit. Caribou were scarce and the fishing was not reliable. First they got hungry and then they began to starve.

When they finally reached the broad Thelon River the paddling got easier, though game was no more plentiful. It was while descending this river that late one evening they pulled ashore and went to sleep on a beach below a fine grove of spruce trees. They awoke the next day to warm sunny weather. The stresses of the preceding months told on them for they were exhausted and malnourished. The trees nearby were novel after so long out on the tundra, the luxury of unlimited firewood a pleasure. The beach sand was warm and comfortable, and there were at least a few fish in their nets. They decided that a rest would do them good, so they stayed for three indolent days. It was the most pleasure they had had on the whole expedition. A few weeks later, on September 26, 1925, their journey ended when they pulled into the trading posts at Baker Lake. From there, they were able to book passage back home, but not before learning that all their furs had been spoiled by moisture and inexpert cleaning.

Before leaving Baker Lake, still grimy with the caked dirt of months in the bush, Hornby began thinking about returning to the Barrenlands, the lovely beach on the north side of the Thelon River much on his mind. He tried to convince Critchell-Bullock to go back with him, despite the frictions of the past year. But Critchell-Bullock, "the only person who ever proceeded on the assumption that Hornby was a competent Northern traveler and survived that curious assumption," wrote Whalley, had more sense. One adventure with John Hornby was enough. Sadly, neither Critchell-Bullock nor Hornby had noted in Hanbury's book the following passage:

> On the main [Thelon] River there is a stretch of country about eighty miles in length into which no human being enters. The Eskimos do not hunt so far west, and Yellow Knives and Dog Ribs from Slave Lake do not go so far east. To penetrate this country in the dead of winter would be to simply court starvation.

The beach on the Thelon was right in the middle of that stretch of country.

Of course, Hornby did go back, and with young and inexperienced partners. One was his nephew Edgar, the other Harold Adlard. This was to have been a grand adventure, their first big wilderness trip in the North. It would toughen them and give them the substance and fiber young English gentlemen needed. For Hornby perhaps the reason for going back was no more complicated than his need to be back in the wilderness.

On July 1 they found themselves at Pike's Portage ready to start the trip into Artillery Lake. Following a route now well known to Hornby they reached the beach on the Thelon on September 5 with fall already in the air. There they immediately started building a cabin up against a small hill slope. In marked contrast to previous expeditions, they had brought no dogs.

We know how the grim and fatal winter unfolded because young Edgar kept a diary. The three men did their best to subsist by hunting, trapping, and fishing, but the caribou never came. By March they were in desperate shape, with barely the energy to carry out chores or hunt. Hornby was shorting his own rations so that the other two had more. As the winter dragged on, with no game to be had near the cabin, the emaciated men were forced to take long trips out from the shelter of the trees onto the tundra looking for caribou. These trips proved futile and the wicked sting of the cold sapped what little remaining strength they had. The crisis came in early April when they were completely out of food, their bodies wasted. Hornby made the last of several noble but futile attempts to find the remains of caribou they had shot earlier in the winter in the deep snow back behind the cabin. He came back shattered, and by the seventh of April he was basically bedridden. On April 9 and 10 he wrote out his will and several letters, then instructed Edgar and Harold on what they should do to survive after his death. On the sixteenth he died.

By April 27 Harold became bedridden. He passed away on May 3, leaving Edgar to face his fate alone. Edgar wrapped Harold's body in a blanket and with effort pulled it outside the cabin, placing it next to Hornby's, which he and Harold had moved outside ten days earlier. The end came for Edgar sometime in early June. He kept up his diary until the end, and in an act that is difficult to even contemplate, wrapped the diary in a cloth, thrust it into the cold ashes of the wood stove knowing it was the only place in the cabin where it would escape moisture and a porcupine. On a separate piece of paper he wrote, "WHOEVER FINDS THIS LOOK IN THE STOVE," placed it in the top of the stove, then lay down on his bunk to die.

A year would go by before a group of four young prospectors traveled down the Thelon River past the cabin. They had been told to look out for Hornby and his party, now overdue. The prospectors saw the little cabin on the north bank of the river above the beach and stopped. They could see that the cabin was dilapidated and weathered, but until they cut a hole in one of the bundles by the door they did not realize that it was a morgue. The door was latched from the inside, so they broke it open, but their examination of the cabin was cut short when one of the men accidentally knocked against the one remaining bunk and a skeletal foot and skull clattered out. Taking a few bundles of papers with them, they fled, failing to see the stained note on the stovetop.

The authorities were already relatively certain that some tragedy had befallen Hornby even before the report from the prospectors was received at Chesterfield Inlet. By the time the confirmation arrived, it was too late in the season to mount an official investigation. The following summer, two years after Edgar died, a three-man RCMP patrol made a rapid descent of the Hanbury and Thelon Rivers, arriving at the moldering cabin in late July.

This time the diary was found. The Mounties buried the three bodies next to the cabin, marking the graves with white wooden crosses. In 1937, Edgar's father had the diary published under the title *Unflinching: A Diary of a Tragic Adventure*. Unflinching indeed!

It was late in the day as we approached Hornby Point. Both Chris and I were intently watching our GPS and straining through the light snow to catch sight of the fuel cache on the north bank. Without that fuel, we weren't going anywhere beyond the Point. With a satellite phone, the danger of starving to death like Hornby was low, but the embarrassment of having to call in an air strike for supplies would have been too much. We needed to find that gas cache. So it was with some relief that we spied the red barrels up on the beach right where they were supposed to be. Just beyond the barrels was a strip of spruce forest that looked sheltered and snug. I drove up into the woods to find a camp spot and quickly discovered there was four feet of soft snow in the trees, a marked contrast with the hard pack on the river. It was the deepest snow we had seen yet and our evening ritual of packing the camp site with the snowmobiles was particularly fun as we all got mired in it at one point or another. Eventually we had a nice spot packed down and all the tents up. As the activity of the long day subsided, Henry and Glen passed out steaming mugs of soup. We could hear the wind blowing hard above the trees, but down between them by the tents, the air was still. It was our first camp in the forest since the Douglas cabin, and it had the same sedative effect on us that it had on Hornby and Critchell-Bullock. Our conversations were muted, our actions slow and contemplative. Despite the cold, a warm and secure feeling pervaded the camp. Dinner was nice, but everyone turned in early. As the tops of the spruce trees swayed in the wind we drifted off to sleep in our three orange tents.

At breakfast there was some talk of spending the day there, a rest day, but perhaps haunted by memories of Hornby we decided it would be better to travel. We planned to leave after lunch. Glen, Chris, and I laid out snow depth lines and started measuring them while the rest of the crew pumped gas from the barrels into our plastic jugs. Our snow line ran from camp farther into

Chris and Dan looking tired after a day on the Thelon River.

the forest toward a low hill, and as I drove the line to pack it down, I kept expecting to see cut logs or even the remains of the Hornby cabin. From the historical documents, I believed this was the right place. I thought I might even see the three white crosses marking the graves near the cabin, but there was nothing. I finally decided that the deep snow was hiding everything. We finished the measurements about noon, packed up camp, and were ready to go by one in the afternoon. We drove out onto the river, which very quickly curved around a distinct point, and headed north. Jon thought this was Hornby Point proper, and moreover, that it looked like a site someone like Hornby might choose if he were building a cabin. The land was elevated above the river and had views north and west. We decided to make one last search for the cabin. Jon and I drove up into the woods and circled back and forth looking, but again, there was nothing to see. After getting stuck a few more times in the deep snow, we finally gave up the search and rejoined our companions waiting patiently down on the river.

Like Hornby, we had not done our homework well. A month later I learned that the cabin was located about a hundred yards upriver from where we had our gas cache, in an unremarkable grove of trees. Henry inadvertently took a picture of the cabin site when he was photographing the fueling operation. It seems like an odd spot for a cabin, with no obvious advantages for hunting or fishing. Perhaps in the summer the appeal of the spot would have been more apparent, or then again, perhaps Hornby had sited the cabin on a whim without any practical reason. That would be just like him.

As Dan pumps fuel, the site of the Hornby cabin on the Thelon River is visible over his right shoulder.
H. Huntington.

I would have liked to have seen the cabin, for I have now come to see Hornby as the quintessential refugee from an increasingly mechanized, globalized, and overbearing world, seeking out the ultimate wilderness for solace and escape. When he first came to the North in 1904, conditions were effectively unchanged from those experienced by Matonabbee and Hearne. Hornby was happy, insulated by time and distance from the wider world. He embraced the solitude, the overpowering presence of nature, and the subsistence lifestyle, even the frequent episodes of hunger and starvation. He gathered the wilderness about himself like a warm and comforting quilt. I am sure he wanted the North to remain unchanged. But it was no longer Hearne's era; not even Warburton Pike's era. The railroads had spanned Canada and paddlewheel steamers were plying the Mackenzie River regularly. Then World War I came, broke the man, and delivered him back to the North along with improved radios and airplanes. In short, Hornby's timing was bad. When he first arrived in the North the place still retained its old power, but by the time he died, technology was rolling back the remoteness of the Arctic. Indeed, had the authorities gotten word of his death just a few weeks earlier than they did, they would have sent the investigating patrol to Hornby Point by airplane. In a few more years the trio would have had trouble starving to death on the Thelon because of regular flights into the Barrenlands.

Of course, Hornby did not plan to meet his death at the Point, but he did not flinch from it when the time came, and his love and solicitude for his companions marked the man with dignity at the end. Also, he seems to have had no regrets for having fully committed himself to the wilderness and dying there.

Sadly, Hornby's short-comings and eccentrici-ties—notably his lack of planning and his impulsive decisions—tend to obscure his underlying commit-ment. That facet of the man was pure and heart-felt. It is worth something today in a world of seven billion people. Perhaps that is the reason for his fame: Hornby stands as a reminder of what the world has lost since the days of Samuel Hearne. I am sure that Hornby would not have liked the seven of us charging around his point on noisy gas-guzzling snowmobiles. For that matter, I suppose that most of the wilderness pilgrims who come to the Point by canoe in summer would not have liked that either, but in our own way we were there to show our respect.

Simple crosses mark the graves of Edgar Christian, John Hornby, and Harold Adlard, seen in a 1979 photo. *Courtesy Prince of Wales Northern Heritage Centre.*

From Hornby Point we continued down the Thelon, crossing two more big lakes. Then we crossed a snowmobile track, the first since we had left Kugluktuk. It could only have originated in Baker Lake, so we carefully fol-lowed it home. Two days later we arrived in town in a blinding snowstorm. It was with no small sense of pride that when asked where we had come from we answered simply, "Alaska." The hospitality in Baker Lake was wonder-ful. Packing up snowmobiles, sleds, and gear to ship home took most of our attention, so there was little time for ruminating on what we had found dur-ing our journey.

It wasn't until some time later that I realized what the trip was really about. We knew the journey was about digging deeper, about finding the soul of the Arctic, but being geologists and physicists, our natural tendency was to think this soul resided in the natural features of the land. So we dug down through the snow, drilled through the ice, walked on the oldest rocks in the world, and tried to puzzle out why the rivers and lakes were distributed in a particular pattern. We looked for the soul in the geology, the permafrost, the taiga, and the tundra.

Not surprisingly, we did not find it in those places. Looking back on the route we chose, the places we visited, and the trip's most memorable experiences, I now realize that to find the soul of the Arctic, one needs to look to the *people* of the Arctic—past, present, and future. Virtually all of the magical moments we experienced on the trip were related to people and the places they live or had lived: Old Crow, Lapierre House, the Douglas cabin, the Diavik mine, and Hornby Point. We got close to the people we met along the way by swapping stories, working on snowmobiles, talking about trails and routes, traveling with them, or sharing potlatches. In historic places where the people are now dead and gone, we got close by standing where they had stood while recounting their stories and exploits. I had so immersed myself in the history of these places that I actually experienced a strange blurring of time during the trip. Rounding one of the bends of the Thelon River, I would find myself wafting back and forth between centuries. Had I come around a corner and seen Hearne and Matonabbee, Franklin and his men, or Hornby, I would not have been surprised. Past and present mixed like saltating grains of snow in my mind, but always it was the people, not the places, I found drawing me in.

Reading and thinking about Hornby in particular helped to bring this real essence of the trip into focus, for there is a bit of Hornby in many arctic residents, including me. Hornby was steeped in the lore of the harsh undeveloped Arctic, a man for whom courage in the face of hardship and privation was the highest calling. He would have disliked the airplanes, helicopters, radios, snowmobiles, ice roads, multinational corporations, and myriad other advances that have flowed North since World War I, because these have eroded the Arctic's wilderness mystique and its lethal edge. Worse, in the eyes of someone like Hornby, the new technology has opened "his" Arctic to the multitudes—people who otherwise would have neither the skills nor the toughness to make a go of it there. And along with technology has come greater regulation and government control, eating away at the unfettered freedom of being completely isolated from society. Hornby must have hated the changes he saw coming and whether through willful or unintended ineptitude, he managed to artificially maintain the old harsh Arctic right up to his death by starvation.

But the reality is that the spread of technology and governmental structure has greatly improved the lives of arctic residents, made them easier, longer, and safer. While I would love to know how Hearne and Franklin felt, traveling with no maps, no way of calling for help, through a pristine country nearly empty of people, I would not want to change places with them. Unlike Hornby, my longing for the past has never been strong enough to eschew the benefits of modern technology. On every expedition, we have traveled with the best and most up-to-date gear: satellite phones, emergency beacons, high-powered snowmobiles, air drops, complete medical kits, and the best maps and satellite images we can get. Most arctic residents I know, Native and non-Native alike, have a similar attitude. We are a pragmatic people. Hornby's choice to turn his back on the modern world is elected by very few, and those who do it are viewed by the rest of us as foolhardy or suicidal.

Perhaps this pragmatism lies at the center of the success of the arctic people: a willingness to embrace new ideas, new ways, new technology, if it makes life in a tough place just a little easier. Consider how quickly the Inuit discarded the bone snow knife the minute something better (steel) came along. Similarly, Matonabbee saw the benefits of dealing peacefully with the whites and other tribes rather than fighting them, and took steps to see that things changed. Part of being a "hardy" people is being able to adapt and grow. This is a trait the people of the Arctic will need even more in the future to meet the coming challenges. The forces of globalization are very powerful and the rich resources of the Arctic are needed by an oil- and mineral-hungry world. Arctic climate change is making it ever easier to access these resources. Evermore technology and change is likely to come to the region. Like Matonabbee, the people are going to need to be clever and wise about how they adapt…embracing what is good and useful, but protecting what they love about the Arctic and what attracts them and keeps them living there.

Are the people of the Arctic up to this challenge? Or have they become too tamed by technology to produce forceful leaders and extraordinary characters like those described in the foregoing chapters? Are there still Hearnes and Hornbys out there? There is no scientific way to answer this, but as I began to recall the many people we met on the trail, and as I thought about the things they had done and their outlooks on life, I found that my answer was a unequivocal "yes." The Arctic is still home to amazing people. From Earl Cadzow, Peter Josie, William Kleedehn and Sol Carriere, to Russell Andre, Sister Joan Liss, the scientists at Daring Lake, the miners at Diavik, and the toothless snow-knife maker in Baker Lake, we found people with a strong love for and a keen interest in the harsh country they lived in. We found warm hearts for strange travelers (us) and willingness to tackle their world with the tools they have.

ACKNOWLEDGMENTS

The long snowmobile trip of 2007 touched me in many ways, surprisingly most of them human. Long before I became a snow scientist, when I was a sailor on the USCGC Northwind, *I was intrigued by the arctic landscape that I saw from the deck of the ship. The mountains, rivers, and tundra prairies were the attractors that lured me north and these natural features still have a powerful draw for me after more than thirty years. Initially, I was unaware of the rich human history and the interesting people who lived in the Arctic. The mountains, volcanoes, glaciers, ice, and snow of the region were the focus of my professional life. But with time I began to learn about and appreciate the people and the culture. For the thirty years during which I've done research in the Arctic, we would stage out of villages and towns to get to our research sites. The locals we met were unfailingly hospitable, had often lived adventure-filled lives, and they would share with us what they knew of the area's history. For example, in 1982 while waiting to fly into Mt. Wrangell at the Copper Center Lodge, the proprietor Mrs. Ashby told us how the gold seekers headed to the Klondike in 1898 were trapped at the site of the lodge for the winter. Behind the lodge, hidden in the woods, the tiny cabins these desperate men built that bitterly cold winter were still standing. Examining these cabins, we came to understand in ways we never could from the history books what those gold seekers must have endured as they waited for the long cold winter to end.*

So, with time, some of my focus began to shift from snow crystals and geology to arctic people, places, and human events. I read more histories, talked to more people, and visited more historical sites. Eventually this interest led to the trip across Alaska and Canada described here. Throughout the trip we were met with warm hospitality and generosity. In village and hamlet, the people shared food, fuel, snowmobile parts, trail knowledge, and stories. They let us sleep in their schools and they escorted us out of town, not to get rid of us but to ensure we did not get lost. We owe them a debt we can only begin to repay by being equally hospitable to travelers we meet. There are far too many people to name individually, but they made the trip for us, and I want to thank them all.

Some special thanks, however, are in order. First, the National Science Foundation generously provided the funds that made the trip possible and supported publication of this book. Logistics for the Alaska segment of the traverse were provided by Polar Field Services, Inc., under the leadership of Marin Kuizenga. In Canada, Environment Canada provided logistics, including the crucial gas cache at Hornby Point. We were fed and housed at the Tundra Ecosystem Research Station on Daring Lake through the great generosity of Steve Matthews, who allowed us to stay even after I had blown the main electrical panel. Our host at the diamond mine was Seth Bohnet, the Environment Information Manager of Diavik Diamond Mines, Inc. The U.S. Army Cold Regions Research and Engineering Laboratory generously gave Jon Holmgren and me the time to make the two-month-long traverse and supported the trip in many ways. Our communications were supplied and maintained by SRI International under a contract with the National Science Foundation.

Writing this book has been something of a journey, too, and like the physical journey it describes, people have made it both possible and rewarding. Joan Braddock of the University of Alaska Press has supported the book from the start. Dermot Cole, the columnist for the Fairbanks paper and author of several books, provided encouragement that a book of this nature would be valuable. His brother Terrence Cole, a Northern historian by training, read

The Crew: (from left) Dan Solie, Chris Derksen, Arvids Silis, Henry Huntington, Jon Holmgren, and Glen Liston at a cairn along the Thelon River.

the Northern Cross chapter and provided the perspective that I ultimately adopted. Mike Burwell, a poet and editor from Anchorage, working with an early draft of the book, helped me find a consistent voice for the narrative and gave me much needed encouragement that I was writing stories people would want to read. Thanks to Christopher Hiemstra of CRREL for creating the maps. Christine Soares edited the book, eliminating crowded writing and giving it a sense of space. She also organized the various pieces of the book in a manner suitable for publication, a task I would have found impossible. My debt to her is large and I want to thank her. But more than anyone, my wife Betsy Sturm has made this book possible. She has endured my many absences on expeditions with unfailing humor and grace, handled the household chores solo while I was gone for months, yet still has encouraged my writing. She has listened with patience to trial paragraphs, read every draft of the book, and has always supported me. With love and affection, I want to thank her.

Lastly, I will be forever grateful for the warm and supportive companionship of the six friends who went along on this trip. Jon, Glen, Dan, Henry, Arvids, Chris: Thanks, guys!

ANOTHER ARCTIC STORY

Two Alaskans started reading books on arctic exploration, and soon they wanted to do a big trip of their own. They weren't dog mushers, and while both could ski, they wanted to go farther than skiing would allow. They decided to take a long snowmobile trip. Their goal would be Anaktuvak Pass, an Iñupiat village nestled in the mountains to the north, about a hundred miles west of the nearest road. The place sounded remote and ancient.

They found two old but serviceable snowmobiles, a wooden sled, and a dark green pyramidal tent that looked like it had last been used in the 1920s. They contacted the village and talked to the mayor, explaining to him in great detail when they would be coming. They loaded their sled with food and fuel and started out.

They got stuck in deep snow, spun out on overflow ice, and at times were lost in the hilly moraines that front the Brooks Range. They rolled their sled, broke it, but fixed it as well. They saw moose and caribou but no human tracks. They felt like explorers.

As they neared the village, they came upon another snowmobile track and followed it. Soon a man driving a far newer and more powerful snowmobile passed them, heading toward the village going fast. He was towing a *komatik*, a traditional-style wood sled on which were piled several bloody caribou. He waved.

Next, they crossed something that looked like a road. This puzzled them because Anaktuvak was supposed to be remote, unreachable by road. Later they learned this was the Hickel Highway—an abandoned 1960s project. At the other end of the road was their home in Fairbanks.

As they neared the village, they passed a dump surrounded by a chain-link fence to keep out the bears. On a pole was a solid-state surveillance camera. They drove over a little rise and landed on a gravel road, where they barely had time to get out of the way of a brand new Ford Aerostar driving to town, which was perhaps two hundred yards away. By the runway they saw a compound full of heavy equipment, most of it new and painted bright yellow. The runway was lighted and stretched almost a mile.

In the village they asked for the mayor to let him know they had arrived safely. His assistant said, "He has flown to Fairbanks for a few hours but he will be back later this afternoon. Who are you?"

They drove around the village. Where were the Iñupiat? They parked in front of a modern building with a sign that said Wash-a-teria. Inside, washing machines and dryers were spinning. The air was warm and humid. One wall of the Wash-a-teria was lined with traditional skin masks. Two elders were sitting on orange plastic chairs drinking coffee from chipped plastic mugs.

The two sat down and talked with them. The old men asked where they had come from. When they said the road, the elders registered neither surprise nor any admiration. The conversation petered out and there was silence. Finally one of the elders, glancing out the window at their snowmobiles said, "Your sled is too short."

They mounted up and headed home feeling somewhat confused.

A few months later, talking to a friend with vast experience in the Arctic, they learned that to have received any comment at all from the elders about their sled meant they were doing something right.

RECOMMENDED READING

Asfeldt, Morten, and Bob Henderson, eds. 2010. *Pike's Portage: Stories of a Distinguished Place.* Toronto: Natural Heritage Books. (HORNBY)

Balikci, Asen. 1970. *The Netsilik Eskimo.* Foreword by Margaret Mead. Garden City: The Natural History Press.

Berton, Pierre. *Prisoners of the North.* 2004. New York: Carroll and Graf Publishers. (HORNBY)

Boden, Jürgen F., and Elke Boden. 1991. *Canada, North of Sixty.* Toronto: McClelland & Stewart.

Burwash, L. T. 1929. "Across Arctic Canada, 1925–1926." *The Geographical Journal* 74(6): 553–568.

Chandler, Graham. 1998. "Shooting Star." *Up Here* 14(1): 16–19. (HELEN FALLS, HANBURY RIVER)

Christian, Edgar. 1937. *Unflinching: A Diary of Tragic Adventure.* London: J. Murray. (HORNBY ON THE THELON)

Cooke, Alan, and Clive Holland. 1978. *The Exploration of Northern Canada, 500 to 1920: A Chronology.* Toronto: Arctic History Press.

DeCoccola, Raymond, and Paul King. 1986. *The Incredible Eskimo Life among the Barren Land Eskimo.* Surrey: Hancock House Publishers Ltd. (KUGLUKTUK)

Douglas, George Mellis. 2008. *Lands Forlorn: A Story of an Expedition to Hearne's Coppermine River,* ed. R. S. Hildebrand. Tucson: Zancudo Press.

Downes, Prentice G. 1988. *Sleeping Island: A Journey to the Edge of the Barrens,* 2nd ed. Foreword by R. H. Cockburn. Ferrisburg, VT: Heron Dance.

Ecogistics Consulting. 1999. "Rampart House Historic Site and Lapierre House Historic Site Management Plan." Wells, British Columbia: Vuntut Gwich'in First Nation and Government of Yukon.

Edinger, Ray. 2003. *Fury Beach: The Four-Year Odyssey of Captain John Ross and the Victory.* New York: Berkley Books.

Franklin, Sir John. 2005. *Narrative of a Journey to the Shores of the Polar Sea in the Years 1819–1822,* Cosimo Classics series, reprint of 1825 edition. New York: Cosimo.

Franklin, Sir John. 1988. *Thirty Years in the Arctic Regions, or The Adventures of Sir John Franklin.* Reprint of 1859 edition. Lincoln: University of Nebraska Press.

Fuller, W. A. 1999. "Samuel Hearne's Track: Some Obscurities Clarified." *Arctic* 52 (3): pp. 257–271.

Gough, Barry. 1997. *First Across the Continent: Sir Alexander Mackenzie.* Norman: University of Oklahoma Press.

Hanbury, David T. 1904. *Sport and Travel in the Northland of Canada.* New York: The Macmillan Company.

Hansen, Thorkild. 1965. *The Way to Hudson Bay: The Life and Times of Jens Munk.* New York: Helen and Kurt Wolff. (CHURCHILL)

Hayes, Derek. 2002. *First Crossing: Alexander Mackenzie, His Expedition Across North America, and the Opening of the Continent.* Seattle: Sasquatch Books.

Iglauer, Edith. 1974. *Denison's Ice Road.* New York: E. P. Dutton & Company. (GREAT BEAR LAKE, ICE ROADS TO DIAMOND MINES)

Jenkins, McKay. 2005. *Bloody Falls of the Coppermine: Madness, Murder, and the Collision of Cultures in the Arctic, 1913.* New York: Random House.

Jenness, Diamond. 1928. *The People of the Twilight.* Chicago: The University of Chicago Press.

Krajick, Kevin. 2001. *Barren Lands: An Epic Search for Diamonds in the North American Arctic.* New York: A. W. H. Freeman/Owl Books.

Llorente, Segundo. 1969. *Jesuits in Alaska.* Portland: Service Office Supply.

Lopez, Barry. 1986. *Arctic Dreams.* New York: Vintage Books.

Mackenzie, Alexander. 1801. *Voyages From Montreal, On the River St. Laurence, Through the Continent of North America, to the Frozen and Pacific Oceans; In the Years 1789 and 1793. With a Preliminary Account of the Rise, Progress, and Present State of the Fur Trade of That Country.* London: Cadell & Davies.

Mackenzie, Alexander. 1966. *Exploring the Northwest Territory: Sir Alexander Mackenzie's Journal of a Voyage by Bark Canoe from Lake Athabasca to the Pacific Ocean in the Summer of 1789.* Edited by T. H. McDonald. Norman: University of Oklahoma Press.

Mallet, Thierry. 1930. *Glimpses of the Barren Lands.* New York: Revillon Frères.

Mallory, Enid L. 1989. *Coppermine: The Far North of George M. Douglas.* Peterborough, Canada: Broadview Press.

Mannik, Hattie, ed. 1989. *Inuit Nunmiut: Inland Inuit.* Altona, Manitoba: Friesen Corporation. (BAKER LAKE)

Marshall, Robert. 1956. *Alaska Wilderness: Exploring the Central Brooks Range.* 2nd ed. Berkeley: University of California Press.

Marshall, Robert. 1991. *Arctic Village.* Originally published in 1933 by H. Smith and Haas. Fairbanks: University of Alaska Press.

May, Wilfred "Wop." "The Hunt for the Mad Trapper of Rat River." 1952 account published by the Northwest Territories & Yukon Radio System History Project. Accessed May 20, 2011. http://www.nwtandy.rcsigs.ca/stories/may.htm.

McGhee, Robert. 2001. *The Arctic Voyages of Martin Frobisher: An Elizabethan Venture.* Seattle: University of Washington Press.

McGhee, Robert. 2005. *The Last Imaginary Place: A Human History of the Arctic World.* Oxford: Oxford University Press, Oxford.

McGill, Jean S. 1974. *Northern Adventure: The Exploration of Great Bear Lake, 1900.* Cobalt, Ontario: Highway Book Shop.

McGoogan, Ken. 2004. *Ancient Mariner: The Arctic Adventures of Samuel Hearne, the Sailor Who Inspired Coleridge's Masterpiece.* New York: Carroll & Graf Publishers.

McPhee, John. 1976. *Coming into the Country.* New York: Farrar, Straus and Giroux. (YUKON RIVER, CIRCLE)

Mishler, Craig. 1990. "Missionaries in Collision: Anglicans and Oblates among the Gwich'in, 1861–65." *Arctic* 43 (2): 121–126.

Mowat, Farley. 1960. *Ordeal By Ice: The Search for the Northwest Passage.* Volume I: *The Top of the World Trilogy.* Toronto: McClelland & Stewart.

Mowat, Farley. 1989. *Tundra: Selections from the Great Accounts of Arctic Land Voyages.* Volume III: *The Top of the World Trilogy.* Salt Lake City: Peregrine Smith Books.

Nagle, Ted, and Jordan Zinovich. 1989. *The Prospector North of Sixty.* Edmonton: Lone Pine Publishing.

Naske, Claus M., and Herman E. Slotnick. 1987. *Alaska: A History of the 49th State.* Norman: University of Oklahoma Press.

Neary, Nash. 1948. "The Mad Trapper of Rat River." Originally published in *Notes of Interest—The Northwest Territories and Yukon Radio System,* October 1948. Reprinted online by the Northwest Territories & Yukon Radio System History Project. Accessed May 20, 2011. http://www.nwtandy.rcsigs.ca/stories/rat_river.htm.

Newman, Peter C. 1988. *Caesars of the Wilderness—The Story of the Hudson's Bay Company,* Volume II. New York: Penguin Books.

Niven, Jennifer. 2003. *Ada Blackjack: A True Story of Survival in the Arctic*. New York: Hyperion.

North, Dick. 1966. *The Mad Trapper of Rat River: A True Story of Canada's Biggest Manhunt*. Guilford: Lyons Press.

North, Dick. 1995. *The Lost Patrol: The Mounties' Yukon Tragedy*. Guilford: Lyons Press.

Pelly, David F. 1981. *Expedition: An Arctic Journey through History on George Back's River*. Toronto: Betelgeuse Books, Toronto. (FRANKLIN)

Pelly, David F. 1996. *Thelon: A River Sanctuary*. Toronto: Dundurn.

Pelly, David F., ed. 1997. *Arctic Cairn Notes: Canoeists' Reflections on the Hanbury-Thelon & Kazan Rivers*. Toronto: Betelgeuse Books. (HELEN FALLS)

Phillips, Carol A., ed. 1995. *A Century of Faith: Centennial Commemorative, 1895–1995, Episcopal Diocese of Alaska*. Fairbanks: Centennial Press.

Pike, Warburton. 1917. *The Barren Ground of Northern Canada*. New York: E. P. Dutton & Co. (HEARNE, DIAMOND MINES)

Powell-Williams, Clive. 2002. *Cold Burial: A True Story of Endurance and Disaster*. New York: St. Martin's Press. (HORNBY)

Raffan, James. 1990. *Summer North of Sixty: By Paddle and Portage Across the Barren Lands*. Toronto: Key Porter Books.

Rasmussen, Knud. 1927. *Across Arctic America: Narrative of the Fifth Thule Expedition*. New York: G. P. Putnam's Sons.

Renner, Louis L. 2005. *Alaskana Catholica: A History of the Catholic Church in Alaska*. Spokane: The Arthur H. Clark Company.

Richardson, John. *Arctic Ordeal: The Journal of John Richardson, Surgeon-Naturalist with Franklin, 1820–1822*. Edited by C. Stuart Houston. Kingston: McGill-Queen's University Press.

Seton, Ernest Thompson. 1911. *The Arctic Prairies: a canoe-journey of 2,000 miles in search of the caribou; being the account of a voyage to the region north of Aylmer Lake*. Toronto: William Briggs.

Sissons, John Howard. 1968. *Judge of the Far North: The Memoirs of Jack Sissons*. Toronto: McClelland & Stewart.

Smith, Phillip S., and J. B. Mertie, Jr. 1930. "Geology and Mineral Resources of Northwestern Alaska." *United States Geological Survey Bulletin 815*. Washington: U.S. Government Printing Office.

Steele, Peter. 2003. *The Man Who Mapped the Arctic: The Intrepid Life of George Back, Franklin's Lieutenant*. Vancouver: Raincoast Books.

Stuck, Hudson. 1914. *Ten Thousand Miles with a Dog Sled: A Narrative of Winter Travel in Interior Alaska*. New York: Scribner. (FT. YUKON)

Tape, Ken D. 2010. *The Changing Arctic Landscape*. Fairbanks: University of Alaska Press. (CLIMATE CHANGE)

Tyrrell, James Williams. 1897. *Across the Sub-Arctics of Canada: A Journey of 3,200 Miles by Canoe and Snowshoe Across the Barren Lands*. Toronto: William Briggs.

Waldron, Malcolm. 1931. *Snow Man: John Hornby in the Barren Lands*. New York: Kodansha International.

Watt, Frederick B. 1980. *Great Bear, A Journey Remembered*. Yellowknife, NWT: Outcrop Ltd. (GREAT BEAR LAKE)

Whalley, George. 1962. *The Legend of John Hornby*. London: John Murray.

Wohlforth, Charles. 2004. *The Whale and the Supercomputer: On the Northern Front of Climate Change*. New York: North Point Press.

Zaslow, Morris. 1971. *The Opening of the Canadian North 1870–1914*. Toronto: McClelland & Stewart.

Zoellner, Tom. 2006. *The Heartless Stone: A Journey through the World of Diamonds, Deceit, and Desire*. New York: St. Martin's Press.

INDEX

Note: Italicized page numbers refer to illustrations and their captions.

Aberdeen Lake, *196* (map), *218* (map)
Aber Resources, 179–180
aboriginal people. *See* indigenous people
Acasta gneiss, 193
Adlard, Harold, 219, 226–227, *231*
airplanes and air travel, 21, 57, 58–59, 66–67
Akaitcho, Chief, 163
Aklavik, 59, 68, 70
Akpatok Island, *199*
Alaska, *2* (map)
Alaska Air National Guard, 21
Alexander family, 37
Alexi, Peter, 67
all-weather roads, 185
Anaktuvak Pass, 239–240
Andersen, Dave, 14–15, *15*, 19, 30
Andre, Leroy, 140–141
Andre, Russell, 78–79, 90
Anglican—Catholic rivalry, 124, 127–133
Antarctic, 12
Anthony, Harry, *45*
archean geologists, 193
Arctic
    abundance of life, 12–13
    blizzards, 97
    climate change and, xii, 233
    communications, 58–59
    dominant themes in stories of, xi–xii
    drowning deaths of snowmobilers, 206–207
    geology of, 106
    hospitality, 137, 231
    as mission field, 123
    people of, *x*, 233 (*See also* indigenous people; Inuit)
    protectors of isolation and mystery, 57
    the soul of, 232–233
    technological advances and, 198, 232–233
Arctic Red River trading post (Tsiigehtchic), *56* (map), 59, 75, *76* (map), 78, *79*
Arima (Indian woman), 221, *221, 222*
Artillery Lake, *218* (map)
Arvids. *See* Silis, Arvids
Athabasca, Lake, 86
aufeis (overflow ice), 17, 23–25, *24*, 71, *71*
Au Sable River Canoe Marathon, 42
axe throwing, 143
Aylmer Lake (*Thoy Kye Lyned*), 195, *196* (map), 204–205

Back, Sir George, 112, *158, 162*
Baker Lake, 1, *2* (map), 147, *196* (map), *218* (map), 231
"Ballad of the Arctic Science Bandits" (Huntington), 11
Balto (dog), 22
Barrenlands
    diamond mining, 185, 193
    expeditions (1888 to 1909), 212–213
    Hornby and, 195, 223–227
    Indians and Inuits on, 141
    Laurentide Ice Sheet and, 177–178
    muskoxen population, 213
    transition zone between taiga and tundra, *205*
Barrow, Alaska, sea ice, *150*
Bathurst Inlet, *154* (map), 157, 185
Bear Rock, 87, *89*
Beaufort Sea, *2* (map)
Beauparlant (Franklin expedition), 162
Belanger, Solomon, 159–160, 163
Belanger Rapids, *154* (map)
Bell, John, 55
Bellanca Pacemaker, 57, 66, *68*
Bell River, *38* (map), *51, 56* (map), 69
Bering Land Bridge, *x*

Bering Strait, *2* (map)
Bernard, Joe, 59
Berton, Pierre, 108
BHP-Billiton, 179–180, 185
Biederman, Bella, 34
Biederman, Charlie, *33, 34*
Biederman, Ed, 34
Biederman's cabin, 33
Big Esker, *116* (map), 117, *120,* 121, *180*
Birch Creek, *18* (map), 30
black ice, Great Bear Lake, 100
Bloody Creek, 140
Bloody Falls, 141, *143, 154* (map), 205
boats, lining, 88, 108
bones, prehistoric, 211
Boundary Waters, 85
Breynat, Bishop, 123–124
British Royal Navy officers, Franklin
    expedition, 156, 160–161, 169
Brooks Range, 58
Burnside River (*Conge-catha-wha-
    chaga*), *154* (map), 159, 204–205

cabin fever, 224
Cadzow, Daniel, 44, *47*
Cadzow, Earl, 37, 127–128
camp sites, SnowSTAR expedition
  below Eagle Summit, 30
  Daring Lake, 180, *180*
  Etacho Point, Great Bear Lake, 98
  on Franklin's route, 164–165, *165*
  Great Bear Lake, 95–96
  Hornby Point, 220, 228
  inside arm of Big Esker, 117, *121,*
    121–122
  near Douglas cabin, 110–111
  Old Woman Creek (*Shanaghàn
    Kòhnjìk*), 45
Camsell Bend, 87
Canadian Shield, 93, 106–107, *107,* 193
cannibalism, 162–163, 168
canoe routes, 85
Cape McDonnell, *94* (map), 101

caribou
  in Barrenlands, 141
  Coppermine River shallows crossing,
    197
  Franklin's expedition and, 157, 161
  migration route of, 159
  Porcupine herd, 55, 72, *72–73*
Carriere, Solomon, 42–43
Catholic church, 93, 127–133
channel fever, 217
Chapman, Henry, 133
Chapman, John, 133
Charles II, King, 199
Charley River, *18* (map)
Chawchinahaw, 200–201
Chena Hot Springs Road, 23
Chena River, North Fork, 17, 24–25
Chena River trail, 19–20
China, trade with, 86
Chipewyan Indians, 140–143, *142,* 197,
    200–205
  See also Matonabbee
Chris. *See* Derksen, Chris
Christian, Edgar, 219, 226–227, *231*
Christianity, 124, 127–133
Christians, muscular, 123
Chukchi Sea, *2* (map)
Circle, *2* (map), 37
climate change
  and the Arctic, xii, 150–151, 185, 233
  snow and, 12–13
Clinton-Colden Lake, 195, *196* (map)
coastal erosion near Drew Point, *151*
coastal sea ice, 150
Cogead Lake, 159
Collier, John, *199*
communications in the Arctic, 58–59
confluence bagging, 97–99, *196* (map),
    213–215, *214*
Conge-catha-wha-chaga (Burnside
    River), 159, 204–205
Conne-e-quese, 201–202
Contwoyto Lake, *154* (map), 159

copper
  Hearne's search for, 140, 200–201, 208
  from Santa Rita pit mine, New
    Mexico, *208*
  Wrangell Mountain deposits, 105
Coppermine River, *154* (map)
  caribou crossing at shallows, 197
  Franklin expedition and, 161
  massacre at Bloody Falls, 141, 205
  navigability, 208
  portage of, 142
Copper Mountains, 109
Cordilleran, 106–107, *107*
Coronation Gulf, 105, *138* (map),
  156–157
Crédit (Franklin expedition), 162
Cree Indians, 140–143, *142,* 201–202
Critchell-Bullock, James C., 212,
  222–223, *223*
Cumberland House, Saskatchewan, 43
Curtain Mountain, 71
Curtain Mountain cabin, *56* (map), 70

Dagoo 340 sled-dog race, 31, 42
Daily News-Miner, 19
Dan. *See* Solie, Dan
Daring Lake, *2* (map), 10, *174* (map), 175
Daring Lake research station, *181*
Dease, Peter Warren, 112–113
Dease Inlet, 108, 124–125, 222
Dease River area, 104, *116* (map), 117,
  118, 125
De Beers Canada, 185
Deline, 87, 93, *94* (map), *134,* 135, 140
Dene Indians, 93, 200–202, 209
  See also Matonabbee
Derksen, Chris, *14, 229*
  background and expedition role, 10
  at cairn along Thelon River, *237*
  Diavik Mine tour, 182, *189*
  gas cache, 217
  at Hornby Point, 228
  ice pressure ridge crossing, *207*

sled of, 180–181
  snow knife of, 145
diamond dust, 183
diamond mines and mining, *174* (map),
  175–180, *184,* 184–186, 190–191, 193
  See also Diavik Mine
diamond rush, 179
diamonds, formation of, 176, 193
Diavik Mine, *172, 174* (map)
  annual output of, 185
  crews and schedules, 188
  fuel tanks, *183*
  garnets, diopsides, and ilmenites
    found near, *178*
  kimberlite from, *177*
  open pit, *191*
  origins of, 180
  security, 182, 187
  tour, 187–190
diopsides, 177, 179
diorite, brown, 142
diptheria epidemic, 22
Discovery (ship), 199
Discovery Channel (television program), 65
Dismal Lakes, 113, *116* (map)
DNA kits, 65
dog teams, 20–21, *69*
  See also sled-dog races
Douglas, George Mellis, 105, *105,* 108,
  113, 124, 221
Douglas, Lionel, 105, 109, *110*
Douglas Bay, *94* (map), 97
Douglas cabin, 101, *110, 111*
Douglas expedition, 108–109
Drew Point, coastal erosion, *151*
Drymeat, Jacob, 59
Dubawnt Lake, *196* (map)
Dubawnt River, *196* (map)
dynamite, 61

Eagle River, *56* (map), *58*
Eagle Summit, 20–21, *23,* 30–31

Eames (Inspector), 62
Eda Lake, *154* (map), 160
Edmond's Island, *45*
education, in the North, 133
Ekati Mine, *174* (map), 180, 185
electron microprobe, advent of, 177
Episcopal Church, 128, 131
eskers
    Big Esker, *116* (map), 117, *120*, 121,
        121, *180*
    climbing, 175
    and diamond mines, 176
    formation of, 178
    near headwaters of Hanbury River,
        224
    near Tundra Ecosystem Research
        Station, *175*
    origins of term, 120–121
Etacho Point (Gros Cap), *94* (map),
    98, 108
expeditions
    Barrenlands (1888 to 1909), 212–213
    Douglas's, 108–109
    science-driven, 4
    through Dease crossroads, 104
    USGS, 57–58
    See also Franklin, Sir John; Hearne,
        Samuel; Hornby, John
extractive enterprises, 84, 154

Fairbanks, Alaska, 1, *2* (map), 19, 105
Far-Off Metal River, 200
field mentality, 26
Fipke, Chuck, 175–176, 178–180
firewood cutting, 95
fishing boats, Plummer's Lodge, *104*
Flaherty, Dick, 19, *29*, 30
folk-art murals, Our Lady of Good
    Hope, 130
Fontano (Franklin expedition), 163
Fort Chipewyan, 80, 89
Fort Confidence, *94* (map), *112*, 112–
    113, *113*

Fort Enterprise, *154* (map), 156, 162
Fort Good Hope, *76* (map)
    overview, 93
    Christianity, 133
    establishment, 90
    missionaries, 129
    Our Lady of Good Hope church,
        129–132, *131–132*
    Rouvière at, 123
Fort Hearne (fishing boat), *136*
Fort McPherson, *2* (map), 44, 55, *56*
    (map), 75
Fort Norman (Telida), 87, 93
Fort of the Forks, 90
Fort Reliance, 222
Fort Simpson, 90
Fort Yukon, *2* (map), 37, 44, 130
Fourth of July raft race, Nome, xi
Fox, Alaska, 211
Franklin, Sir John
    1821 expedition, 153, 155–164
    1845-1848 expedition, 168–169
    Bloody Falls artifacts, 142
    Coppermine River portage, 142
    Hudson's Bay Company and, 112
    portrait of, *155*
    risk-taking by, 170–171
    route taken by, *154* (map), 156, *161*,
        164–168
Fremmerlid, Mark, 65
French fishermen, 198
Frobisher, Martin, 198–199
frost flowers, *71*
fumarole sample collection, Mt.
    Wrangell, 6–7
fur trade, 84, 199–200

Gamètì (Tlicho village), 193
Garland (Constable), 63
garnets, 177, *178*
Garry Island, Mackenzie Bay, 88
gas shortages, 137, 217
General Clinton Canoe Regatta, 42

geologists, archean, 193
geology field camp, 143
geology of the Arctic, 106
glacial erratics, *106*
Glen. *See* Liston, Glen
global warming. *See* climate change
gold deposits, 105
Gold Rush days, 20
Golovin Bay, 207
GPS (global positioning system), 101,
    214–215
granites, 106
Gray's Bay, 185
Great Bear Lake, *94* (map)
    blowing snow, *102*
    crossing, 95–104
    Hornby and Melvill expedition,
        220–221
    saltating snow, *97*
Great Bear River, 87–88, *94* (map)
Great Depression, 59
Great Lakes system, 106
Great Slave Lake, 87, 208
Grollier, Henry, 130
Gros Cap (Etacho Point), *94* (map), 98,
    108
Guggenheim syndicate, 105
Gwich'in people, 44, 51, 55, 93

Haghe, Louis, *155*
Hanbury, David, 113, 225–226
Hanbury River, 195, *196* (map), *212*
Hasskjold, Sigvald Pederson, 65
HBC. *See* Hudson's Bay Company
    (HBC)
Hearne, Samuel, *197*
    in Barrenlands, 195
    country wife of, 203
    expeditions on behalf of HBC,
        200–201
    Inuit massacre account, 141–142
    on Kathawachaga Lake, 158–159
    at Lac de Gras, 197

link to 1990s diamond rush, 198–199
marker erected by, 205
route traveled by Matonabbee and,
    202–204
search for copper, 140, 208
significance of journey by, 208–210
Helen Falls, Hanbury River, *212*
helicopters, 21
Hepburn (Franklin expedition),
    162–163
Hersey (RCMP Sergeant), 68
Hickel Highway, 239
Hodgson, Joe, 108
Hodgson's Point, *94* (map)
Holmgren, Jon, *4*
    axe marks discovered by, 121–122
    background and expedition role, 3–5
    at cairn along Thelon River, *237*
    Diavik Mine tour, 182, 188, *189*
    and Douglas cabin, 110
    drilling through ice on Great Bear
        Lake, *13*
    role in confluence bagging, 214
    Rosebud Summit, 26–27
    search for Hornby cabin, 229
    snow and ice studies, 98
    snowmobile maintenance and repair,
        39–40, 138, 180
    traveling in whiteout, 167
Hood (Franklin expedition), 162–163
Hood River, *154* (map)
Hopkins, Frances Anne (Beechey), *50*
Hornby, John
    with Arima and dogs at cabin near
        Fort Confidence, *221*
    Barrenlands expeditions, 195, 223–
        224, 226–227
    as Father Rouvière's wilderness
        guide, 221
    grave site and marker, *231*
    at Great Bear Lake with Melvill,
        220–221
    life and death of, 219–227

muskoxen sightings, 212

near starvation of, 222

as refugee from mechanized world, 230

remains buried by RCMP, 227–228

return route from Barrenlands,
224–225

Rouvière and, 123–125

in Tulita (Fort Norman), *220*

in World War I, 221–222

Hornby Bay, *116* (map), 123

Hornby cabin site, 229, *230*

Hornby Point, 217, *218* (map), 219, 228

Hudson, Henry, 57, 199, *199*

Hudson Bay, *2* (map), 106, *196* (map),
218 (map)

Hudson's Bay Company (HBC)

acquisition of North West Company,
90

Fort Confidence, 112–113

Fort McPherson, 55

fur traders and, 84

Hearne's expeditions on behalf of,
140, 200–201

Matonabbee and, 203

missions co-located with, 123

New Rampart trading post, 44

Old Rampart trading post, 46

origins and expansion of, 200

Hudson Strait, *199*

Hunter, James, 130

Huntington, Henry, *10, 41*

background and expedition role, 6–9

Bloody Falls and, 139–140, *143*

at cairn along Thelon River, *237*

Diavik Mine tour, 182, *189, 192*

filling fuel jugs, *19*

Glen's birthday celebration, 101

Hornby cabin site, 229

at Hornby Point, 228

muskoxen sighting, 215

snow and ice measuring, 98–99

snowmobile driving, 19

snowmobile maintenance, 180

ice

bare of snow, *101*

black, 100

drilling through, *13*

drill rig on Lac de Gras, *184*

edge danger, 169–170

Laurentide Ice Sheet, 106, *107, 161,*
177–178

Mackenzie River crossing, *185*

overflow (*aufeis*), 17, 23–25, *24*, 71, *71*

pressure ridges, 207, *207*

rafted, *99*

sea, *150*, 150–151, *151*, 185

shelf, *77*, 77–80, 90

shorefast, *13*

thickness concerns, 99

ice age, 106

ice bridges, 119

ice roads, 184–185, *185*

ice-snow roads, *82*, 82–83, 93

ice studies, 13

Great Bear Lake, 98

Iditarod, Alaska, 22

Iditarod Trail Sled-Dog Race, 20, 22

igloos, 144–145

ilmenites, 177

inconnu (sheefish), *201*

Indian country, 141

Indians

of Barrenlands, 141

Chipewyan, 140–143, *142*, 197,
200–205

Cree, 140–143, *142*, 201–202

Dene, 93, 200–202, 209

taiga, 105

See also names of individuals

indigenous people, 97, 140–150, 197,
200, 240

See also Gwich'in people; Inuit people; Sahtu people

industrial dormitories, 187–188

International Boundary Survey (1909–
1912), 45

International Polar Year 2007–2009
  (IPY), 12
Inuit country (Nunavut), 141
Inuit people
  of Barrenlands, 141
  Bloody Falls massacre, 140, *142, 204*
  of Canadian Arctic Archipelago, 168
  of Coronation Gulf, 105, 156
  Father Rouvière and, 124–125,
    127–133
  girls and story knives, 149
  igloos and, 144–146
  and inuksuk, *148*
  and Northern Cross, 112–113
  pragmatism, 233
  spiritual world, 133
inuksuk, 148, 164
Iñupiat people, 133, 240
Inuvialuit encampments, 88
Irissari, Bob, *x*

Jackson Brothers, 51
Jenness, Diamond, 128, 133
Jette (Father), 133
Johnson, Albert. *See* Mad Trapper of
  Rat River (Albert Johnson)
Johnson, Johnny, 65
Jon. *See* Holmgren, Jon
Josie, Peter, 46, *49*
Junius (Inuit guide), 162
Jupiter Bay, 108

Kaasen, Gunnar, 22
Kassi, Danny, 46, 51
Kathawachaga Lake, *154* (map), 158
Keith Arm, Great Bear Lake, *94* (map)
Killik River, 58
kimberlite, *177,* 190
kimberlite pipes, 176–178, 186, 188–189
King, Alfred, 59–60
Kippe, Carl, 170
Klamath (USCGC), ix
Kleedehn, William, 31–33, *32,* 42

Klondike, 105
knife throwing, 143–145, 147
KNK radio, Fairbanks, 66
KNK radio station, Fairbanks, 66
komatik, 239
Kugluktuk, *2* (map), 125, 150, 153, *154*
  (map), 205, 213
Kuparuk River, 5–6

Lac de Gras, *174* (map), 180, 183, *184,*
  186, 197
La Chute River, 55
La Chute River trail, 70
lake crossings, Great Bear Lake, 95–99
LaNauze, Denny, 126–127
Lands Forlorn (Douglas), 105
Lapierre House, 51, *52, 56* (map), 70
Laurentide Ice Sheet, 106, *107, 161,*
  177–178
Lawrence, Thomas, *87*
Le Pointe de Misère, *174* (map), 179,
  196 (map)
LeRoux, Guillaume, 125–126, 129
Linklater family, *45*
Liss, Sister Joan, 240
Liston, Glen
  background and expedition role, 5–6
  on bare ice, *101*
  birthday celebration, 101, *102*
  at cairn along Thelon River, *237*
  Diavik Mine tour, *189*
  at Hornby Point, 228
  ice bridge collapse, 119
  ice pressure ridge crossing, *207*
  muskoxen sighting, 215
  on overflow ice, *24*
  relaxing in cook tent, *7*
  snowmobile maintenance, 180
  souvenir hunting, 139–140
  tour of Deline, 135
  whiteouts, 167
Little Chicago, *76* (map), 78–79, 90–91
Lower Wilberforce Falls, *158*

MacKay Lake, *196* (map)
Mackenzie, Alexander, 80–84, 86–90, *87, 89*
Mackenzie River, *76* (map), *81, 92*
  drainage, 55
  high-water line, 80
  origins, 87
  shelf ice, 77
Mackey, Dick, 22
Mackey, Lance, 22
Mad Trapper of Rat River (Albert Johnson)
  cabin remains following siege, *61*
  death photo, *69*
  death site, *56* (map), *58*
  guns and axe of, *65*
  landscape of, 72–73
  manhunt for, 57, 59–68
  mystery of, 64–65
  Richardson range crossing by, 55, 66–67
  snowshoes used by, *64*
mail delivery, 34
Mallory, George, 33
Marconi, 58
martens, *86*
massacres, 140–143, *142*, 205
Mathias, Joseph, *155*
Matonabbee, 197, 202–205, 233
May, Wop, 57, 66, *68*
McDowell (Constable), 60
McKinley, Mount, 128
medicine, in the North, 133
Melvill, James Cosmo, 220–221
Mertie, J. B., Jr., 57–58
Methye Portage, 49–51
Métis voyageurs, 43, 48–51
Michel (Franklin expedition), 162–163
Millen, Edgar, 59, 63
Millen, Mount, *56* (map), 66
mineral indicators of diamonds, 177–179, 190–191
mines and mining

diamonds, *174* (map), 175–180, 184–186, 190–191, 193
  open-pit, 188–190
  radium, 93
  uranium, *134*
  See also Diavik Mine
missions and missionaries, 93, 122–123, 128–129
moraines, 166, *169*
mosquitoes, 87
moulins, 120–121
mushers, 20–21, 31, 42
muskoxen, 211–215
muskox skull, *211*
mutiny, aboard *Discovery,* 199

Naedzo, Joseph, 135
Narakay Islands, *94* (map), 101, *102*
National Postal Museum, 34
Native land claims, Canada, 140–141
Nerysoo, William, 59
New Rampart, *38* (map), 44, *45*
Neyelle, Charlie, *135*
Nome, Alaska, xi, 22, 105
Nonsuch (ship), 199
Norman Wells, *2* (map), *76* (map), 88, *90*
North, Dick, 65
Northmen (*les hommes du nord*), 85
North West Company, 84, 89–90, 93
Northwest Game Act (1917), 213
Northwest Passage
  explorations in search of, 112–113, 155–156, 168, 171, 199
  Northwind's traverse of, iv
  Pond and, 86
Northwest Territories, *2* (map), 82, *83*
Northwind (USCGC), ix, *x*
Nunavut, *2* (map), 148

Oblate of Mary Immaculate, 122
Obstruction Rapids, *154* (map), 162
Ocean Station Papa, ix

oil, near Fort Good Hope, 93
oil and gas field rigs, *90*
Old Crow, *2* (map), 37, *38* (map), 40–44, *43*, *56* (map), 130
Old Crow Range, *42*, 43
Old Rampart, *38* (map), 44, 128
Old Woman Creek (*Shanaghàn Kòhnjìk*), 45
One Man's Wilderness (Proenneke), 219
open-pit mining, 188–190
Our Lady of Good Hope church, 129–132, *131–132*
overflow ice (*aufeis*), 17, 23–25, *24*, 71, *71*

Page, Dorothy, 22
panak (snow knives), 139, 144–148, *149*
peace journeys, 141
Peel River, 55, *56* (map)
Peltier (Franklin expedition), 160, 162
permafrost, 12–13, 211
Perrault (Franklin expedition), 163
Pike, Warburton, 197, *198*
Pleasant Valley Store, *16*
Pleistocene ice age, 106
Plummer's Great Bear Lake Lodge, 103
Point Barrow, 112
Point Lake, *154* (map), 156, 161
Point Separation, 88
polar bears, 151
Pond, Peter, 86
Porcupine River, 37, *38* (map), 43
portages, 46–51, 142
Portugese fishermen, 198
potlatch in Old Crow, 41–42
Precambrian granite, 104
Prince of Wales Fort, *196* (map), 208
Proenneke, Dick, 219
Providence, Lake, 161, *174* (map)
pusher tugs, shallow draft, 83, *83*

quarantine camp, Edmond's Island, 45
quartz crystals, 142

radios, 58–59, 62, 66
radium mining, 93
Rae, John, 113
rafted ice, Great Bear Lake, *99*
raft race, Fourth of July, xi
Rasmussen, Knud, 133, 146
Rat River, *56* (map)
RCMP. *See* Royal Canadian Mounted Police (RCMP)
Redington, Joe, Sr., 22
religious competition, 127–133
religious icons, Deline shrine, *134*
resource extraction, 84, 151
Richardson, Sir John, 156, 162–163
Richardson Mountains, 55, *56* (map), 62, 67, 69–70, 72–73, *73*
Riddell (Constable), 63
rime plumes, *31*
Rio Tinto, 185
riparian zones, 118–119
risk and reward, cultural differences, 169–171
Ritch Island, 104
roads
    all-weather, 185
    building, 29–30
    ice, 184–185
    winter, *82*, 82–83, 93
rock tripe (*tripe de roche*), 157–158, *159*
Roman Catholic church, 93, 127–133
Rosebud Summit, *18* (map)
    ascent, 25–26
    challenges of, 17
    descent toward Birch Creek, *30*
    mushers and, 32
    snowmobiles and sleds, *27*, *28*
Rouvière, Jean-Baptiste
    cabin location, *122*
    and competition between Catholic and Anglican churches in the North, 127–133
    at Douglas Cabin, *123*
    at Fort Good Hope, 129

as missionary, 122–126
murder of, 126
Rouvière, Lake (Lake Imaerinik), *116* (map), 117, 124
Royal Canadian Corps of Signals, 60
Royal Canadian Mounted Police (RCMP)
  burial of Hornby, Christian, and Adlard remains, 227–228
  Historical Collections Unit, 65
  hunt for Sinnisiak and Uluksuk, 126–127
  and Mad Trapper of Rat River, 57, 60–63, 67
  visit paid to Hornby and Critchell-Bullock, 224
Royal Navy officers, on Franklin expedition, 156, 160–161, 169

sacred spots, 219
Sahtu people, 87, 101, 112–113, 135, 140
saltating snow, 96, *96*
Samandre (Franklin expedition), 162
Sandberg (Swedish geologist), 105
Sandvik House, 3
Sanford, Mount, 3
Sarren, Bobby, *13*
sastrugi (rhythmic snow dunes), 207
Scented Grass Hills, 97
Schultz Lake, *218* (map)
science-driven expeditions, 4
scrub spruce flat, *51*
sea ice, *150*, 150–151, *151*, 185
Seppälä, Leonhard, 22
shallow draft pusher tugs, 83, *83*
Shanaghàn Kòhnjìk (Old Woman Creek), *45*
sheefish (inconnu), *201*
shelf ice, *77*, 77–80, 90
shift work in northern Alaska, 188
shipping routes, Arctic climate change and, 150–151

shorefast ice, *13*
Siberian hunters, 57
Silis, Arvids, *14*
  background and expedition role, 10
  at cairn along Thelon River, *237*
  Diavik Mine tour, 188, *189*
  ice pressure ridge crossing, *207*
  sled, 180–181
  snow knife, 145
Sim, Vincent C., 128–129
Simpson, George, 112
Simpson, Thomas, 112–113
Sinnisiak, 126–127, *127*
sintering, 144–145
Sittichinli (Special Constable), 60
Skidoo snowmobiles, 39
Slave River, 87
sled-dog races
  Dagoo 340, 31–32
  Iditarod Trail Sled-Dog Race, 20, 22
  Yukon Quest International, 17, 20–21, *31*, 32–34
smallpox outbreak, 44, 45
Smart Lake, 225
Smith, Gilbert, 45
Smith, Philip S., 57–58
Smith, Shirleen, *52*
Smith Arm, Great Bear Lake, *94* (map)
Snap Lake Mine, 185
snow
  blowing, *102*
  drifting, 96
  and global climate, 12–13
  properties of, 144–145
  saltating, *96*, 97
  soft, in trees, *70*
  suspended load, 96
  thermal conductivity, 144
snow-ice, 100
snow knives (*panak*), 139, 144–148, *149*
snowmobiles
  Chris's and Arvids's, *181*
  driving, 19

and drowning deaths, 206–207
hittings rocks, 164
Jon's, *183*
maintenance and repair, 39–40,
   138–139, 180
rough-locking sleds, 21
Skidoo clutches, 39
tough sledding, *166*
snow-on-ice roads, *82,* 82–83, 93
SnowSTAR expedition, *xiv,* 1
appearance of, 103
snow studies
digging pits for, 139, 143
elements of, 13
Great Bear Lake, 98–99
at Hornby Point, 228
on Lac de Gras, 183
near Bloody Falls, *144*
science-driven expeditions, 4
with snow knife, 139
soapstone carving, polar bear, *140*
Solie, Dan, *9, 229, 230*
background and expedition role, 6–8
Bloody Falls trip, 139–140
at cairn along Thelon River, *237*
concerns about ice thickness, 99
on Franklin's trail, 164–165
ice bridge collapse, 119
muskox sighting, 211, 215
near-death experience on Mt.
   Wrangell, 6–8
snowmobile breakdown, 39–40
snowmobile driving, 19
traveling in whiteout, 167
and William Vittrekwa, 70
South Pole 300° club, 5
Spearfish Lake, 204
spill piles, 189
starvation and near-starvation, 160–
   162, 222
Starvation Lake, 162
starvation trail, 155
Steese Highway, 30

Stefansson, Vihljalmur, 113
St. Germain (Franklin expedition),
   161–162, 164
stories of the Arctic, dominant themes,
   xi–xii
story knives, ceremonial, 149
Stuck, Hudson, 37, 123, 127–128, *129*
Sturm, Matthew
background, ix–xi
on board *Northwind, x*
at confluence, *214*
examining snow near Bloody Falls, *144*
expedition role, 4
Superior, Lake, 85
Swenson, Rick, 22

taiga, *208*
taiga—tundra transition zone, 115
Tanana River, *18* (map), 58, 128
tank traps, 118–119
technological advances, and the Arctic,
   198, 232–233
Telida (Fort Norman), *76* (map), 87, 93
Thanakoie Narrows, 213
Thelon River, *2* (map), 195, *196* (map),
   217, *218* (map), 225–226
Thomas, Eira, 180
Thoy Kye Lyned (Aylmer Lake), 195,
   204–205
Tidd, Claude, *48*
Togo (dog), 22
topographic sense of indigenous
   people, 97
tracking, from the air, 67
trade goods, movement of, 48–49,
   84–85
trading posts, 44, 46–48, 55, 90
   See also Fort *entries*
trading system, triangular, 86
trail-hardening, 26
tripe de roche (rock tripe), 157–158, *159*
Tsiigehtchic (Arctic Red River trading
   post), *56* (map), 59, 75, *76* (map), 78, *79*

tugs, shallow draft pusher, 83, *83*
Tuktoyaktuk, 87
tundra, *209*
Tundra Ecosystem Research Station, *154* (map), *174* (map)

Uluksuk, 126–127, *127*
umiaks, x–xi, *xii*
Unflinching (Christian), 228
uranium mining and cancer deaths, *134*
US—Canada boundary, *48*
US Coast Guard (USCG) cutters, ix
US Geological Survey (USGS) expedition, 57–58

Vaillant (Franklin expedition), 160, 162
Verville (Constable), 63
Victorian era, class and racial structures, 168–169
Vikings, 198
Vittrekwa, Ernie, 55, 70–71, *72,* 75
Vittrekwa, William, 59, 70
volcanism across the Canadian Shield, 176
voyageur canoes, paintings by Hopkins, *50*
voyageur crews (*les allants et venants*), 85
Vuntat Gwich'in (People of the Lakes), 44, 51, 55

wars, among indigenous people, 140–150

Water River, confluence with Bell River, *51*
Wekweèt, *154* (map)
whale fisheries, Hearne and HBC, 200
whales, and sea ice, 151
Whitefish Lake, 204
White Man's burden, 122
whiteouts, 166–167, 206–207
Wilberforce Falls, 157, *158*
wilderness stories, xi
Willow Island, *45*
willows (shrub jungle), 117–118
Winnipeg, Lake, 85
winter roads, *82,* 82–83, 93, 184–185
woolly mammoths, 211
World War II, 135, 230
Wrangell, Mount, 6–8, 105
Wright Brothers, 58

Xahweguweh Financial Corporation, 93

Yamba Lake, *154* (map), 160, 168, *174* (map), 175
Yamoga Land Corporation, 93
Yellowknife (town), 87, 198
Yellowknife Indians, 156, 163
Yukon, *2* (map), 55
Yukon Quest International Sled Dog Race, 17, 20–21, *31,* 32–34
Yukon River, *18* (map), 20, 34, 37, 128

zircons, 193
Zzeh Gittlit, Chief, 44